ADVICE & DISSENT

SARAH A. BINDER AND FORREST MALTZMAN

ADVICE & DISSENT

The Struggle to Shape the Federal Judiciary

BROOKINGS INSTITUTION PRESS

Washington, D.C.

Copyright © 2009
THE BROOKINGS INSTITUTION
1775 Massachusetts Avenue, N.W., Washington, D.C. 20036
www.brookings.edu

Library of Congress Cataloging-in-Publication data

Binder, Sarah A.
    Advice and dissent : the struggle to shape the federal judiciary / Sarah A. Binder and Forrest Maltzman.
        p.   cm.
    Includes bibliographical references and index.
    Summary: "Explores the state of the federal judicial selection system. Reconstructs the history and contemporary practice of advice and consent, identifying political, institutional causes of conflict over judicial selection and consequences of such battles. Advocates pragmatic reforms of the institutions of judicial selection that harness incentives of presidents and senators together"—Provided by publisher.
    ISBN 978-0-8157-0340-2 (pbk. : alk. paper)
    1. Judges—Selection and appointment—United States. I. Maltzman, Forrest, 1963–
II. Title.
    KF8776.B56 2010
    347.73'14—dc22   2009026626

9 8 7 6 5 4 3 2 1

Printed on acid-free paper

Typeset in Minion

Composition by Cynthia Stock
Silver Spring, Maryland

Printed by R. R. Donnelley
Harrisonburg, Virginia

For Noa and Mica

Contents

Foreword

It's a safe guess that the Framers of the Constitution would have serious concerns about how the third branch of government is faring in the early twenty-first century. It would be hard for them to square their ideal of judges as neutral arbiters with the often intense partisan and ideological scrutiny of nominations for every level of the federal judiciary.

In *Advice and Dissent,* Sarah Binder, a senior fellow in Governance Studies at the Brookings Institution, and Forrest Maltzman, a professor of political science at George Washington University, review more than six decades of the practice of advice and consent on Capitol Hill. In addition to providing a useful, lucid look backward, they provide a guide to conflicts and controversies now in the headlines and offer fresh insights into how the U.S. political system—and, in particular, the Senate—might better serve society in its treatment of judicial nominations for trial and appellate courts.

Given the stakes involved, the process whereby candidates for lifetime positions on district courts and the U.S. courts of appeals are considered is far less understood than it should be. Sarah and Forrest provide a timely corrective for that shortcoming in civic knowledge. While partisan pique and ideological polarization of the parties are part of the problem, they do not fully explain the fate of appointments to the bench. Sarah and Forrest show how senators are increasingly resourceful in their exploitation of new and inherited rules of the game for advice and consent. Digging deep into Senate archives, the authors locate the origins of key institutional practices and show how those practices have been used to derail nominations. In their view, the very structure of the federal bench has become a product of the legislative process.

The authors point out that many defend the current practice of advice and consent on the grounds that careful scrutiny of potential judges' legal and policy views is necessary before granting lifetime tenure on the bench. Sarah and Forrest acknowledge that the concept of prospective accountability is valid for unelected judges. However, they warn of the consequences of unbridled partisan and ideological attacks on candidates for federal judgeships. They propose innovations to improve the practice of advice and consent, including reforms that would harness a president's interest in filling vacant judgeships swiftly and senators' interest in retaining influence over the selection of nominees while at the same time ensuring the public's faith in unelected judges.

In short, the book is a model of what we at Brookings regard as our core mission: rigorous, high-quality, empirical, nonpartisan research that identifies ways in which the U.S. system of governance is falling short—and imaginative, pragmatic suggestions on how the nation can do better. I join Sarah and Forrest in gratefully acknowledging financial support for this project from the National Science Foundation, the Carnegie Corporation of New York, and the law firm of O'Melveny and Myers.

STROBE TALBOTT
President
Brookings Institution

Washington, D.C.
June 2009

Acknowledgments

We are in debt to the generosity and creativity of many friends and colleagues who have aided us in writing this book. It is a much better book than we could have written by ourselves.

We appreciate first and foremost the scrupulously careful reading by Russell Wheeler, who read the manuscript from start to finish and provided detailed comments and tough questions throughout. We are grateful as well for advice from many colleagues and friends: Stan Bach, John Baughman, Rick Beth, Robert Bradley, Rachel Paine Caufield, Chris Deering, Melinda Hall Gann, Shelly Goldman, Greg Huber, Robert Katzmann, Eric Lawrence, Tony Madonna, Tom Mann, Pietro Nivola, Dave Primo, Don Ritchie, Jim Rogers, Elizabeth Rybicki, Jeff Segal, Martin Shapiro, Chuck Shipan, John Sides, Lee Sigelman, Elliott Slotnick, Steve Smith, Mitch Sollenberger, Mark Spindel, Paul Wahlbeck, Kent Weaver, and Ben Wittes. The book also benefitted from helpful feedback we received in seminars in the political science and government departments at Harvard, SUNY Albany, Stony Brook, Swarthmore, Temple, University of Minnesota, University of Wisconsin–Madison, Washington University in St. Louis, William and Mary, and Yale.

Bruce Ragsdale from the Federal Judicial Center's History Office was critically important in helping us to launch our nominations dataset; Jessie Kratz at the Center for Legislative Archives at the National Archives provided invaluable assistance in seeking out archival records related to Senate blue slips; and Steven Schlesinger, Cathy Whitaker, and John Golant at the Administrative Office of the United States Courts were instrumental in helping us to build a dataset on court performance. We also wish to thank Jim Duff, director of the Administrative Office of the U.S. Courts, for answering all of our questions on courts and judges on early weekend mornings in his mud-covered, dog-park clothing.

At the Brookings Institution, we thank Sarah's research assistants who toiled for years over more than two centuries of nominations data: Grace Cho, Alan Murphy, Mark Hiller, and Molly Reynolds. They were aided by Brookings interns Ravi Gupta and Emily Zametkin. Will Adams and Mitch Killian from George Washington University also provided excellent research assistance. We also greatly appreciate the careful work of our tag-team Brookings verifiers, Andrew Rubenstein and Georgina Druce, and the assistance of Gladys Arrisueno in Governance Studies. Finally, we appreciate all the efforts of Chris Kelaher, Susan Woollen, Janet Walker, and Anthony Nathe at the Brookings Press in shepherding the book from manuscript to publication so carefully and swiftly.

Funding for this project was generously provided by a number of sources, and we acknowledge their support: The Carnegie Corporation of New York's Carnegie Scholars program, the National Science Foundation's POWRE grant program (SES-D9805772) and O'Melveny and Myers (Washington, D.C.).

We dedicate this book to our two daughters, Noa (forever offering advice) and Mica (always happy to consent). Few coauthors are so fortunate to share so much.

ADVICE & DISSENT

1

The Struggle to Shape the Federal Judiciary

For better or worse, federal judges in the United States are asked today to resolve some of the most important and contentious public policy issues. Although some hold onto the notion that the federal judiciary is simply a neutral arbiter of complex legal questions, the justices and judges who serve on the Supreme Court and the lower federal bench are in fact crafters of public law. In recent years, for example, the Supreme Court has bolstered the rights of immigrants, endorsed the constitutionality of school vouchers, struck down Washington, D.C.'s ban on hand guns, and most famously, determined the outcome of the 2000 presidential election. The judiciary clearly is an active partner in the making of public policy.

As the breadth and salience of federal court dockets has grown, the process of selecting federal judges has drawn increased attention. Judicial selection has been contentious at numerous junctures in U.S. history, but seldom has it seemed more acrimonious and dysfunctional than in recent years. Fierce controversies such as the battles to confirm Robert Bork and Clarence Thomas to the Supreme Court are emblematic of an intensely divisive political climate in Washington. Alongside these high-profile disputes have been scores of less conspicuous confirmation cases held hostage in the Senate, resulting in declining confirmation rates and unprecedented delays in filling federal judgeships. At times over the past few years, over 10 percent of the federal bench has sat vacant. Although Senate parties reach periodic agreements to release their hostages, conflict over judicial selection continues to rise. All the while, the caseload of the federal judiciary over the past two decades has expanded to an exceptionally heavy level.

This book explores the state of the nation's federal judicial selection system—beset, as we perceive it, by deepening partisan polarization, obstructionism, and a deterioration of the practice of advice and consent. We set aside the more celebrated Supreme Court to focus on the selection of judges for the U.S. courts of appeals and the U.S. district courts. We do so for several reasons. First, the lower federal courts are the workhorses of the federal judiciary, with more than 380,000 cases filed in the appellate and district courts in 2007.[1] Moreover, the Supreme Court issues opinions in only a small percentage of the cases filed by parties seeking redress from decisions of the federal courts of appeals. For the Supreme Court's October 2006 term (running from October 1, 2006 through September 30, 2007), for example, the Court issued full opinion decisions in 73 cases, approximately 1 percent of the more than 7,100 appeals for *writ of certiorari* that emerged that term from decisions of the federal courts of appeals.[2] More often than not, these are the courts of last resort for plaintiffs seeking justice in the federal courts. Who sits on the trial and appellate court benches is thus highly consequential for the shape of public law.

Second, although these courts issue decisions on some of the most important economic, social, and political issues of the day, a typical nomination to the lower federal courts receives far less scrutiny than would a nomination to the Supreme Court. Out of the public spotlight, a nominee's detractors have a far easier time blocking appointments they oppose. Senators understand the latitude they have to block nominations, and they often do so surreptitiously by exploiting the Senate's formal rules and informal practices. Given the potential impact of lower court appointments and given how little scrutiny these appointments often receive, we focus exclusively on appointments to the lower courts.

Third, indicators of the health of the nomination and confirmation process suggest that something has gone astray in the Senate's practice of advice and consent. If we compare confirmation rates for nominees to the Supreme Court and to the courts of appeals since 1947, their success rates are roughly the same: about 80 percent of both sets of nominations confirmed. If we narrow our focus to the period after 1992, however, the likelihood of confirmation for Supreme Court nominees remains high (80

Figure 1-1. *Confirmation Rates for U.S. District Courts and U.S. Courts of Appeals, 1947–2008*

Percentage confirmed

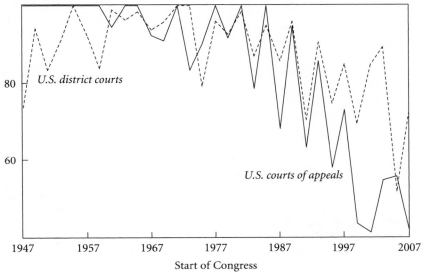

Source: Data for the 80th to 107th Congresses compiled by authors from U.S. Senate, Committee on the Judiciary, *Legislative and Executive Calendar,* final edition. Data for 108th to 110th Congresses (through December 18, 2008) compiled by the Department of Justice, Office of Legal Policy (www.usdoj.gov/olp/ [December 18, 2008]).

percent confirmed), but the confirmation rate falls to under 60 percent for nominations to the appeals courts.[3] The broader pattern can be seen in figure 1-1, which shows confirmation rates for nominations to the federal district and appeals courts. The bottom has clearly fallen out of the confirmation process, with confirmation rates dipping below 50 percent during some recent Congresses. Moreover, perhaps most often missed in discussions of confirmation patterns is that conflict over the selection of federal judges has not extended equally across all twelve circuits.[4] As seen in table 1-1, nominations for some appellate vacancies attract very little controversy, such as the Midwest's Seventh Circuit. Not so for the Courts of Appeals for the District of Columbia and for the Fourth and Sixth Circuits, for which roughly half of all appellate nominations have failed since 1991. By focusing on the lower federal bench, we aim to explain both the marked

Table 1-1. *Confirmation Failure Rates for the Courts of Appeals*[a]

Circuit	Percentage of nominations that failed
District of Columbia	61
1st	29
2nd	12
3rd	35
4th	65
5th	50
6th	59
7th	14
8th	14
9th	46
10th	31
11th	42

Source: Data for the 80th to 107th Congresses compiled by authors from U.S. Senate, Committee on the Judiciary, *Legislative and Executive Calendar*, final edition. Data for 108th to 110th Congresses (through December 18, 2008) compiled by the Department of Justice, Office of Legal Policy (www.usdoj.gov/olp/ [December 18, 2008]).
a. Pooled data, 1991–2008.

temporal trend as well as the disparate treatment of the circuits that we see in recent decades.

Not only has conflict become more pronounced over time and in certain places, the duration of the nomination and confirmation processes has stretched out in recent decades. From the 1940s to the 1980s, a typical court of appeals nominee was confirmed within two months of nomination. By the late 1990s, the wait for successful nominees had stretched to about six months. Since the beginning of George W. Bush's presidency, even successful nominees to the U.S. courts of appeals have waited on average more than six months to be confirmed (see figure 1-2). That number may be misleading, however, since many nominees were submitted during more than one session of Congress before achieving Senate confirmation. These average waits, moreover, pale in comparison to the experiences of nominees who failed to be confirmed during the Bill Clinton and George W. Bush administrations. Since the mid-1990s, the typical nomination that failed to be confirmed (at least the first time he or she was nominated) has lingered before the Senate for almost a year and a half. As the confirmation process has

Figure 1-2. *Nominations to the U.S. Courts of Appeals: Length of Time from Nomination to Confirmation, 1947–2008*

Number of days

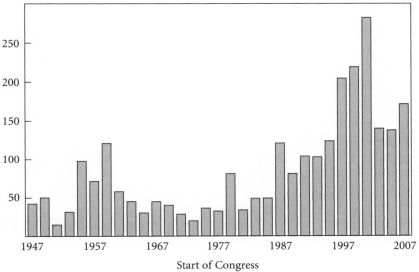

Start of Congress

Source: Data for the 80th to 107th Congresses compiled by authors from U.S. Senate, Committee on the Judiciary, *Legislative and Executive Calendar*, final edition. Data for 108th to 110th Congresses (through December 18, 2008) compiled by the Department of Justice, Office of Legal Policy (www.usdoj.gov/olp/ [March 29, 2009]).

dragged on in recent years, some candidates have become increasingly reluctant to wait it out. Numerous nominees for these cherished lifetime appointments pull themselves out of the running after waiting months and often years for the Senate to act. As Miguel Estrada said in 2003 upon abandoning his two-year-long quest for confirmation, "I believe that the time has come to return my full attention to the practice of law and to regain the ability to make long-term plans for my family."[5]

Delays in filling vacant judgeships, however, do not lie solely with the Senate. The time it takes for nominees to be chosen by the president to fill the nation's trial courts has also increased in recent decades. At the end of the 1950s, it took an average of about 200 days, or just over six months, for presidents to select nominees once a vacancy occurred. By the end of the

Figure 1-3. *Nominations to the U.S. District Courts: Length of Time from Vacancy to Nomination, 1947–98*[a]

Number of days

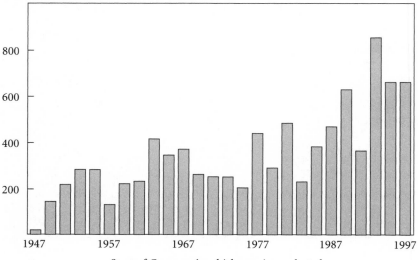

Start of Congress in which nominee selected

Source: Data for the 80th to 105th Congresses compiled by authors from U.S. Senate, Committee on the Judiciary, *Legislative and Executive Calendar,* final edition (through December 1998).

a. Duration of vacancy is calculated as the number of days elapsed between the original vacancy for a judgeship and the referral of a nomination to the Senate. Vacancy dates for nominations announced before the opening of a vacancy are set to one day before the nomination date. Vacancy dates for vacant judgeships inherited by a new presidential administration are kept at the original vacancy date.

1990s, it took more than 600 days, or roughly twenty months, from vacancy to nomination (see figure 1-3). More recently, a typical judicial vacancy for the U.S. district courts during the One Hundred Ninth Congress (2005–06) lasted more than seven months before a nominee was named. Despite the low salience of so many of the nominations to the lower courts, senators clearly take stock of these nominees and often exploit the rules of the game to derail the nominations on their way to confirmation. These multiple indicators of a judicial selection system near its breaking point deserve concerted attention, and their variation cries out for explanation.

Our Contribution

Although we detect signs of conflict over federal judges as early as the 1970s, scholars have yet to offer a comprehensive treatment of the politics and processes of judicial selection. The topic of lower court judicial selection has certainly attracted interest. Legal scholars have questioned the growing importance of ideology in confirmation hearings, while judicial scholars have examined how presidential ambitions shape the selection of judges and how interest groups succeed in derailing nominees they oppose.[6] Such studies provide excellent, but partial, portraits of the forces shaping the contemporary politics of advice and consent.

To the extent that scholars have attempted to provide a broader explanation of patterns in judicial selection, two alternative accounts have been proposed—neither of which, we argue, fully captures the political and institutional dynamics that underlie contemporary advice and consent. One account—which we will call the *big bang theory* of judicial selection—points to a breaking point in national politics, after which prevailing norms of deference and restraint in judicial selection have fallen apart. The result, according to partisans of the big bang, is a sea change in appointment politics, evidenced by the lengthening of the confirmation process and the rise in confirmation failure. A strong alternative account—which we will call the nothing-new-under-the-sun theory of judicial selection—suggests that ideological conflict over the makeup of the bench has been an ever-present force in shaping the selection of federal judges and justices. Judicial selection has always been political and ideological as senators and presidents vie for influence over the bench.

Adherents of the big bang account typically point to a cataclysmic event in Congress or the courts that had an immediate and lasting impact on the process and politics of judicial selection thereafter. Most often, scholars point to the battle over Robert Bork's nomination to the Supreme Court in 1987 as the event that precipitated a new regime in the treatment of presidential nominations by the Senate. As John Maltese has argued about Supreme Court appointment politics,

> The defeat of Robert Bork's 1987 Supreme Court nomination was a watershed event that unleashed what Stephen Carter has called "the confirmation mess." There was no question that Bork was a highly

qualified nominee. He was rejected not because of any lack of qualifi-
cation, or any impropriety, but because of his stated judicial philosophy: how he would vote as a judge.[7]

The president's willingness to nominate a strong conservative deemed
outside the mainstream by the Democratic majority and the Senate Democrats' willingness to challenge a qualified nominee on grounds of how he
would rule on the bench together are said to have radically altered the practice of advice and consent for judicial nominees. Adherents of the big bang
account have also argued that the Bork debacle spilled over into the politics
of lower court nominations, significantly increasing the politicization of
selecting judges for the lower federal bench.[8]

Other versions of the big bang theory point to alternative pivotal events,
including the Supreme Court's 1954 *Brown* v. *Board of Education* decision.
As Benjamin Wittes has argued, "We can reasonably describe the decline of
the process as an institutional reaction by the Senate to the growth of judicial power that began with the *Brown* decision in 1954."[9] Still other versions
of the big bang account point to the transformation of party activists (from
seekers of material benefits to seekers of ideological or policy benefits) and
the mobilization of political elites outside the Senate seeking to affect the
makeup of the bench.[10]

No doubt, each of these forces—the Bork debacle, the changing character of elite activists, and the emergence of the courts as key policymakers—
have shaped to some degree the emergence of conflict over nominations in
the postwar period. Still, these explanations do not help us to pinpoint the
timing or location of conflict over judges. The increasing relevance of the
Warren court on a range of controversial issues certainly must have played
a role in increasing the salience of judicial nominations to senators. Had
the Court avoided engaging in controversial social, economic, and political
issues, senators would have had little incentive to try to influence the makeup
of the bench. But neither do we see large changes in the dynamics of advice
and consent until well after the 1954 decision and until well after the emergence of more ideological activists in the 1960s. And certainly the no-holds-
barred battle over the Bork nomination may have shown both parties that
concerted opposition to a presidential choice was within the bounds of
acceptable behavior after 1987. Still, isolating the impact of the Bork fight

cannot help us to explain the significant variation in the Senate's treatment of judicial nominees before and after the One Hundredth Congress. It is also important to recall that executive branch appointments also experienced a sea change beginning in the late 1980s and through the 1990s, taking much longer to secure confirmation. Thus evidence to support the big bang account remains incomplete. More likely, as we suggest later in the book, episodes like the Bork confirmation battle are symptoms, rather than causes, of the more taxing road to confirmation during the past decades.

Lee Epstein and Jeffrey Segal's nothing-new-under-the-sun alternative suggests instead that "the appointments process is and always has been political because federal judges and justices themselves are political."[11] As these scholars argue, presidents have always wanted to use the appointment power for ideological and partisan purposes, and senators have always treated appointees to "help further their own goals, primarily those that serve to advance their chances of reelection, their political party, or their policy interests."[12] We certainly share these scholars' views of legislators, judges, and presidents as strategic political actors. We should expect to see legislators and presidents engage in purposeful behavior shaped by their prevailing goals. But that is a starting—not ending— point for attempting to explain the dynamics of advice and consent. It is quite difficult to account for variation in the Senate's treatment of judicial nominees—both over time and across circuits—if we simply maintain that the process has always been politicized. Thus we recognize the political nature of advice and consent but also seek to identify the ways in which the players' changing incentives interact with the Senate's institutional rules and practices to encourage senators to target appointees who would most shift the ideological tenor of the federal bench.

In the chapters that follow, we do not limit ourselves to arbitrating between the alternative accounts by means of confirmation statistics. Instead, our book promises a broader investigation of the constitutional processes of advice and consent. First, most recent studies have focused on the confirmation stage, which occurs after the critical stage of selecting nominees.[13] Studying only the confirmation process risks missing considerable conflict over the makeup of the bench that plays out as senators and White House officials vie for the right to name judicial nominees. We also include within our purview the contests within Congress and between Congress and the president over where newly created federal judgeships should be located.[14] One aim of this book is to broaden our field of vision in studying judicial selection, with an eye to understanding the wider landscape over which politicians attempt to mold the federal bench.

Second, a key contribution of this book is our institutional perspective. We examine the constitutional provisions, formal chamber rules, and informal Senate practices that sustain advice and consent; we determine the origins of home state senators' privileged role in reviewing nominees; and we explore the consequences of the Senate's rules and practices for the selection and confirmation of federal judges. Most recent studies pay only passing attention to the institutional maze that nominees must maneuver to make it onto the bench.[15] Once nominated, a candidate for the federal bench normally needs to gain the approval of the Senate Committee on the Judiciary, of both home state senators for the vacant judgeship, of the majority party that wields control over the nominations agenda, of those senators who would be able to sustain a filibuster against the nominee, and of course the up or down support of the median senator. Potential vetoes are widely distributed across the Senate, begging questions of why advice and consent has evolved in this way and under what conditions institutional rules and practices afford senators effective vetoes over the selection and confirmation of nominees. We also look briefly at selection mechanisms used by senators to identify candidates for the bench and consider whether the ways in which senators lend advice to the president affects the fate of nominees.

Third, most recent studies, with the exception of Sheldon Goldman's *Picking Federal Judges,* begin their analysis in the late 1970s and conclude that increased partisanship since that period is to blame for increasing confirmation delays and falling confirmation rates. Because evidence is lacking from before the recent past, these conclusions about contemporary confirmation politics are premature. In this book, we recreate the history of judicial selection reaching back to 1789 and use the period after World War II to model how rising partisan polarization has encouraged senators to exploit formal and informal rules of advice and consent to affect the fate of judicial nominees. Our historical sweep allows us to put into perspective arguments about appointment politics that are typically based on the period after the 1970s.

Marshalling decades of data on nomination and confirmation outcomes, we offer an institutional account of advice and consent politics. We show that partisan pique and the rise of ideological disagreement are necessary, but insufficient, to explain the fate of appointments to the bench. One must also account for the array of institutional vetoes that senators are increasingly willing to exploit to shape judicial selection. Moreover, we show that such resistance is not a costless endeavor to senators, as senators narrowly target their opposition where they perceive it to matter the most: The courts of appeals are targets more often than the district courts, and appellate courts that are evenly balanced between the parties are more often targeted than appellate courts that have already tipped to one party or the other. We provide further evidence of the impact of institutions in our analyses of two recent congressional efforts to create and locate new judgeships for the federal district courts. The placement of new judgeships corresponds to judicial demand but also to the electoral and institutional preferences of the legislators who create them.

Finally, others have examined the causes of conflict over filling federal judgeships. To our knowledge, however, the consequences of conflict over judicial selection have escaped systematic attention. In this book, we examine two ways in which controversy over judicial nominations may have harmful effects. First, we explore the impact of prolonged vacancies on the federal bench—vacancies that occur when presidents and senators delay filling federal judgeships. There is reason to suspect that empty judgeships are one of the key causes of heavy court dockets, delays for litigants, and diminished morale on the federal bench. In harnessing more than three decades of performance measures for the federal appellate courts, we explore whether and to what degree vacant judgeships limit the efficiency and capacity of the federal courts. Second, we explore the broader impact of confirmation conflict on the public's trust of federal judges and their decisions. We offer evidence from a survey experiment that suggests that partisan differences over judicial nominees may be undermining the perceived legitimacy of the federal judiciary—a worrisome development for an unelected branch in a system of representative government.

Before turning to a plan of the book, a brief aside about the concept of judges as political actors is in order. We assume throughout the book that senators and presidents perceive judicial nominees and lower court judges in general—primarily those on the appellate courts—to have ideologies or sets of policy views that can be discerned with some degree of certainty. We are not claiming that judges' votes on the appellate bench are solely based on the set of policy views that judges bring to the bench. Clearly, a range of ideological, philosophical, institutional, and case-specific forces shape judges' voting behavior.[16] Nor do all—nor most of, for that matter—the decisions released by the lower federal courts lend themselves to categorization as liberal or conservative. Still, the concept of ideological voting has adherents among legal scholars, such as Cass Sunstein, as well as among political scientists, given the evidence that Democratic-appointed judges tend to vote more often in a liberal direction than do their Republican-appointed colleagues. We assume throughout the book that judges (and thus nominees) can be considered as political actors who hold a set of policy views and who reach their decisions in part by applying those views of the world to the cases before the court. Certainly the concept fits less well for judges than it does for legislators, and less well for judges who serve on federal trial courts compared with those who serve on federal appellate courts. Still, the increased presence of district judges among nominees to the appellate courts and appellate judges among nominees to the Supreme Court in recent years means that senators may increasingly have come to scrutinize both trial and appellate court nominees for their policy views. The decline in confirmation rates for both levels of federal courts in recent Congresses certainly suggests such a change has occurred in senators' priorities in reviewing potential candidates for lifetime appointments to the federal bench.

Plan of the Book

Our goals in this book are threefold: We seek to reconstruct the history and contemporary practice of advice and consent, to identify the causes of conflict over the makeup of the federal bench in the post–Second World War period, and to explore the consequences of battles over appointments to the federal courts. We take up the first task in chapter 2, assessing how decisions made at the Constitutional Convention and by legislators serving in the first Congress in the late eighteenth century shaped the future politics of judicial selection—in particular setting the stage for home state senators to exercise disproportionate power over the selection of nominees to judgeships in their states. We reconstruct the history of confirmation outcomes back to 1789 and use this history to explore patterns in judicial selection.

This history leads us to raise questions about why and when formal and informal veto rights over the fate of nominees have been distributed so widely across the Senate. In particular, we burrow deep inside the Senate's institutional past to determine the origins of the advice and consent practice known as the *blue slip*—the informal practice maintained by the Judiciary Committee that grants senators a special voice in the consideration of judicial appointments to judgeships in their states. We conclude chapter 2 with a sketch of the institutional maze through which appointees today must maneuver to secure nomination and confirmation—including the need to avoid confirmation traps set by committee, filibuster, and party players.

We turn in chapter 3 to explain patterns in nomination outcomes, explaining why presidents select some nominees swiftly, while other vacancies linger months or years before a nominee is selected. We pay particular attention to the role played by home state senators from the president's party, challenging the conventional wisdom that home state senators through the practice of senatorial courtesy dominate the selection of nominees. In chapter 4, we explore the dynamics of confirmation, identifying the forces that affect the fate of nominees in the Senate. We show how players' exploitation of the rules and practices of advice and consent limit the president's influence over the shape of the bench, even given his "first mover" advantage in selecting nominees. We conclude with a review of the "nuclear option" scenario in the Senate in 2005. We consider why the impasse over nominations in the Bush administration led Republicans to propose such a contentious reform of Senate debate practices and why their plan failed.

Having shown that the confluence of partisan incentives and institutional arrangements alters the course of nomination and confirmation processes alike, we argue in chapter 5 that the distribution of power within Congress also helps to explain the allocation of new federal judgeships across the states. Not surprisingly, legislators' incentives to shape the makeup of the federal bench also encourage them to make their mark on the structure of the bench. Although new judgeships are located in part to help existing courts deal with overloaded dockets, legislators' partisan, institutional, and electoral interests also come to the fore in determining where new judgeships are placed and thus how the bench expands.

We conclude our analysis by examining the consequences of conflict over judicial selection. In chapter 6, we explore the impact of vacant judgeships on the performance of the federal courts, showing that judgeships that sit empty contribute to rising caseloads for sitting judges and slow down their ability to dispose of cases on their dockets. We then report the results of an experimental study of the impact of confirmation conflict on individuals' perceptions of federal judges, showing that citizens' trust in federal judges is directly affected by what they know about a judge's road to confirmation. Divisive confirmation contests reduce confidence in those federal judges and their decisions, suggesting that the legitimacy of the unelected branch is put at risk when senators and presidents go to battle over the records and qualifications of potential jurists. There is a cost, we argue, to the break-down in advice and consent—even if debate over the views of judicial candidates may be desirable for those seeking greater prospective accountability of unelected judges with lifetime appointments to the bench.

We conclude in chapter 7 with proposals for reforming the institutions of judicial selection with an eye to encouraging greater efficiency and account-ability in the practice of advice and consent. We advocate reforms that har-ness the incentives of presidents and senators together. We consider pragmatic reform of advice and consent to be a key challenge for those con-cerned not only about the health of the Senate as a partner in the separation of powers, but also about the legitimacy of an unelected judiciary in a rep-resentative political system.

2

The Origins and Evolution
of Advice and Consent

I've been a judge for most of my public legal career, and I just haven't been that familiar with how these things work. I didn't have a clue what a blue slip was, or how it would affect you. I just think a judge should present himself with the best possible qualifications, and then you just have to step back and watch the process work.

—JUDGE JAMES A. WYNN JR.,
North Carolina State Court of Appeals, 2001.[1]

Unfortunately for Judge James Wynn, nominated twice by President Bill Clinton for a vacancy on the United States Court of Appeals for the Fourth Circuit, the blue slip does matter. A blue piece of paper distributed by the Senate Judiciary Committee to the two home state senators for each nomination, the blue slip allows senators to register their objections to judicial nominees slated to fill vacant federal appellate court judgeships designated for their home state. In the case of Judge Wynn, Senator Jesse Helms (R-N.C.) availed himself of the blue slip in 1999. Signaling his intention to block the nomination, Helms's opposition encouraged the Republican-led Judiciary panel to shelve Wynn's nomination.[2]

Judge Wynn was not the only Fourth Circuit nominee who failed to navigate his or her way to confirmation: between 1991 and 2006, the Senate confirmed only ten of the twenty-five nominations sent to the Senate to fill vacancies on the circuit. Nominations to fill judgeships on the Fourth Circuit that were reserved for the state of North Carolina were especially hard hit. Between 1981 and 2002, not a single judge was confirmed from North Carolina for the Fourth Circuit. Even though North Carolina is the most populous state within the circuit (which includes South Carolina, West Virginia, Virginia, and Maryland), North Carolina had lost all of its representation on the circuit by 2003.[3] Not until 2003, when George W. Bush nominated Allyson Duncan—an African American, moderate Republican woman—was a new federal judge from North Carolina confirmed for the Fourth Circuit bench.

Why did successive presidents from Ronald Reagan through George W. Bush find it so difficult to secure confirmation of their nominees to the Fourth Circuit and to North Carolina seats in particular? The blue slip plays a central role in explaining the fate of nominations for this bench. One of several methods of delay that can prevent nominees from securing committee hearings and floor consideration, the blue slip takes its place along with other Senate practices that devolve influence over the fate of nominees to numerous Senate players. Technically, nominations must gain the consent of a Senate majority to secure confirmation. Practically, multiple actors influence the series of decisions that lead to an up or down confirmation vote. These additional, influential senators include the members of the Senate Judiciary Committee and its chair, home state senators for the judgeship holding the blue slips, any other senator or senators seeking to place holds on nominees or to sustain a filibuster, and the majority party leader who determines whether or not to go into executive session for the full Senate's consideration of a nomination.[4] The politics of advice and consent today are shaped by these multiple potential veto points in the confirmation process.

In this chapter, we offer a historical account of the development of advice and consent. Why look backward if we care primarily about the contemporary politics of judicial selection? Myths about the Senate's constitutional origins and historical practice of advice and consent abound. Senatorial courtesy (or deference to the home state senators from the president's party) is held to have taken root in the very first Senate in 1789. Partisan scrutiny of nominations is said to be a consequence of the failed nomination of Robert Bork to the Supreme Court in 1989. Judicial filibusters are claimed to be the invention of Senate Democrats in 2003, eager to block President

George W. Bush's appointments to the appellate courts. Some argue that judicial filibusters are in fact unconstitutional. We find slim empirical support for the conventional wisdom about the history of advice and consent. Thus we offer a sketch of how advice and consent was constructed by the Framers of the U.S. Constitution and how it has evolved to place our understanding of advice and consent on firmer historical ground.

We make three key observations. First, embedded in a constitutional framework, the pathways of advice and consent involve informal Senate practices as well as formal chamber rules. Because multiple rules and practices collectively and sequentially affect the dynamics of judicial selection, Senate consideration of nominees is unlikely to take a single form over time or across nominees at a particular point in time. This evolving and complex web of potential veto points is consequential, as it spreads blocking power to multiple actors across the Senate. Moreover, because some elements of advice and consent entail informal practice—as opposed to formal standing rule—how pivotal senators interpret such practices affects other senators' strategies for treating nominees. Understanding the politics of judicial selection requires us to think broadly about the institutional framework of the Senate.

Second, although there is a partisan cast today to the treatment of judicial nominations, the pivotal players for much of the history of advice and consent have been the home state senators for each nomination. How and why home state senators secured influence over the selection and fate of nominees thus merits attention. We explore the emergence of two sources of home state senator power. First, we offer an account of the state-based design of the federal court system and assess the politics that gave rise to federal courts whose jurisdictions are contained within state boundaries. Second, we explore the adoption of the blue slip in the early twentieth century, a practice that institutionalized the Senate Judiciary Committee's consultation with home state senators as part of the process of considering nominations.

Third, we use the evolving influence of home state senators to make a broader observation about the institutional development of the Senate and potentially other legislative bodies. It is often tempting to explain the origins of Senate rules and practices by looking to the preferences of sitting senators. If we see a rule that broadly distributes influence, we typically assume that it was created to serve the chamber's commitment to individual and minority party rights. The evolution of advice and consent, however, offers a different portrait of the dynamics of institutional change. At times, institutional evolution is the unintended consequence of choices made for other reasons, as we show in explaining the adoption of the blue slip. Other times, the choice of an institutional practice is the result of bargaining and compromise, and thus it represents the constructed response of the Senate in light of disagreements about how institutional practices should work. As we show in this chapter, the idea that federal court districts should not cross state boundaries—thus making home state senators the natural arbiters of who sits on the bench—is the result of compromises secured at the Constitutional Convention and again in the first federal Congress. The story of how advice and consent has evolved raises doubts about the preordained character of judicial selection in the Senate and suggests that the practices are not set in stone; institutional reform remains a plausible possibility.

We start by exploring the design of advice and consent during the Constitutional Convention, a debate that took place even before the delegates knew what shape the future federal judiciary would take, and then we take a look at the design of the lower federal courts as conceived in the late eighteenth century. Next, we sketch the evolution of advice and consent over the course of the nineteenth century, explore the creation of the blue slip in the early twentieth century, and consider how the practice has evolved to modern times. The transformation of advice and consent during the modern period, we argue, is not just a matter of the rise of partisan divisions over the courts. It is equally a story about the ways in which inherited rules both advantage and constrain senators seeking to influence who sits on the federal bench.

Advice and Consent at the Constitutional Convention

The Framers' decisions about the process of selecting officers to fill government positions appear in Article II, section 2 of the U.S. Constitution:

> . . . and he shall nominate, and by and with the advice and consent of the Senate, shall appoint ambassadors, other public ministers and consuls, judges of the Supreme Court, and all other officers of the United States, whose appointments are not herein otherwise provided for, and which shall be established by law. . . .

We seek an understanding of the Framers' expectations for how the Senate would provide the president with advice and consent, as those expectations can serve as a baseline against which to measure the quality of advice and consent processes today. What were the intentions of the Framers in crafting the advice and consent clause? Why did the Framers design a confirmation process that vests power in both the president and the Senate? What can we discern from the record of constitutional debates about alternative methods of selecting judges and other federal officers?

Throughout this discussion, it is important to keep in mind that the Framers' debates about judicial selection in 1787 proceeded without knowing for sure whether or not there would be any federal courts other than the Supreme Court (and possibly some admiralty courts). Nor was it known at that stage whether any lower courts that might be created would be tied directly to the states. Also, inasmuch as the advice and consent clause provides an identical process for considering both judicial and executive appointments, much of the debate about advice and consent was ultimately about appointing officers generally. Although we read Article II, section 2 today knowing that a federal judiciary was created in 1789, which then evolved considerably over the course of the nineteenth century—and that the salience of federal judgeships grew considerably in the period after World War II—delegates to the convention obviously operated without a clear sense of how a national judiciary would be designed beyond the basic outline of a Supreme Court.

We begin our examination of advice and consent by dropping in on the convention's first consideration of judicial selection—debate of a proposal by Edmund Randolph of Virginia in the spring of 1787 (as part of a broader plan of government) to empower the legislature to establish "a National Judiciary."[5] The first debate and vote on the proposal were held on June 5 and ended in the rejection of Randolph's plan for legislative appointment.[6] James Wilson of Pennsylvania and James Madison both were opposed, with Wilson favoring appointment by the executive and Madison "rather inclined to give it to the Senatorial branch."[7] Both saw "intrigue and partiality" as likely components of legislative appointments, a prediction that would resurface repeatedly at the convention. Benjamin Franklin suggested that the convention consider options beyond investing the appointment power entirely in the executive or the legislature, given the importance of finding an acceptable means of selecting judges.

On this first day of debate, Madison moved to strike from Randolph's resolution the provision that the legislature appoint judges, arguing that the issue of judicial selection could be decided later "on maturer reflection." The motion passed with only two state delegations voting to retain legislative appointment: Connecticut and South Carolina.[8] That both were less populous states was no accident, as presidential selection by the Electoral College, seen by small states as adequate protection against the election of an executive solely by large-state voters, had not yet been introduced.[9] In the same debate of June 5, John Rutledge of South Carolina criticized Wilson's proposal for executive authority over appointments by warning that citizens would nearly perceive a single individual with such great power as a monarch.[10] As will become apparent, the population differences between states would have a significant impact on the debate about advice and consent.

The convention returned to judicial selection on June 13 in response to a motion by Charles Pinckney of South Carolina and seconded by Connecticut's Roger Sherman to reinvest the national legislature with appointment power. Accounts differ on whether Pinckney specified that the "second branch" of the legislature appoint judges.[11] In his debates at the convention, Madison recorded that he objected to appointment by the whole legislature and that he ultimately succeeded in having the motion withdrawn without a vote. In arguing against legislative appointment, Madison repeated his earlier objections about legislators' "partialities" and also expressed concern— for the second time, as well—that many legislators would not prove capable of properly assessing the qualifications needed to hold a judgeship. They would select, he claimed, a candidate without those qualifications over an accomplished candidate if the former were present at that moment, had proven a talented legislator, or personally had assisted the legislators.[12]

Appointment by the Senate, Madison argued, was the solution to these shortcomings. To Madison, the Senate would provide a defense against both the risk of assigning such a critical role to a single person (the executive) and the likelihood that many legislators would prove incompetent in selecting good judges. Coming from the smaller and more selective chamber of the two, Madison reasoned, senators would be more likely to make wise appointments. After Pinckney and Sherman withdrew their motion, delegates followed Madison's lead and approved appointment by the Senate on a unanimous vote.[13] There is no record of debate on the proposal, apart from

Madison's speech, nor is there any evidence of why the delegates from South Carolina and Connecticut voted in its favor.

The convention's consideration of judicial selection had not ended, however. Madison himself turned against his idea of placing appointment power in the Senate. Between the June 13 debate and the next discussion of judicial selection, most issues at the convention receded to the background as delegates negotiated the details of legislative representation. Just over a month after the vote for Senate appointment, the "Great Compromise" established the apportionment of representatives and senators by population and state, respectively. Despite its familiar name, the compromise squeaked through on a 5 to 4 vote, with many delegates from large states rejecting equal representation by state in the Senate. Afterwards, many of these same delegates, including Madison, revised or reversed their earlier position that special powers like judicial appointments should be lodged in the Senate.[14]

Debate on July 18 made apparent the impact of the Great Compromise on the earlier agreement that the Senate would choose the judges. Nathaniel Ghorum led off debate on whether judges should be appointed by the legislature's "second branch" by proposing a new mechanism for selecting judges: executive appointment "with the advice & consent of the 2d branch, in the mode prescribed by the constitution of Masts. [Massachusetts]." Massachusetts was Ghorum's home state, which he viewed as successful in choosing judges.[15] Later in the debate, Madison proposed executive appointment with a one-third vote of the Senate. Given the weak role provided here for the Senate, Madison's proposal represented a major shift from his earlier advocacy for Senate appointment as a defense against the dangers of appointment by a single executive. Although Madison argued that a one-third Senate vote would provide a sufficient check against "incautious or corrupt nomination by the Executive," gone from this speech was his earlier praise for the selective Senate as the ideal seat for the appointment power.[16] In its place, both in this debate and the next on July 21 stood a new assertion that the executive likely would select better candidates than would the Senate.

In defending his plan, Madison explicitly invoked the Great Compromise and made clear the central role it played in shaping the debates over judicial selection. Madison noted that the Senate "was very differently constituted" during the pre-compromise debates when he had proposed giving it sole appointment power. The Senate apportionment decision required, he claimed, that delegates come to another compromise between representation by the people and by the states, this time over shared powers of judicial appointment.[17] More than any other statement in the convention, Madison's brought into light the undercurrent of interstate politics that drove debates over appointment power after the Great Compromise.

Madison seems to have been trying to exploit tensions between northern and southern states in speaking for his revised plan. He warned that northern senators, who would hold a majority of seats in the Senate but represent a minority of the nation's population, could select all the judges, and "a perpetual ground of jealousy & discontent would be furnished to the Southern States."[18] The extent to which regional differences (as opposed to the differences based on state population) influenced the judicial selection debate is unclear, as no other statements of this sort were recorded. Still, Madison's statement reinforces the importance, more broadly, of interstate politics in shaping the delegates' deliberations about the proper form of the appointment power.

Both July debates and their accompanying votes suggest that interstate politics played a central, though likely not dispositive, role at this stage in the discussion of judicial selection. James Wilson and Gouverneur Morris, both of Pennsylvania, moved on July 18 that judges be appointed by the executive. The vote failed 2 to 6, with only Massachusetts and Pennsylvania, two of the more populous states, approving the measure. Nathaniel Ghorum garnered greater support for his motion that nominations be made by the executive with the advice and consent of the Senate, but even this compromise failed on a tie vote of 4 to 4. In addition to Virginia, another populous state, only Maryland joined Massachusetts and Pennsylvania in voting for the advice and consent formulation.[19]

With the convention stalemated, Madison moved that the delegates approve his plan for executive appointment with the support of one-third of the Senate.[20] After debate on the plan three days later, a vote yielded only three delegations in support—predictably, the large-state trio of Massachusetts, Pennsylvania, and Virginia—with six opposed, including Maryland, which previously had agreed to "advice and consent" and the greater role it provided for the Senate. The next vote reaffirmed the delegates' commitment to appointment by the Senate, as six of nine states elected to retain the selection mechanism originally proposed by Madison before the convention reached a decision on Senate apportionment.[21]

The two July debates included some discussion of the crucial population-based division between states, but they also illuminated the delegates' other major considerations regarding appointments. In calling for sharing the appointment between the executive and the Senate, Madison cited the major arguments made for executive appointment—"responsibility"—and legislative appointment—"security."[22] On the subject of personal responsibility, delegates repeatedly questioned whether individual legislators would be held sufficiently accountable for their appointments to the bench. Proponents of executive appointment and Ghorum, who introduced the "advice and consent" option, argued that senators would not make wise selections, as the diffusion of responsibility for appointments throughout the body would give each individual little incentive to pay careful attention to the nominees' "character." The lack of accountability also would allow senators' selfish, and even corrupt, motives to permeate the process. The executive, in contrast, would shoulder sole responsibility for his choices and would be open to public criticism.

The issue of character and fitness for the bench figured prominently in the debates as well. Delegates repeatedly asserted that one or the other branch of government would best evaluate those qualities, yet they provided little evidence to make either case. Moreover, there never even was a detailed discussion of the qualifications judges ought to have.[23] On "character," Ghorum raised the point that senators might have little interest in judicial appointments outside of their own states, making them poor judges of a candidate's character.[24] Edmund Randolph of Virginia defended senators' local attachments, claiming that selection by the Senate would help ensure a broad geographic distribution of judges, while Randolph's fellow Virginian George Mason reinforced the point by claiming that the "local & personal attachments" formed by the executive within the national capital area would give potential appointees in that region an unfair preference.[25]

In addition to considering the "responsibility" of the executive, "security" was high on many delegates' minds, some of whom expressed deep suspicion of investing such a substantial power as judicial appointments in one individual, even if he would be restrained in part by a one-third Senate vote for confirmation. Oliver Ellsworth of Connecticut feared that under such circumstances, "The Executive will be regarded by the people with a jealous eye."[26] Other delegates made more substantive critiques of strong executive power, focusing on the heightened risk of corrupt appointments made under such a system and the subsequent influence an executive might wield over judges who owed their positions solely to him. The fear of corruption ran deep at the convention. The theme of "security" also encompassed the fears of small-state delegates that an executive might make the bulk of his appointments from the more populous states. Involvement of the Senate, they believed, was critical to protecting, if not enhancing, the influence of small states and their interests in the staffing of the judicial branch.

The judicial appointment power remained vested in the Senate until nearly the end of the convention. The Committee of Eleven—formed of one delegate from each represented state to consider matters in dispute— returned to the full body on September 4 with a revised article assigning the president the authority to nominate and appoint judges "by and with the advice and consent of the Senate."[27] Three days later, after minimal debate, the convention unanimously passed the advice and consent provision for Supreme Court justices and approved by a 9 to 2 vote (with Pennsylvania and South Carolina opposed) advice and consent for "all other officers of the U.S."[28] The Constitution's final wording did not vary in its substance from the committee's version, providing for the president and the Senate to share the appointment power for (among other officers) "Judges of the supreme Court, and all other Officers of the United States, whose Appointments are not herein otherwise provided for, and which shall be established by law."[29]

As the final pair of votes makes clear, the appointments clause now separated Supreme Court justices from lower court judges, who were placed in the catchall category of "all other officers." The Committee of Eleven implicitly clarified an earlier ambiguity on this point. The July debates had not distinguished between the two levels of the judiciary, and the Committee of Detail, which met after the debates but before the Committee of Eleven, had treated the issue in two different ways over the course of its meetings.[30] As delegates ultimately left to Congress whether even to create lower courts, the convention predictably featured little discussion of how lower court judges would be selected. The final constitutional text leaves little doubt, though, that all federal judges, whether on the Supreme Court or lower courts, must be appointed by the president with the Senate's advice and consent.

The significant shift late in the convention from Senate appointment, which the delegates had approved on a 6 to 3 vote, to an "advice and consent" structure begs explanation. Unfortunately, the historical record is quite thin on this point. The Committee of Eleven did not keep a record of its proceedings, which were conducted in secret.[31] Compromises on a range of issues were made during this period, most likely between the more and less populous states given the convention's pattern of negotiations. Most likely, the decision of the Great Compromise that turned the Senate from an upper chamber based on population (as conceived in Madison's Virginia Plan) to one based on equal state representation altered Madison's and other large state delegates' views of the Senate and its special powers.[32] Once states gained an equal footing in the Senate, the independence and national perspective that Madison intended for the Senate were undermined. Not surprisingly then, his support for Senate control of judicial appointments was undermined as well.

The only direct evidence of how the Committee of Eleven reached its decision comes from Gouverneur Morris, the sole member of the committee to speak during the September 7 debate on the revised appointments clause. (James Wilson, Charles Pinckney, and Elbridge Gerry expressed their opposition to advice and consent during this discussion, but none were members of the Committee of Eleven.[33]) Echoing the major arguments made throughout the convention for executive or legislative appointment, Morris stated that "as the President was to nominate, there would be responsibility, and as the Senate was to concur, there would be security. As Congress now make [*sic*] appointments there is no responsibility."[34] No further debate was recorded before votes were taken.

As Morris gave the only statement on judicial appointments by a member of the Committee of Eleven, his word must be given substantial weight in determining the role that the committee—and, by extension, the Constitutional Convention—intended the president and the Senate to play in the appointments process.[35] By providing a clear rationale for involving both branches, Morris seemed to indicate that he envisioned a substantive role in the process for the Senate, which would not serve merely as a rubber stamp for the president's nominees. When delegates returned home to lobby for the new Constitution's ratification, they seemed to suggest the same.[36] Moreover, it would be difficult to square a weak Senate role with the convention's repeated earlier decisions to give the power of appointments entirely to one or both legislative chambers. Such a complete turnaround would be highly improbable. We can also infer from the Committee of Eleven's decision to increase the threshold of Senate consent from Madison's one-third to the implied majority vote that more than a token expression of Senate support was intended to be secured by the president. By the same token, we can infer that the lower threshold for judicial appointments compared with that for treaties reflected the delegates' different views of the types of interests at play in treaty deliberations in contrast to the selection of judges. Of course, it could also be that the requirement for a majority of the Senate to confirm a nominee was pitched as a compromise between Madison's one-third threshold and the two-thirds threshold elsewhere in Article II.

With a reasonable degree of certainty, then, we can conclude from the constitutional text that emerged from the Committee of Eleven, from Morris's speech on its behalf, from delegates' earlier votes during the convention, and from their later statements during the ratification debates, that the Senate was to play a central role in judicial appointments at least by defending against presidential corruption and abuse of power. The delegates' intentions are clear, even if we cannot with certainty re-create the set of compromises that led them to agree to embed a shared power of judicial appointments in the Constitution. Most important, the provision for advice and consent was itself emblematic of the compromises forged in Philadelphia, many of them evolving in response to the delegates' other compromises over the essential structure of Congress and the new American system.

Constructing the Federal Courts

Delegates to the convention also confronted the issue of what a potential federal court system might look like, although they left much of the design of a judiciary to the new government they were constructing. The Framers wrote into Article III, section 1, a bare outline for the structure of a federal judiciary: "The judicial Power of the United States, shall be vested in one supreme Court, and in such inferior Courts as the Congress may from time to time ordain and establish." The Framers agreed quite readily to the establishment of an independent judiciary whose powers would be exercised by the Supreme Court and to life tenure for federal judges, while the establishment and jurisdiction of lower federal courts were far more controversial at the convention. At issue—in the most general of terms—was whether to create additional federal courts and, if so, what the jurisdictions of such courts would be.

Delegates who preferred a stronger national role for the new government—most notably James Madison of Virginia—supported a system of inferior courts with broad jurisdiction. States-rights delegates led by Roger Sherman of Connecticut, who feared the centralization of power beyond state control, argued for a more limited federal judicial power so that the power of state courts could be preserved and strengthened.[37] Madison's position prevailed, however. Congress was empowered in Article III to create lower courts if it saw fit and to specify their jurisdiction within limits prescribed in the Constitution. Moreover, in theory at least, a broad scope of judicial power was authorized in Article III for the inferior courts that Congress might subsequently create. Whether and when the lower courts might accrue such jurisdiction, however, would depend on decisions made by Congress after ratification of the Constitution.

The constitutional debate over the desirability of a national judiciary continued when the first Congress convened and began work on what would become the Federal Judiciary Act of 1789. That act is best conceived as a compromise between state-centered legislators who saw no need for inferior courts (other than admiralty courts) and nation-focused Federalists who did not want to see national judicial power arbitrated in state courts.[38] The solution in the 1789 act was to create a system of lower courts that ran parallel to existing state courts. The act created thirteen judicial districts and located eleven of them within one of three circuits. Each district was composed of a minor trial court known as the district court that was to be staffed with a part-time district court judge. A major trial court known as the circuit court met in each district of the circuit and was staffed by the district court judge and two Supreme Court justices "riding circuit." In other words, unlike the courts of appeals—which were not created until the Evarts Act of 1891—the original circuit courts were trial courts and had no judges of their own. The Evarts Act created the courts of appeals, which redirected the appellate caseload burden away from the Supreme Court and assigned it to the new courts of appeals that were to be staffed with full-time appellate judges.

Debates about the structure of the courts extended to the jurisdiction to be granted to the lower federal courts. Anti-Federalists preferred to leave trial adjudication to the states, limiting federal jurisdiction to questions arising from admiralty law and treaties. Federalists preferred to fully empower the inferior courts with the authorities elaborated in Article III of the Constitution, including diversity jurisdiction (generally speaking, jurisdiction over cases that arise between citizens of different states) and a general jurisdiction over federal questions (that is, questions that arose in legal disputes over the application of the federal Constitution and statutes). Anti-Federalists succeeded in limiting the lower courts' jurisdiction, largely requiring cases arising under the interpretation of the Constitution or federal law to be filed in state courts. Indeed, it was not until 1875 that Congress would create general federal law jurisdiction for the federal courts.[39] Instead, in 1789 Congress allowed for only limited diversity jurisdiction for the federal circuit courts and jurisdiction over admiralty and minor civil and criminal cases for the district courts.

For understanding the development of advice and consent, perhaps the most important decision made in the Federal Judiciary Act pertained to the structure of the lower federal courts. By aligning the boundaries of the new federal judicial districts with state lines and by requiring that district judges reside in their states and that the courts follow state procedural rules unless they conflicted with federal law, the act in effect ensured that the lower federal courts would be largely creatures of the politics and legal culture of the states in which they were located.[40] As historians of the federal judiciary have noted, Congress could have devised an alternative structure that might have attenuated the connections of the states and the federal courts. Consider, for example, the effort of the Federalists in passing the ill-fated Judiciary Act of 1801—soon thereafter repealed by the victorious Jeffersonians. In drafting the initial version of their bill, Federalists expanded the number of circuit courts, allowed for the appointment of circuit court judgeships (rather than the assignment of Supreme Court justices "riding circuit"), and, most important in this context, created a system of judicial districts whose boundaries bore no relation to state lines.

Had the Federalist plan succeeded, the practices of advice and consent might have evolved differently. Unbound to state lines, the practice of judicial selection might have produced a much diminished role for particular

senators. Without a clearly designated set of home state senators, no senator or senators would naturally have been able to lay claim to the right to be
involved in selection of judges for particular openings on the federal bench.
That is speculation of course, but the broader point is important. The whole
idea of the involvement of home state senators for judicial vacancies is a consequence of political compromises made at the outset in the creation of the
federal judiciary. Moreover, over two centuries later, it reflects the staying
power of the ideas of the anti-Federalists and others who challenged Madison's design for the new national locus of political power. Although the
broad scope and independence of the federal judiciary today certainly look
little like the vision held by the anti-Federalists, these Framers' imprint on
judicial selection was long lasting.

Advice and Consent in the Nineteenth Century

Perhaps not surprisingly, little has been written about the lower federal
courts in the early nineteenth century. No doubt, the extremely restricted
jurisdiction of the courts and the small role of the federal government before
the Civil War together limited the role of the federal courts in economic,
political, and social life. Most important, the federal courts lacked broad
authority to hear "federal question" suits until 1875, meaning that conflicts
over federal law were heard in state courts and litigants had limited ability
to remove their cases into federal courts. Although the Supreme Court's
Swift v. *Tyson* decision in 1842 allowed federal courts to create a federal
common law when hearing diversity cases—a decision not overruled until
1938—the legal doctrine in *Swift* was applied primarily to questions of commercial law in the antebellum period.[41] Only after the Civil War did the
courts broaden the range of federal law for which federal judges were freed
from the constraints of local and state law. Before the Civil War, "the perceived utility of federal judicial power," Howard Gillman observes, "was very
issue-specific, and all antebellum efforts to expand the general significance
and power of federal courts in the political system were ignored or
rebuffed."[42]

In a legal culture that favored state adjudication of disputes and an institutional context that limited the involvement (and therefore the dockets) of
federal courts, judicial selection in the antebellum period rarely elicited

much attention or conflict. Given the size of the federal bench in this era, and given that the circuit courts were staffed until 1891 primarily by circuit-riding Supreme Court justices, the Senate considered relatively few nominations each Congress.[43] To reconstruct the historical record of judicial selection, we turned to the *Senate Executive Journals* that record for each Congress the actions of the Senate on nominations. From 1789 until the onset of the Civil War in the Thirty-seventh Congress (1861–62), 159 nominations were submitted to the Senate for U.S. district court judgeships, or less than one nominee per year.[44] Recorded roll call votes on nominations in the antebellum period were also rare; the Senate conducted just thirteen floor votes on those district court nominations, in other words subjecting less than 10 percent of total nominations before the war to a recorded vote.[45]

Although recorded votes were infrequent, relatively few nominations were made overall, and the jurisdictions of the trial courts were clipped, it would be a mistake to interpret the historical record of judicial selection as completely devoid of conflict. As suggested in figure 2-1, conflict over judges varied during the nineteenth century, with John Quincy Adams and the presidents before the Civil War encountering rougher sledding. Still, 92 percent of the district court nominees were confirmed during the antebellum period, a rate that essentially remained unchanged over the subsequent eight decades.

Given the low salience and size of the federal court dockets before the Civil War, one might surmise that presidents typically deferred to the views of home state senators in selecting nominees for judgeships in their states. Such a pattern might help account for the generally high confirmation success for appointees in this era. Indeed, the conventional wisdom about judicial selection points to the almost overnight emergence of *senatorial courtesy*—the expectation that senators would support a colleague who objected to an appointment to a federal office in his state, assuming that the president and the senator were from the same party. Although presidential deference to interested senators and to senatorial courtesy are not strictly the same thing, a strong norm of senatorial courtesy would enhance the influence of home state senators when dealing with the president over the selection of appointees. If a president knows that other senators will defer to the views of the home state senators from the president's party, his ability to secure controversial appointments is diminished.

Figure 2-1. *Percentage of Nominations to the Lower Federal Courts That Failed, by Congress, 1789–1946*[a]

Percent

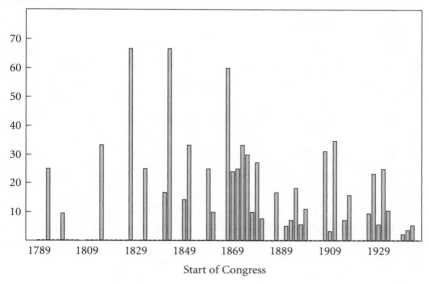

Start of Congress

Source: Codebooks of Senate roll call votes for each Congress from 1789 to 1946 (http://vote view.com).

a. Data include nominations to the U.S. district courts (1789–1946), U.S. circuit courts (1801–1890), and U.S. courts of appeals (1891–1946).

The received wisdom about senatorial courtesy merits closer attention. Almost every account of senatorial courtesy places its origins in the very first Congress and points to the failed nomination of Benjamin Fishbourn.[46] President George Washington had nominated Fishbourn for the post of a naval officer at the Port of Savannah. Fishbourn was said to be superbly qualified for the position, and yet the Senate rejected the nomination—reportedly as a courtesy to Georgia's two senators who opposed confirming Fishbourn. The next day, Washington withdrew Fishbourn's nomination, instead selecting the preferred candidate of the two Georgia senators—early evidence of the prominence of senatorial courtesy in the practice of advice and consent.

Still, there is slim evidence for the opposition of the Georgia senators, William Few and James Gunn, to the appointment.[47] Moreover, Few and

Gunn were aligned with the anti-administration faction, and thus they could hardly represent a case of presidential deference to home state senators from the president's party. And yet, the account of the Fishbourn nomination has taken on legendary status in Senate lore. To be sure, Senate histories by Joseph Harris in 1953 and Clara Kerr in 1895 suggested that the application of senatorial courtesy was uneven for the rest of Washington's presidency. But most accounts, including theirs, still assume that senatorial courtesy was inscribed in Senate practice in the first Congress and soon thereafter sealed into Senate norms.[48]

Our sense is that senatorial courtesy had a much rockier foundation than Senate lore suggests. The most extensive historical treatment of judicial selection, written by Kermit Hall, raises doubts about the strength of senatorial courtesy before the Civil War.[49] As President Andrew Jackson once noted, "[I] regretted in [my] nominations, to have to differ with Senators of a State." But, as Hall relates, Jackson felt that "duty often compelled such action."[50] Presidential resistance to the Senate continued episodically well into the 1850s, with senatorial courtesy, according to Hall, only taking root after the emergence of well-defined Democratic and Republican parties after the Civil War.

The roll call record for nominations in the antebellum period provides some evidence of the Senate's uneven deference to the preferences of the home state senators from the president's party for vacant judgeships in their states. One case from Andrew Jackson's presidency is particularly illustrative. Only one of Jackson's eighteen nominations to the U.S. district courts was rejected. The nomination was killed by recorded vote in May 1834, when the Senate voted on a resolution to appoint Benjamin Tappan to a judgeship in the Ohio Federal District Court after the expiration of Tappan's recess appointment.[51] Eleven Democrats voted in favor, with three defecting to join the anti-Jackson Whigs in opposition. In this case, despite the support of a Democratic senator from Ohio for Tappan's appointment, Senate Democrats—as well as the Senate opposition—were unwilling to defer to the interests of the home state senator. To be sure, senatorial courtesy explicitly refers to the Senate's unwillingness to buck a fellow senator who states his or her objection to a nominee. But surely senatorial courtesy demands that when a home state senator from the president's party advocates confirmation, the rest of the Senate should defer to the interested home state partisan. Although lore places the roots of senatorial courtesy in 1789, it seems clear that it was not uniformly accepted nearly half a century later.

We see similar problems twelve years later during the administration of President James Polk over the nomination of John Kane for a judgeship on the federal District Court for Eastern Pennsylvania. In this case, although the president prevailed on a floor vote confirming Kane's appointment, the vote again showed significant party fissures.[52] This time, one Whig joined twenty-seven Democrats voting to confirm Kane, but five Democrats defected to join eighteen Whigs to oppose the appointment. One of the five dissenting Democrats was the home state senator of the president's party, Simon Cameron (D-Pa.). Despite Cameron's plea to his colleagues to reject Polk's appointment, senatorial courtesy was clearly not strong enough to induce senators to defer to the expressed interests of the home state senator from the president's party. Refusal of the opposition party to support Cameron's views also suggests the weakness of senatorial courtesy as a chamber practice at that time. Granted, most nominations did not move to a recorded vote. But if senatorial courtesy worked as seamlessly as commonly believed, recorded votes should be even rarer than the three dozen votes we observe before the modern period.

The fitful development of senatorial courtesy was accompanied by variation in the criteria used by presidents to select appointees.[53] Certainly personal relationships, family ties, and party support came to influence presidents in choosing nominees. But presidents were also clearly considering potential judges' policy views when making choices for the federal bench—even with the relatively constrained jurisdictions of these trial courts. Given the interest in potential judges' views about the constitutionality of a national bank, the concern about the treatment of bankruptcy petitions after Congress granted bankruptcy jurisdiction to the federal district courts around the time of the Panic of 1837, considerations about the enforcement of the Fugitive Slave Act and the subsequent *Dred Scott* case, presidents in the antebellum period appear to have queried their potential appointees on their views on these and other salient issues. Despite the low profile and limited dockets of federal judges, their decisions on these issues—particularly the treatment of slaves in the states and the territories before statehood—had immediate policy consequences and political ramifications in the antebellum period.

Over the course of the two decades after the Civil War, a transformation of the federal courts took place. Republican Congresses during Reconstruction expanded the diversity jurisdiction of the federal courts and enlarged the power of litigants to remove cases from the state courts into federal courts. At first, such efforts to enhance the reach of the federal courts were aimed primarily at providing more neutral ground for litigation over Freedmens' rights and the protection of federal officers in the South.[54] By the mid-1870s, however, Republicans' incentives to increase litigants' removal powers were fueled more heavily by the party's ties to economic interests and the incentive to protect corporate interests in the East from unfriendly juries and judges in the South and West when debtors tried to sue industrial and banking interests in state courts. The Judiciary and Removal Act of 1875 cemented the expanded power of the federal courts, as it ensured that civil litigation involving national commercial interests could be removed from state courts to federal courts. Although Democrats attempted to curtail the expanded federal judicial powers, they were ultimately limited by the persistence of divided party government and the frequent turnover in control of the chambers of Congress and the White House at the end of the nineteenth century.[55]

The growing importance of the courts can be seen in their expansion during and after the Civil War. Between 1861 and 1890 (before the courts of appeals were created by the Evarts Act in 1891), the Senate considered 134 district court nominations—roughly five nominations per year and a five-fold increase over the nominations during the antebellum period. Creation of new judgeships for the circuit court trial courts in 1869 further expanded the federal bench, with twenty-seven such nominations considered by the Senate after the antebellum era.[56]

Between 1891 and 1946, the Senate considered a total of 679 nominations—roughly twelve nominations each year—including 492 nominations to the district courts and 187 nominations to the new U.S. courts of appeals.[57] Still, despite the expansion and growing salience of the federal courts, presidential success in securing confirmation of their appointees remained pretty much unchanged after the Civil War—averaging over 90 percent for both trial court and the new appellate court nominees between 1890 and the end of World War II. Nor did confirmation rates vary with much predictability, showing similar levels of success between periods of unified and divided control (this is not surprising given how seldom divided government occurred at the turn of the century and through the world wars).

It would be a mistake, however, to conclude that judicial selection remained a story of senatorial deference to the president during this long period. If we isolate the period of a highly competitive two-party system from the late 1860s through the realignment of 1896 that secured a robust Republican majority, confirmation failure for all lower court nominations averaged roughly 15 percent over a thirty-year period (1867–96), which is similar to overall rates of confirmation failure for the period since the 1970s. Senate scrutiny of presidential appointments is clearly not a modern phenomenon, even if we see only isolated episodes of Senate challenge of judicial nominations before the contemporary period. As the federal courts became central players in sustaining Republicans' political and policy agendas during the latter half of the nineteenth century, not surprisingly we see their party's nominees receive more scrutiny—and face tougher sledding—when sent up to the Senate for confirmation.[58] Derailing a president's nominees is hardly a modern phenomenon.

Why Create a Blue Slip?

Perhaps the most striking—if not puzzling—development in the history of advice and consent is the adoption of the blue slip practice by the Senate Judiciary Committee. To understand why the adoption of the blue slip strikes us as puzzling, consider the mechanics of the blue slip today. Each time a president makes an appointment to the lower federal bench, the Senate refers the nomination to the Senate Judiciary Committee. The panel's counsel then sends a blue slip to each of the two home state senators for the nomination. Literally a blue sheet of paper, the blue slip asks each home state senator for his or her opinion regarding the nominee. A senator who signs and returns the blue slip with an endorsement signals the senator's support for the nominee. Returning the slip with a note objecting to the nominee or failing to return the blue slip signals the senator's intention to oppose the nominee. Because the chair of the Judiciary panel has historically heeded the views of the home state senators, scholars of judicial selection have come to share the views of Judiciary Committee staff, who in 1979 argued that the blue slip was a mechanism for "institutionalizing senatorial courtesy within the [Judiciary] committee as an automatic and mechanical one-member veto over nominees."[59]

Numerous students of judicial nominations have relied upon this characterization of the blue slip, arguing that the blue slip institutionalized senatorial courtesy by creating a routine practice for soliciting the views of home state senators during the confirmation process.[60] But the blue slip did more than institutionalize senatorial courtesy: it transformed it in two important ways. First, the blue slip today empowers home state senators regardless of party. No more could senators from the president's party—under the guise of senatorial courtesy—hold disproportionate influence over the fate of nominees.[61] As Joseph Harris notes in his history of advice and consent, there was at best "uneven extension" of the norm to opposition party senators—not surprising given that there was no expectation that such senators would be afforded the opportunity for patronage.[62]

Allowing opposition party senators to weigh in on judicial nominations is puzzling, as the blue slip potentially undercuts the privileged role of the president's partisans in shaping the selection and confirmation of new federal judges in their states. Moreover, the blue slip today increases the influence of the opposition party regardless of whether party control of the White House and Senate is unified or divided. In periods of divided control, the blue slip provides a veto tool that opposition party senators can use to block nominees they oppose. In periods of unified control, opposition party senators may still exploit the blue slip to slow down the confirmation of nominees they might oppose. Given the value of senatorial courtesy to home state partisans of the president, it seems especially puzzling that the blue slip would have been extended to senators of both political parties.[63]

The blue slip transformed senatorial courtesy in a second way as well. Senatorial courtesy is typically conceived of as an informal norm of deference within the Senate chamber.[64] In contrast, the blue slip leaves a paper trail. By creating the blue slip practice, the views of home state senators became known in writing to the Judiciary Committee chair and his panel colleagues, and by extension to the home state senators' chamber colleagues. By creating a routine paper trail of correspondence between the committee chair and the home state senators, the blue slip altered the flow of information—reducing uncertainty about the nominee's confirmation prospects. It also reshaped senators' expectations regarding the confirmation of federal judges.

Senators came to expect that their objections to nominees recorded via the blue slip would be heeded by their chamber colleagues. In short, by creating the blue slip, senators manufactured a potential veto tool for home state senators regardless of whether or not they hailed from the president's party. The story of the inability of successive presidents to confirm new judges to the Fourth Circuit in the 1980s and 1990s attests to the power of ideological foes of the president to use the blue slip to block nominees they oppose.

If the blue slip can be exploited by ideological foes of the president and his party, particularly in periods of divided government, why did the Senate transform senatorial courtesy in this way? This is both a theoretical question about the forces that bring change in political institutions and an empirical question about the development of advice and consent practices in the Senate. We consider four potential explanations that might account for the adoption of the blue slip. We then turn to the historical record to uncover the creation of the blue slip and to determine the fit of the competing accounts to the origins of this Senate practice.

Competing Accounts

The first account suggests that institutional choices reflect short-term instrumental action of players seeking political advantage. According to this view, the blue slip was the brain child of senators seeking to increase their leverage over the selection of judges in their home states. Because senators from the president's party could rely upon senatorial courtesy, we would expect the blue slip to be an invention of opposition party senators in a period of divided government. Controlling the Senate, the opposition party might have created the blue slip to intentionally undercut senatorial courtesy, allowing the opposition party during divided government to challenge the president over the makeup of the bench. The limitation of this account, however, is that it cannot explain why the blue slip would have been extended to senators of both political parties. If the intention was to challenge the influence of the president's party over the bench by undercutting senatorial courtesy, dealing in the president's partisans in the Senate minority party would make little sense.

The second account suggests that politicians might consider their long-term parliamentary needs, rather than their immediate short-term interests, in choosing the rules of advice and consent. To be sure, scholars who have studied the extension of procedural rights in the House of Representatives to minority party members have found little support for models in which legislators alter the rules in anticipation of their future parliamentary status.[65] Given uncertainty about the future, actors are likely to discount that future and thus make choices about institutions based on short-term distributional advantage.[66] And unless both parties can make credible commitments to protect such rights in the future, current majorities cannot count on the protection of new rights.

Still, given the broad and lasting impact of federal judges with life tenure, senators might think about their future needs in designing the practice of advice and consent. If so, and given a moderate level of uncertainty about whether or how long their party will control the Senate, we might expect majority party senators to create and give blue slips to both majority and minority party senators. Granting blue slips to the minority would serve the current majority's longer-term influence over the makeup of the bench, should the majority lose control of the chamber. Thinking prospectively about the rules of advice and consent might make sense in the Senate given senators' six-year terms and the life tenure of federal judges. Both of these two accounts in sum paint the blue slip as a consequence of interparty competition over the makeup of the bench, predicting the creation of the blue slip in a period of divided government.

The third account suggests that intraparty differences may have motivated adoption of the blue slip. President Theodore Roosevelt, for example, in making an appointment to the Seventh Circuit Court of Appeals in 1901 took sides in a dispute between the two Indiana senators (Albert Beveridge and Charles Fairbanks). Representing opposing factions in the Indiana Republican party, the senators advocated competing candidates for the vacant judgeship.[67] Roosevelt selected the candidate of the senator more closely aligned with himself, rejecting the candidate of the senator aligned with one of Roosevelt's potential challengers. Intraparty disputes also arise over policy. Disagreements between Woodrow Wilson and midwestern Democratic senators arose, for example, over appointments to fill appellate court vacancies when senators preferred candidates who lacked progressive credentials.[68] Wilson routinely selected the nominee with the best record on progressive issues, including salient labor and antitrust issues of the early twentieth century.[69]

Under this account, the blue slip might have been the institutional response of senators seeking to make their party's president more responsive to their interests during periods of unified party control. Instead of undercutting senatorial courtesy, senators might have intended to improve it. Creating a formal paper trail of senators' views about nominees, the blue slip would allow senators to expand the scope of conflict over disputed nominees. Rather than confining the disagreement to a senator and the president's staff, the blue slip would have been a means for, in E. E. Schattschneider's terms, socializing conflict over judicial vacancies.[70] Senators from the "wrong" state party faction might have envisioned the blue slip as a means of increasing the visibility of their objections to appointees supported by their own party's president or by the other home state senator from the president's party. Still, the intraparty account has a hard time explaining why the blue slip was granted to the minority party if the majority's goal was to enhance their fellow Senate partisans' influence over White House selections.

The fourth account conceptualizes the blue slip as a mechanism of agenda control in the Senate. Before the advent of the blue slip, given the informality of senatorial courtesy and its applicability only to senators from the president's party, there was no guarantee that a senator's views about a nominee would be known to the Senate Judiciary Committee chair or the party leader before a nomination was considered on the Senate floor. Moreover, the lack of a majority cloture rule—let alone any cloture rule before 1917—left Senate leaders vulnerable to obstruction by the opposing party when calling up nominees on the Senate floor.

After advent of the blue slip, senators were forced to reveal their positions early in the Senate's consideration of a nomination. By creating a paper trail that revealed the preferences of the home state senators—regardless of party—the blue slip altered the flow of information and reduced uncertainty about the nominee's confirmation prospects. Blue slips revealing senators' opposition enabled the Judiciary chair to avoid potentially costly legislative battles—costly to the president seeking to fill the bench, costly to the president's party seeking to keep peace in the family, and costly to the Senate party and committee leaders seeking to protect their institutional reputations by managing the uncertainty inherent in legislative life. Given the potential of nominations to trigger filibuster fights and the potential for senators to take other legislative measures hostage to gain leverage against a confirmation, a premium would be placed on reducing uncertainty about a nominee's prospects before expending resources and time on a potentially risky appointee.

For the blue slip to reflect an innovation of committee or party leaders seeking to improve their management of the Senate's executive session, the practice would have been created during a period of unified party control. Presumably chamber leaders would primarily want to reduce uncertainty about the prospects of confirmation when their own party controlled the White House. Given that senatorial courtesy would mean that most of those nominees would be the choice of the president's partisans, the blue slip only makes sense as a product of unified government. Moreover, we might also expect under this account that the blue slip would be offered to members of the opposition party (namely, the minority party during a period of unified control). Extending the blue slip to minority party senators would grant the majority an early warning to flag contested nominees—a tool that the inherited practice of senatorial courtesy would not have provided. Most important, if inventers of the blue slip only intended to increase information flow about pending nominations, offering a blue slip to minority party senators was unlikely to have been considered a new procedural right for the minority. Transformation of the blue slip into a veto power for the minority would thus be a future and unintended consequence of an effort to improve control of the agenda.

Archival Evidence

With these four potential accounts of why the blue slip might have been created, we turn to the history of the blue slip. Existing treatments of judicial selection often note the existence of the blue slip practice, but none provides an account of why the practice was created. Nor do such accounts tell us much about when it was adopted. Joseph Harris's 1953 treatise on senatorial courtesy makes no reference to the blue slip. Nor does Harold Chase's 1972 examination of judicial selection.[71] Among the few who have examined the use of the blue slip, little is said about its origins.

One scholar who has dated the origins of the blue slip suggests that it was invented in the early 1950s, but he provides no supporting evidence.[72] The chair of the Senate Judiciary Committee at that time was Senator James Eastland (D-Miss.), but empirical support for Eastland's role in creating the blue slip is slim. Except for a single reference in a Judiciary Committee staff study in 1979, we find no evidence of Eastland's hand in its creation. According to that staff report, "the blue slip has been used for over 25 years, according to former committee staff members."[73] Simple arithmetic leads to the conclusion that the process was created around 1954, just before Eastland took control of the committee in 1956.

Coverage of judicial nominations in the *New York Times* and *Washington Post* raises doubts about the 1950s genesis of the blue slip. Granted, the first explicit reference to the blue slip does not appear until 1967, when Senator Jacob Javits (R-N.Y.) held up a judicial nominee who had been recommended by his fellow New York senator, Robert F. Kennedy. "Senator Javits said in an interview," the *Times* reported, "that he had not returned the so-called 'blue slip'—the required form stating that he has no objections to the nomination—to the Senate Judiciary Committee."[74] In the 1940s, however, *Washington Post* coverage of Senator Wilbert (Pappy) O'Daniel's (D-Tex.) opposition to a Roosevelt judicial nominee notes that O'Daniel "returned to the Judiciary Committee the formal notification it sends all senators who might be interested in nominations, with this single notation: 'This nomination is obnoxious to me.'"[75] This suggests that the use of blue slips predates the 1950s.[76]

To identify the origins of the blue slip, we use the archival records of the Senate Judiciary Committee.[77] Available in the committee papers at the National Archives are notes from committee business meetings, the committee's executive dockets, and nomination files for individuals referred to the committee before 1956.[78] The committee meeting notes reveal nothing about the committee's decision to create the blue slip. Nor do the nomination files appear to be reliable for dating the origins of the blue slip. Although the first evidence of the use of blue slips appears in the nomination files for the Sixty-fifth Congress (1917–19), the executive docket books suggest that the blue slip practice was already in place by that time.[79]

Extending from the Thirty-ninth Congress (1865) through the Seventy-seventh (1943), the committee's executive docket books track the passage of nominations into and out of the committee and typically record the final confirmation outcome. According to the docket books, it appears that the practice of soliciting the views of home state senators, recording their stated reasons for supporting or opposing the nominee, and noting the dates on

Figure 2-2. *Executive Docket, Senate Judiciary Committee, 63rd Congress, 1913–15*

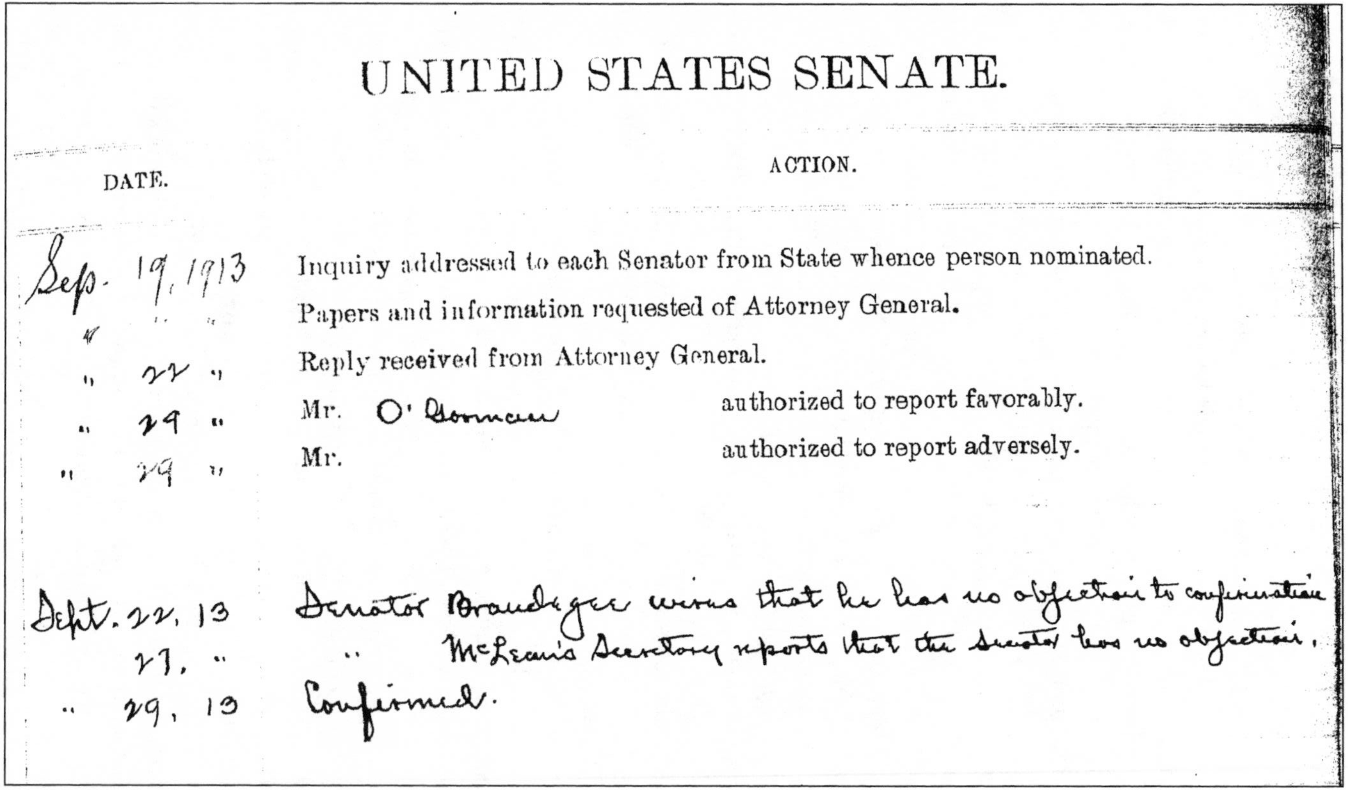

UNITED STATES SENATE.

DATE.	ACTION.
Sep. 19, 1913	Inquiry addressed to each Senator from State whence person nominated.
" 22 "	Papers and information requested of Attorney General.
" 29 "	Reply received from Attorney General.
" 3? "	Mr. O'Donnell authorized to report favorably.
	Mr. authorized to report adversely.
Sept. 22, 13	Senator Brandegee wires that he has no objection to confirmation
" 27, "	" McLean's Secretary reports that the Senator has no objection.
" 29, 13	Confirmed.

which senators were contacted by and responded to the committee became routine in 1913 at the start of the Sixty-third Congress. On the left-hand side of each page of the docket book, the committee clerk pasted in a pretyped strip of paper copying the *Senate Executive Journal* notice that a nominee for a federal judgeship had been referred to the committee. The docket also shows the appointment of a subcommittee to review the nomination. On the right-hand side of each docket book page (see figure 2-2), another pretyped form is pasted into the book with space left for indicating the dates on which home state senators were consulted ("Inquiry addressed to each Senator from State whence person nominated"), the attorney general was contacted ("Papers and information requested of Attorney General"), the committee and chamber acted, and the home state senators responded. The docket also records the reactions of the senators to the nominee.

Examination of the complete series of docket books reveals that the process of consulting with home state senators (regardless of party) and documenting the dates and content of their responses was routinized beginning in 1913. Starting in the late 1890s, the docket books periodically record that the home state senators had been contacted about a nomination, but senators' views and responses were not uniformly solicited and documented until 1913. Because the committee regularly solicited the views of the attorney general before 1913 (and recorded such action in its docket book), it is unlikely that regular reporting of senators' blue slip responses in 1913 was simply an artifact of better record keeping by a new and more fastidious clerk. Before 1913, the clerks were already recording the transmittal of papers between the attorney general and the committee.

The blue slips recovered from the nomination files of the Sixty-fifth Congress provide a glimpse of the likely format of the Sixty-third Congress blue slips (see figure 2-3).[80] The appointee was George W. Jack, nominated by President Woodrow Wilson on March 8, 1917, to fill a vacancy on the federal District Court for Western Louisiana. Soliciting the views of the two Democratic senators from Louisiana, Robert Broussard and Joseph Ransdell, the committee sent each of the home state senators a blue slip signed by the panel chair, Charles Culberson (D-Tex.), on March 9, 1917. The preprinted form (with blank space left for the committee clerk to type the name, judgeship, and departing judge) asked "Will you kindly give me, for the use of the Committee, your opinion and information concerning the nomination of . . . ." Both

Figure 2-3. *First Surviving Senate Blue Slip, 65th Congress, 1917*

UNITED STATES SENATE
COMMITTEE ON THE JUDICIARY.

March 9, 1917.

Sir:

Will you kindly give me, for the use of the Committee, your opinion and information concerning the nomination of George W. Jack, of Shreveport, Louisiana, to be United States district judge, western district of Louisiana, vice Aleck Boarman, deceased.

Respectfully,

[signature]

Chairman.

Hon. ROBERT F. BROUSSARD,

U. S. Senate.

REPLY:

March 10th, 1917.

The appointment of Mr. George W. Jack as U. S. Dist. Judge for the Western District of Louisiana is entirely satisfactory. An early favorable report will be greatly appreciated

[signature]

senators returned positive endorsements on March 10. "The appointment of George W. Jack," Senator Broussard noted for the committee, "is entirely satisfactory. An early favorable report will be greatly appreciated."[81] The committee swiftly heeded Broussard's request, reporting Jack's nomination favorably on March 14, with Senate confirmation following on March 16.

Why 1913?

Why 1913? It was a pivotal year for the Democratic Party, having won back control of the Senate and control of the White House in 1912 in a three-way race against Old Guard Republican William Taft and Bull Moose Teddy Roosevelt. With Democrats winning the House, Senate, and White House in the 1912 elections, 1913 marked the first year of unified Democratic control of government since 1895. A full slate of progressive issues topped the Democrats' agenda after eighteen years of Republican rule, including reform of the tariff, currency, and antitrust laws. Progressives also took aim at the federal courts, after the Republican Party's successful transformation of the federal courts during the previous five decades into a bastion of conservative economic nationalism.[82]

Given the electoral context of unified party control, we can safely reject the two potential accounts that mark the blue slip as a product of interparty competition during a period of divided party government. The blue slip does not appear to have been created by a majority party intent on undermining an oppositional White House's control of judicial selection. The blue slip today provides the opposition party with a tool for diluting the president's influence over the selection of nominees for the bench, but partisan intentions could not have motivated Wilson's Democratic majority when they took office in 1913. Nor does it appear that the blue slip was an invention of an opposition party seeking to prepare for its parliamentary future once it lost control of the Senate. To be sure, the Senate Democratic majority was slim after the 1912 elections—holding fifty-one of the chamber's ninety-six seats. But an account predicated on interparty competition leading a tenuous majority to make plans for its future parliamentary needs is not a good fit for an innovation created in a period of unified control.

Given the appearance of the blue slip in a period of unified government, we need to take a closer look at the fit of the two accounts in which institutional innovation is not predicated on competitive party pressures. We consider first the account that suggests intraparty divisions may have motivated factions to institutionalize home state senators' role in the confirmation process and then turn to the final account predicated on the desire of leaders to reduce uncertainty about outcomes when the Senate went into executive session to consider confirmation of the president's judicial appointments.

Wilson and Democratic Factions

There is not much evidence to suggest that intraparty rivalries motivated Democrats to create the blue slip in 1913. In fact, numerous developments in 1913 signaled Senate Democrats' willingness to coalesce behind Wilson. The new president was aggressively setting the agenda, using his constitutional power to call Congress immediately into special session after inauguration in 1913. The Senate Democratic Caucus that year returned to its occasional practice of designating binding caucus votes upon a two-thirds vote of the caucus, and Democrats for the first time in 1913 designated their new caucus leader, John Kern (D-Ind.), as the majority leader and created a party whip position.[83] Given the electoral imperative of holding the Democratic Party together and expanding its base in anticipation of the presidential election in 1916, we would not expect Democrats to adopt new practices that intentionally challenged presidential control of the agenda.[84] Nor would we expect Democrats in such a context to extend the blue slip—and thus a potential veto power—to the minority party Republicans.

Had Wilson cared little about the makeup of the courts, then we might have seen Senate Democrats attempt to increase their leverage over appointments—knowing that the president would acquiesce to a stronger Senate role in filling vacant judgeships. But Wilson did care about the policy consequences of his appointment power.[85] Wilson encouraged his advisers to view federal judgeships as a means of advancing his policy agenda. He directed his attorney general to scrutinize potential judges with an eye to their progressive credentials, to the point that senators' choices were occasionally rejected. Recognizing the entrenched economic conservatism of the federal courts, facing the first opportunity in eighteen years to select federal judges, and understanding the president's intention to use the courts to advance and protect progressive goals, it seems unlikely that Democrats would have rewritten confirmation practices with the intention of diluting the president's appointment power.

To be sure, the Judiciary Committee from which the blue slip emerged in 1913 was hardly a microcosm of the Senate Democratic Caucus. Chaired by Culberson (D-Tex.), the Senate Judiciary Committee in 1913 was home to ten Democrats—seven of whom hailed from the South.[86] Given that the Judiciary Committee was the locus of fights over revisions to federal antitrust and currency reform in the Sixty-third Congress, policy differences between Wilson and the panel's Democrats might have led Democrats to seek a way to increase their leverage over the appointment of new federal judges to the southern federal courts.[87] By creating a committee process for registering objections to nominees, southern Democrats who served on the committee might have calculated that the use of the blue slip would have the effect of preserving local and regional biases of federal courts in the South.

That said, Wilson was by birth a southerner, not all southerners were conservative, and scholars disagree about the extent of Wilson's differences with the South.[88] Even on the highly salient issue of antitrust reform, Wilson and Judiciary Committee Democrats from the South were largely in agreement throughout 1913 on how the Sherman Act might be revised. It was not until spring 1914 that Wilson essentially sold out agrarian Democrats by moving toward the progressives' proposal of creating a federal trade commission.[89] This is at least suggestive that differences over public policy issues were unlikely to have motivated Judiciary Committee Democrats in 1913 to create the blue slip as a means of protecting southern federal judgeships from the White House's progressive interests.

Managing Senate Uncertainty

Did Democrats in 1913 invent the blue slip as a means of reducing uncertainty about the fate of their president's judicial nominees? We lack a smoking gun with which to test this account thoroughly and to draw definitive conclusions. Several pieces of evidence, however, are strongly consistent with the institutional account.

First, as suggested above, the uncertainty account fits best in a period of unified party control. Under such conditions, the Judiciary Committee chair would have had an incentive to smooth the way for confirmation of the president's nominees. Second, the uncertainty account leads us to expect that the blue slip would have been extended to both majority and minority party senators. If the goal in creating the blue slip was to provide a clear record of the views of home state senators about pending nominees, then the majority party should have wanted to know the views of minority party senators as well. Given that the president was unlikely to have consulted with opposition party senators in selecting lower court nominees, but given the lack of a cloture rule that the majority party could rely on to swiftly call for a vote on confirmation in face of opposition from the minority party, routine solicitation of the views of home state senators would have served the majority's goals well.

Third, several institutional innovations by Senate Democrats in the Sixty-third Congress suggest that the new Democratic majority was struggling to gain some greater degree of control over the flow of business on the Senate floor—precursors, of course, to the adoption of cloture in the Sixty-fifth Congress (1917–19). These innovations collectively suggest that the newly empowered Democrats were concerned about their ability to hold their party together as they steered Wilson's legislative priorities through the Senate.

One of these innovations was the formal election of a Democratic floor leader in 1913. Granted, Democrats had been selecting a chairman of the Democratic Caucus as early as 1890, a colleague who was expected to be the leader of the caucus and by extension the party's chamber leader. But when John Kern was elected majority leader for the Democrats in 1913, he became the first Senate leader who was consistently referred to as the Democrat's "majority leader."[90] The change in 1913 surely reflects a gradual transformation of the office of the party leader, but Democrats appear to have had stronger expectations for Kern as the first Democratic leader in a period of unified Democratic control after nearly twenty years in the minority.

In addition to consolidating their expectations about their floor leader in 1913, Democrats in 1913 created the new office of party whip, formally electing J. Hamilton Lewis (D-Ill.) as the "assistant" to majority leader Kern.[91] According to contemporary accounts, the Democratic Caucus created the whip's office "as a further precaution against a snap division in the Senate by which the Democrats might find themselves in the minority. . . . Mr. Lewis's chief duty will be to see that Democrats are present or paired at every roll call."[92] Sources at the time spread the view that Democrats invented the whip office out of a "general dissatisfaction with Mr. Kern's leadership."[93] Whatever the reason, it seems clear that Democrats in 1913 were experimenting with new ways of managing the president's policy agenda in the Senate, with an eye to eliminating costly surprises on the chamber floor.

A third institutional innovation in the Sixty-third Congress also suggests that the majority party was seeking to improve its control of the floor agenda. Before 1914, although unanimous consent agreements (UCAs) had become a regular feature of how the Senate managed the floor agenda, several modern features of UCAs had not yet been adopted, thereby allowing confusion to reign on the Senate floor over the modification and enforcement of these time agreements.[94] Contradictory Senate precedents about the adoption and enforcement of UCAs came to a head in January 1913 and led to a Senate committee to recommend formal revision of the UCA practice in 1914. With that innovation, UCAs became formal orders of the Senate and set the chamber on the path to making UCAs a predictable and reliable tool for leaders seeking to reduce uncertainty about the offering of amendments and timing of floor votes.

Innovations in Democratic leadership and in the treatment of UCAs in 1913 and 1914 together suggest that inherited leadership and floor management practices were proving insufficient to advance and secure the Democratic agenda—even under the most auspicious conditions of unified Democratic control. Creating a blue slip to increase the flow of information about home state senators' views (regardless of party) would have been consistent with the tenor of other institutional innovations in the Sixty-third Congress. Moreover, given the relative ease in filibustering in 1913 (before the adoption of the Senate cloture rule in 1917), Democrats might not have thought they were giving up much to the minority in exchange for gaining information. The cost of the blue slip to the majority probably increased after the adoption of the cloture rule, as the opposition party found itself with a quasi-veto even after the cloture rule had limited the ability of very small groups of senators to obstruct the majority.[95]

The timing of the blue slip seems consistent with the Democrats' institutional imperatives to improve control of the agenda upon regaining control of the Senate in 1913. The incentive to anticipate potential obstruction would have been particularly acute for the new Democratic majority, as Republican leaders in the previous Congress had to deal with Democrats' success in blocking appointments of outgoing President William Taft.[96] Eight of Taft's twenty-three judicial nominations were blocked, yielding a 35 percent failure rate for his nominees. And more generally, adoption of the blue slip fits neatly with other accounts of the transformation of Congress at the turn of the century as workloads burgeoned and organizations more generally became professionalized and institutionalized.[97]

One final consideration about the initial use of the blue slip provides even stronger corroboration that the practice was likely intended to reduce uncertainty about confirmation prospects for the president's nominees. According to one careful study of the nomination files kept by the Senate Judiciary Committee for nominees referred to the committee, no chair of the Judiciary panel allowed an objection from a home state senator (that is, a negative blue slip) to automatically block a nomination in committee before 1956. It was not until Senator James Eastland (D-Miss.) took the helm of the panel in 1956 that negative blue slips came to be treated as an absolute veto—a practice that Senator Edward Kennedy (D-Mass.) tempered, upon becoming chair of the committee in 1979.[98]

Before 1956, it appears from the records of the Senate Judiciary Committee and the *Senate Executive Journal* that negative blue slips were treated as advisory to the committee and the full chamber, rather than as a single-handed committee veto exercised by a home state senator. To understand how a negative blue slip could be advisory, it is helpful to examine the fate of the first nominee apparently subject to a negative blue slip. Within weeks of the opening of the first session of the Sixty-fifth Congress (1917–19), the chair of the committee, Charles Culberson, received a negative blue slip from one of the two Democratic senators from Georgia, Thomas Hardwick, for the nomination of U. V. Whipple for a federal district judgeship in southern Georgia (see figure 2-4). The committee subsequently reported the nomination adversely to the full Senate, which proceeded to refuse to provide its advice and consent.[99] In short, a negative blue slip provided information to the chair about the potential for strong floor opposition should the nominee be reported favorably from the Judiciary Committee. Given the Senate's practice of senatorial courtesy, the home state senator of the president's party could have expected his colleagues to vote down the nominee had he been reported favorably from committee.

Figure 2-4. *First Surviving Negative Blue Slip, 1917*

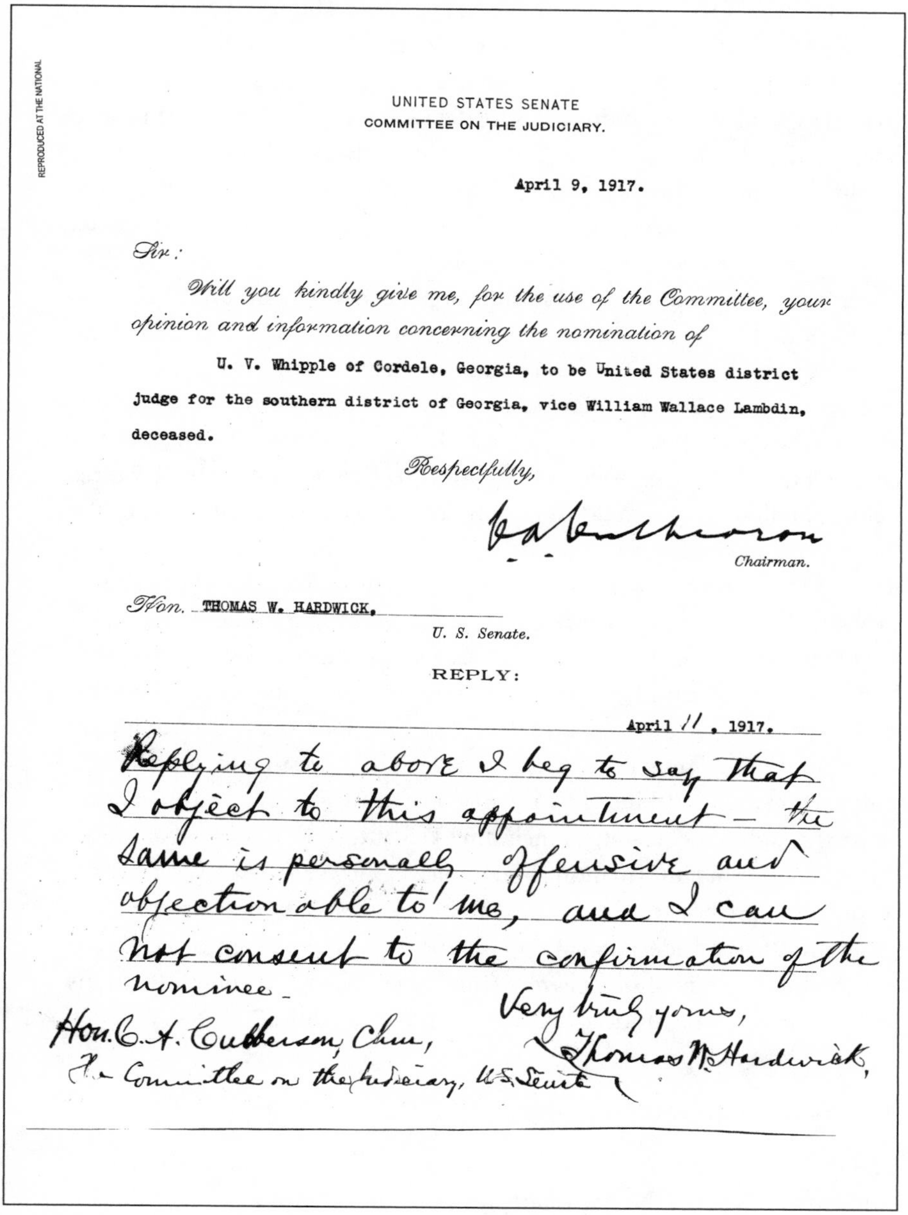

UNITED STATES SENATE
COMMITTEE ON THE JUDICIARY.

April 9, 1917.

Sir:

Will you kindly give me, for the use of the Committee, your opinion and information concerning the nomination of

U. V. Whipple of Cordele, Georgia, to be United States district judge for the southern district of Georgia, vice William Wallace Lambdin, deceased.

Respectfully,

[signature]
Chairman.

Hon. THOMAS W. HARDWICK,
U. S. Senate.

REPLY:

April 11, 1917.

Replying to above I beg to say that I object to this appointment — the same is personally offensive and objectionable to me, and I can not consent to the confirmation of the nominee.

Very truly yours,

Thomas W. Hardwick,

Hon. C. A. Culberson, Chm,
Committee on the Judiciary, U.S. Senate.

Nor was this an isolated incident. Three months later, Wilson submitted a new nominee for the same vacant judgeship, W. E. Thomas. This time, both home state senators returned the same negative blue slip, stating their simple opposition to confirmation (figure 2-5). Once again, rather than be treated as an absolute committee veto, the two negative blue slips appear to have led the committee to report the nominee adversely—a signal received by the full chamber, which rejected the nomination later that day. One month later, Wilson tried again, this time selecting a nominee who proved acceptable to the two home state senators.[100]

Objections registered on blue slips appear to have had high informational value for the committee chairman, allowing him to anticipate and, most important, avoid opposition to the president's favored nominees on the Senate floor. Because the Senate lacked a cloture rule that would have allowed the committee chair—should he have wanted—to call for a vote on confirmation, having in place a system for detecting opposition to nominees before the floor stage would have been a valuable improvement from the perspective of Senate leaders. The original blue slip, it would seem, was devised to be an early warning system, not an absolute veto. That helps to explain, of course, why senators might have been willing to allow opposition party senators to fill out blue slips. Democrats did not believe they were handing over a committee veto to the minority party; they likely believed they were improving their ability to manage the floor and to reduce uncertainty about upcoming floor action. Finally, it is interesting to note that the Judiciary panel used blue slips for many of the other appointments that came through the committee, including U.S. attorney and marshal nominations. Acquiring information about senators' views of these appointments would also have bolstered the chair's ability to forecast floor outcomes during committee consideration of the nominees. Senators' intentions in devising the blue slip, in short, bear a strong resemblance to the motivations underlying other institutional reforms in the Sixty-third Congress.

Theoretical Implications

The transformation of the blue slip from an advisory tool to a potential confirmation veto of the other party's nominees has strong implications for

Figure 2-5. *Second Surviving Negative Blue Slip, 1917*

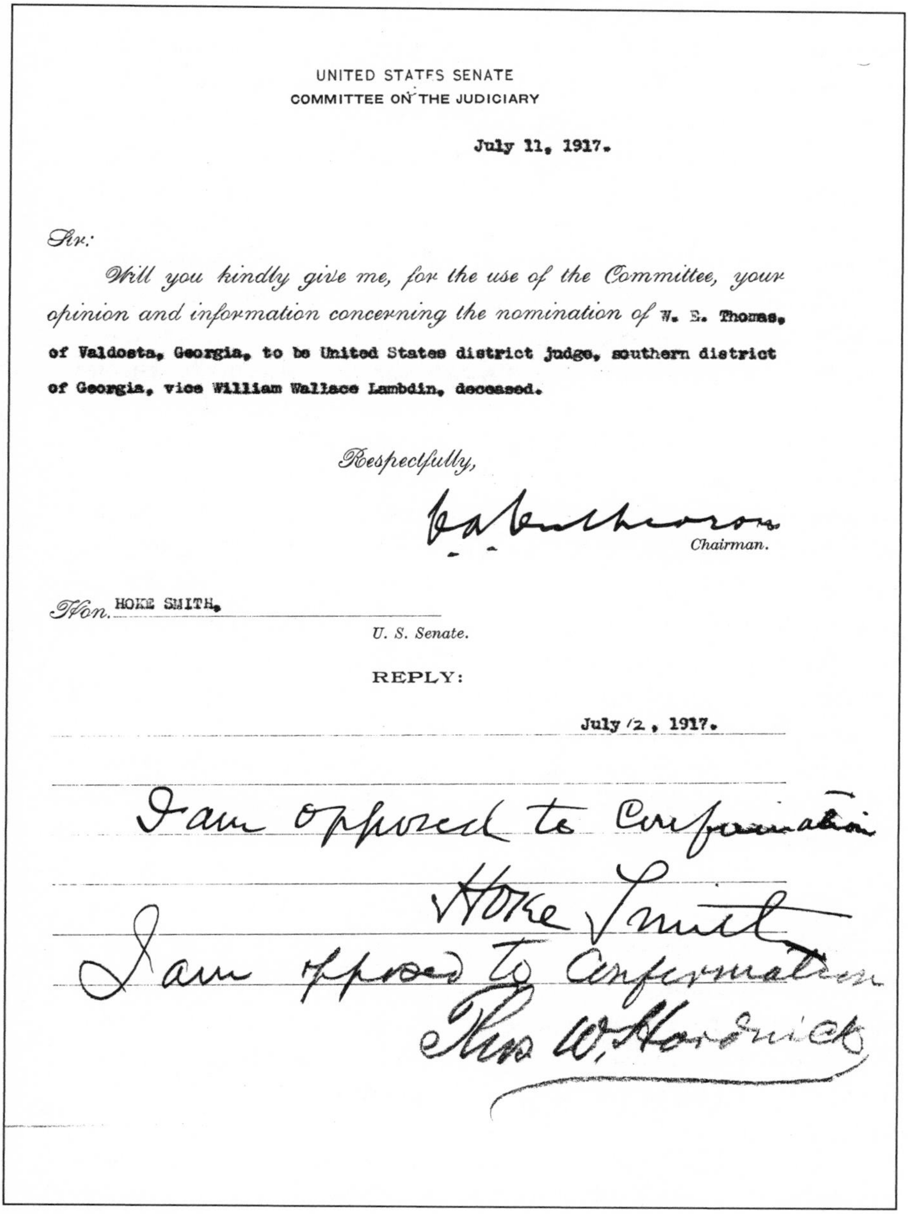

UNITED STATES SENATE
COMMITTEE ON THE JUDICIARY

July 11, 1917.

Sir:

Will you kindly give me, for the use of the Committee, your opinion and information concerning the nomination of W. E. Thomas, of Valdosta, Georgia, to be United States district judge, southern district of Georgia, vice William Wallace Lambdin, deceased.

Respectfully,

[signature]
Chairman.

Hon. HOKE SMITH,

U. S. Senate.

REPLY:

July 12, 1917.

I am opposed to Confirmation

Hoke Smith

I am opposed to Confirmation

Thos. W. Hardwick

how we build theories of institutional choice and change. Where do institutions come from, and why and when do they evolve? One prominent approach to answering such questions entails what Paul Pierson pointedly terms *actor-centered functionalism*: explanations of institutional choice are made through "reference to the benefits these actors expect to derive from particular institutional designs."[101] If an institution secures a particular basket of benefits, scholars often reason that the institution must have been created to provide those benefits for the actors who created the institution.

Despite the prominence of such economic modes of thinking about institutional choice, there are many reasons to doubt the easy fit of such a functionalist account to episodes of institutional choice. As Pierson's critique of actor-centered functionalism suggests, unanticipated consequences, changes in the social environment of an institution, and forces that promote institutional resilience as well as change may intervene over the course of an institution's development. Such dynamics should limit our confidence in accounts that reason backward from contemporary effects of an institution to rational motivations for the institution's selection. Rational calculation may certainly be at work, but snapshots of institutional choice, Pierson suggests, may generate incomplete and potentially misleading accounts of institutional design.

An alternative account recognizes that institutions, once adopted, tend not to be fixed in stone. As Edward Sait observed, "Institutions rise out of experience. . . . A borrowed institution will change in character to the extent that the new environment differs from the old."[102] Institutions inherited from the past may come to have new consequences once the political environment shifts. Moreover, new practice may interact with existing rules and over time come to change the use and impact of both. In other words, although the blue slip today is often exploited to undercut the influence of the president's partisans in selecting new judges, such use of the blue slip appears not to have been obvious to the political actors who created it. Exploitation of the blue slip by the president's foes appears to have emerged only as senators began to innovate with old practices under new circumstances. In other words, key institutional consequences of the blue slip do not appear to have been anticipated and thus could not have driven the adoption of the practice. Answers to the question "where do institutions come from?" require us to explore the path along which the institution has evolved.[103]

The Contemporary Practice of Advice and Consent

The evolution of advice and consent did not end with adoption of the blue slip. As the brief history above suggests, the treatment of blue slips by the Senate Judiciary Committee has varied over time. At first, blue slips appear to have been advisory, offering early warning signals of senators' discontent with a nominee. Later, blue slips were treated as absolute vetoes, allowing a single negative response from a senator to block further consideration of a nomination. Most recently, for a period beginning in 2003 when Republicans gained unified control of the White House and the Senate and lasting until they lost control in 2007, the chair of the Senate Judiciary Committee declared that an objection to a nomination by a single senator would be insufficient to block action on a nominee. In practice, the chair, Orrin Hatch (R-Utah), at times refused to heed the views of Democratic home state senators, even if both opposed a nominee.[104] Of course, once such nominations cleared the committee over the objections of the home state senators, those Democratic senators convinced their party caucus to filibuster the nominations on the Senate floor, preventing the Senate from offering its consent and thus killing the nominations.

As such episodes suggest, perhaps most striking about the contemporary practice of advice and consent for lower court nominations are the multiple and evolving tactics of obstruction that opponents pursue in their efforts to derail nominees. Why multiple tactics? Opponents' choice of tactics is conditioned by the salience of judgeships to senators, presidents, and organized interests, by the partisan context, and by the simple fact that rules and practices get embedded by senators into chamber routines and are inherited, adapted, and sometimes transformed by future senators. We conclude this chapter with a very brief treatment of why these forces are relevant in our efforts to understand and explain the modern practice of advice and consent.

As we show in subsequent chapters, so long as attention to the decisions of federal courts remained uneven across the Senate—as it did before the more forceful entry of the courts into pointed social issues in the 1960s and 1970s—few beyond the home state senators cared terribly much about the selection of new judges for the district and appellate courts.[105] In such a context, the leverage afforded by the blue slip was typically sufficient for senators to exercise influence over the fate of vacant judgeships. Not surprisingly, given the subterranean character of the blue slip, any disputes over judicial nominees in such an era typically took place below the media's (and political scientists') radars. It took charges of dubious ethics and extreme politics to elicit broader interest in the selection of judges, as became clear in the attempted filibuster of the elevation of Abe Fortas to chief justice of the United States in 1968.

In contrast, greater awareness of the decisions of the federal courts in the 1970s and beyond altered the landscape on which judicial selection took place. As scholar Martin Shapiro and others have written, the emergence of the federal courts as active participants in the molding of public policy—on issues relating to health, the environment, economic regulation, abortion, and criminal rights starting in the late 1960s and early 1970s—awakened a broader audience to the potentially pivotal roles played by the courts across a host of salient issues on the national agenda.[106] As Shapiro has argued, "The judges could have stayed out, but they chose to be in."[107] Various political players—activists concerned about the makeup of the courts, senators both pulling and responding to fire alarms about the ideological orientation of nominees given the tendentious questions pending in the federal appellate courts, and a media eager to highlight conflict between the parties over federal judges—each sought better means of influencing the course of judicial selection.

The choice of means, as we show in subsequent chapters, is even today clearly conditioned on the partisan context. In periods of divided party government, when the opposition party to the president controls the Senate Judiciary Committee and fields the majority party leader, opponents can slow down the path to confirmation by encouraging the Judiciary panel to drag its feet in scheduling hearings, by refusing to return positive blue slips to the panel chair, and by placing anonymous holds on nominations that discourage the majority leader from asking for unanimous consent to call up nominations in executive session. Raising the salience of nominees for the party caucus and encouraging the caucus to take a stand against the nominees are key strategies in periods of divided control.

In contrast, in periods of unified party control, when the president's party leads the Senate, tactics of obstruction are more limited and closely shaped by senators' institutional position in the minority party. First, opposing senators can refuse to return blue slips to block action on the president's nominees. Second, as recent experience has suggested, when informal avenues of obstruction such as the blue slip are blocked by the president's party in the Senate, tactics formally protected by chamber rules allow minorities to filibuster and thus in theory derail a president's nominees. Granted, large majorities could outvote minorities, rendering filibusters a costly means of opposing a nominee. In addition, minority parties do not always want to absorb the costs of actively opposing a popular president's nominees. Still, no filibuster-proof majorities have controlled the Senate for more than thirty years, reducing substantially the costs to the minority of seeking to derail presidential nominees.

These multiple and evolving tactics of obstruction raise key questions about the politics of advice and consent that will guide our analysis throughout the rest of the book. Who holds power over the fate of judicial nominees? Given the wide array of senators potentially advantaged under Senate rules and practices, how effective are these procedural powers in shaping the makeup of the federal bench? To put the analytical challenge simply, the availability of tools of obstruction does not mean that these are effective tools. Determining the conditions under which political actors can affect the selection of nominees and their confirmation is the key analytical challenge we take up in the ensuing chapters. And what advantages do presidents retain in a system that so widely disperses influence over the outcomes of judicial selection? Ultimately, we want to be able to explain why advice and consent has become so contentious and what the consequences of such conflict have been for the Senate, the public, and for the performance of the courts themselves. Finally, how the path to the bench might be made less arduous for judicial candidates seeking to serve their country is the focus of our concluding treatment of potential reforms of advice and consent and its practice on both ends of Pennsylvania Avenue.

3

How Senators Influence
the Choice of Nominees

In the spring of 2008, more than forty federal judgeships sat vacant. For roughly 40 percent of the vacancies, President George W. Bush had yet to submit a nomination—even though some of the vacant judgeships were located on courts with the largest caseloads and backlogs of the federal judiciary.[1] Presidential sluggishness in naming nominees in 2008, a pattern we see stretching back many years, is puzzling. Why, if the makeup of the federal bench is such a central component of the policy agendas of recent administrations, would a president ever fail to swiftly nominate a candidate for the federal bench? To be sure, some vacancies are quickly filled, with a candidate ready to be nominated on the day a judge formally retires or takes senior status. Some nominations are even made after the incumbent judge announces his or her impending retirement but before the judge actually retires. Still, other vacancies linger on for months, often years—raising the question of why we see such variation in the disposition of vacant judgeships.

Despite renewed scholarly interest in judicial nominations, the politics of selecting nominees for the bench has largely escaped systematic attention. In this chapter, we focus on the selection of nominees for the U.S. district courts, a decision that is often written off as a matter of patronage. As the *New York Times* summed up nomination dynamics in 1980, "Instead of giving advice and consent on a President's nominee, senators block all but their own. Once the President yields to their choices, they are then easily wheeled to confirmation."[2] The received wisdom suggests that presidents have historically

deferred to the home state senator or senators from their party when nominating judges to serve on a federal trial court within that state. If such choices
are truly matters of patronage and deference, then we should see little variation in how long it takes presidents to select nominees and thus little that
has to be explained.

In this chapter, we challenge the inherited view of nomination politics
and suggest that focusing exclusively on the views of home state senators
risks missing broader dynamics at play when presidents vet candidates for
trial court judgeships. Given our exploration in chapter 2 of the multiple
practices that constitute the Senate processes of advice and consent, we argue
that structural incentives motivate presidents to broaden the selection
process beyond the parochial interests of the home state senator of his party.
Presidents, assuming they favor swift confirmation of their nominees, have
strong incentives to consult broadly when choosing nominees. To test our
notions about the forces that shape the selection of judges, we take advantage of variation in how long it takes for the president to select nominees for
different federal judgeships, taking account of variation both over time and
across federal courts in a given year. Our data sweep from the postwar period
starting in 1947 and run through 1998, a sufficiently long period over which
to estimate the impact of institutional and electoral forces on the selection
of judges. We focus exclusively on vacancies on the U.S. district courts, given
the conventional wisdom that presidents follow the dictates of home state
partisans in selecting trial court judges. In contrast, presidents are perceived
to have greater leeway in choosing nominees for the appellate bench.

Patterns over five decades lead us to conclude that the differences between
the views of presidents and home state senators cannot fully account for
the variation in how long it takes presidents to select nominees. Such variation suggests that existing explanations of the dynamics of judicial selection—whether the big bang or nothing-new-under-the-sun accounts
surveyed in chapter 1—leave much to be explained about how nominees are
chosen for the federal bench. The wide array of procedural rights that char-
acterize the Senate's practice of advice and consent, coupled with the increase
in partisan polarization between Democratic and Republican senators, has
come to shape the selection process in indelible ways—empowering the
opposition party as it attempts to challenge both home state senators' and
the president's influence over the choice of nominees.

Politics of Senatorial Courtesy

Political observers often invoke the concept of senatorial courtesy to describe the process for selecting judges to the federal trial courts. As Harold Chase explained in 1972,

> For a good part of our history, "senatorial courtesy" could be defined accurately as a custom by which senators would support one of their number who objected to an appointment to a federal office in his state, provided the senator and the president were of the same party. . . . In our day, senatorial courtesy has come to mean that senators will give serious consideration to and be favorably disposed to support an individual senator of the president's party who opposes a nominee to an office in his state.[3]

The norm of courtesy in other words reflects senators' deference to their colleagues over matters internal to their home states. As a result of senatorial courtesy, the conventional wisdom holds that presidents are severely restricted in their capacity to choose judges for the district courts.[4] Because home state senators can back up their threat to block a nominee with a blue slip, home state senators from the president's party have typically been said to hold a veto over a president's choices. Nor are senators shy about claiming the right to impose their choice of a nominee on the White House. "I'm given the power to make the appointment," Senator Phil Gramm once boasted, "the people elected me to do that."[5]

The perceived status of district court judgeships as political patronage for home state senators encouraged other senators to defer for a vacant judgeship to the home state senator who hailed from the president's party. To be sure, judgeships are decreasingly considered patronage, as presidents have become more assertive in selecting nominees who are in concert with the president's policy views and legal philosophies—even at the trial court level. Still, the leverage of home state senators from the president's party is perceived to be pronounced. In the absence of a home state senator from the president's party, the conventional wisdom suggests that other actors from the president's party, such as House members and party leaders, wield influence over the selection of nominees. The received wisdom thus suggests that senators and their fellow partisans outside the chamber influence and often dictate the choice of nominees to the White House.

The simplicity of the senatorial courtesy account stands in sharp contrast to what we know about the politics of Senate confirmation for judicial nominees: Presidents are likely to face a number of constraints in seeking swift confirmation of their nominees for the lower federal courts. As we will show in chapter 4, it is clear that institutionally empowered senators and party coalitions exploit their procedural advantages to delay and thus often derail confirmation of appellate court nominees. Although generally high confirmation rates for federal district court nominees fuel the perception that senators defer to the interests of the president, it is equally plausible that presidents anticipate the interests of relevant Senate players at the nomination stage. Given the constraints that presidents face during the confirmation process, the president likely confronts a similar set of structural incentives at the nomination stage that encourage him to navigate and negotiate his way through a broad array of Senate interests in filling judicial vacancies.

Do home state senators from the president's party have unfettered influence over the choice of nominees for vacant judgeships in their home states? Or do presidents face an array of interested actors in making judicial appointments to these vacant trial court seats? We certainly have empirical evidence of a more complex selection process, as Sheldon Goldman notes numerous times in his historical treatment of the appointments process in which the choice of nominees was not a simple dictate of home state senators—even when both senators hailed from the president's party. Goldman, for example, notes that Attorney General Robert Kennedy (charged with the command of judicial appointments for his brother, President John Kennedy) once estimated that roughly 20 percent of the recommendations he received from Democratic senators were unacceptable, and "the result was a struggle with senators to secure a nominee measuring up to the administration's standards."[6]

Conflict also emerges when the home state senators for an appointment are not from the president's party. Goldman recounts episodes in which a Republican administration faced off against Democratic home state senators over the choice of a nominee.[7] When the Nixon administration ignored the recommendation of Florida's two Democratic home state senators over a Florida district court appointment, the administration learned its lesson: the nominee was never confirmed. Two months later, the administration accepted an alternative choice of the Democratic senators, and he was subsequently confirmed. More recently, Republican senator Orrin Hatch of Utah (at the time chair of the Judiciary Committee) held up all nomination hearings until President Bill Clinton would agree to appoint one of Hatch's former aides to a district court vacancy in Utah.[8] Because the nominee was opposed by environmental groups, a long standoff ensued before Clinton agreed to the appointment—again suggesting that the received wisdom about the selection process may mask critical political dynamics.

Forces Shaping the Selection of Nominees

Our task is to delineate the types of challenges that presidents face in filling trial court vacancies and to determine whether these forces systematically affect the selection process. We focus primarily on the duration of the nomination process, as a proxy for the debates, disputes, and conflicts that may emerge over the course of selecting a nominee for a vacant judgeship. For some judicial vacancies, nominees are swiftly identified and announced; for others, the process drags on for months—sometimes even years— before nominees are announced. Arguably, the fewer the constraints faced by the president in making judicial appointments, the quicker the administration should be to announce its nominees. Conversely, the greater the number of political actors with the potential to influence the selection of the nominee (and the greater the potential disagreement across them), the longer it should take for the president to announce his choice.

The duration of the nomination stage thus serves as a proxy for the extent of bargaining, negotiating, or just plain old consulting that occurs between White House and Department of Justice staff and senators over the choice of nominees. If the inherited view of judicial selection is correct, which suggests the dominance of home state partisans of the president in selecting nominees, then a simple pattern should emerge when examining how long it takes presidents to announce nominees. When at least one home state senator for the vacancy hails from the president's party, a nominee should be announced more swiftly than when neither home state senator is from the president's party. If the inherited view of judicial selection provides only a partial portrait, we should find other forces that systematically affect how long it takes presidents to select nominees over the postwar period.

We focus on institutional and political forces likely to affect the president's ability to select a nominee of his choosing: the leverage afforded to home state senators and the chair of the Judiciary Committee, the impact of political parties, and bargaining advantages held by an engaged and popular president. As we explore below, each of these forces yields testable predictions about the duration of the nominations process.

The Impact of Home State Senators

The received wisdom of senatorial courtesy suggests that presidents defer to home state senators of the president's party because their power to object to potential nominees is backed up by the Senate blue slip practice. If a senator opposes a nominee slated for a federal judgeship in his state, according to the conventional wisdom, the senator need only threaten to withhold the blue slip to block a candidate from being nominated. Although senators technically only extend courtesy to home state senators from the president's party, as we explored in the previous chapter, both senators can potentially blue slip the president's choice.[9] Indeed, as early as 1972, judicial scholars noted that the concept of senatorial courtesy had spread to senators regardless of whether they hailed from the president's party: "It must be understood," observed Harold Chase, "that senatorial courtesy extends beyond a senator of the president's party who objects to an appointment to office in his own state. Senators will sympathetically hear objections of a senator of the state who is not of the president's party."[10]

Because either senator can potentially block a president's choice, presidents are likely to take into account the preferences of *both* home state senators, *regardless of party*. In other words, the blue slip procedure may empower senators who, according to the traditional partisan view of senatorial courtesy, have no role in the nomination process. The blue slip practice thus creates a structural incentive for the president to recognize the interests of even ideologically distant home state senators during the process of selecting nominees. As the Nixon administration learned in the example above, failure to do so risks defeat of the nominee.

Democratic senators sought such consultation in 2001 as the George W. Bush administration readied its first slate of nominees for the Senate after Democrats won back control of the chamber that spring. Warning that they would filibuster nominees unless the administration consulted with both

Republican and Democratic home state senators, Democrats boxed the White House counsel into promising to engage in "pre-nomination consultation."[11] As Patrick Leahy, chair of the Senate Judiciary Committee explained at the time, it would not be acceptable to Democrats if they were informed of the president's choice "two hours before [White House spokesman] Ari Fleischer announces it."[12] Such anecdotes suggest that traditional notions of senatorial courtesy may fail to explain the dynamics of how nominees are chosen, particularly when control of the White House and Senate is divided between the parties.

We can go even further to suggest that we should expect even longer delays in selecting nominees when a home state senator is an ideological foe of the president. Disagreement over the legal and policy views of potential candidates should be greatest as the senator and the president diverge ideologically. Threatened by an ideological foe's potential to block the nomination—either by withholding the blue slip or threatening a filibuster—a president would have an incentive either to negotiate with that senator or to defer action on filling the vacancy until an accommodation could be reached or an opponent outfoxed. Either action on the part of the president would stretch out the length of time it takes to select a nominee.

To be sure, we are not arguing that the array of Senate rules and practices that encourage involvement by opposition party home state senators grants such senators the power to select nominees. We are arguing that a president who only has to accommodate the choices of home state partisans—as the received wisdom suggests—would swiftly appoint the candidate preferred by the senator from the president's party. Even in those cases when the president might resist the pick of a home state partisan, the nominee should still be selected more swiftly than if the preferences of senators from the opposition party were to affect the president's choice. More generally, any evidence of delays in selecting nominees that can be attributed to the involvement of rival senators bolsters our argument that the received wisdom fails to capture the dynamics of selecting nominees. In short, in this chapter we seek to test for the impact of home state senators on the selection process in two different ways:

Senatorial courtesy. If a home state senator for a vacancy hails from the president's party, the vacancy will be filled more quickly.[13]

Blue slip power. If a home state senator for a vacancy is ideologically distant from the president, the vacancy will take longer to fill.

Impact of the Judiciary Committee Chair

The threat from a home state senator to block a nominee with a negative blue slip is affected by the behavior of the Judiciary Committee chair when he or she considers the home state senator's preferences. Given the panel chair's procedural control over the committee's agenda, the effectiveness of a blue slip veto depends in large part on the chair's willingness to defer to the views of that home state senator. If the chair is willing to use his or her procedural prerogatives that grant leverage over the committee agenda to block the nominee from being considered in committee, then the force of a threat to use a blue slip veto is strengthened. If the chair is disinclined to defer to the views of the home state senator, then the force of the threat is diluted.

Chairs of the Judiciary Committee have varied in their exercise of their control of the committee's nomination calendar. By most historical accounts, for much of the twentieth century after the advent of the blue slip, Judiciary chairs respected objections from home state senators. As we noted in chapter 2, between 1917 and 1956, it is believed that successive chairmen of the committee forwarded nominations with an adverse report if they lacked support from a home state senator. When Senator James Eastland (D-Miss.) took the helm of the panel in 1956, it is reported that negative blue slips came to be treated as an absolute veto.[14] But the automatic veto appears to have been diluted somewhat when Senator Edward Kennedy (D-Mass.) took up the reins of the committee in 1979. Senator Kennedy made it known at that time that negative blue slips would no longer automatically block committee action on pending nominees. More recently, Judiciary Committee chairs have elucidated their own blue slip policies at the start of each Congress, laying out their expectations for White House consultation with home state senators.

The potential leverage of the panel chair over the fate of nominees should increase the president's incentive to consult broadly in selecting a nominee. If the president and panel chair are ideological allies, there should be fewer grounds on which the panel chair would exercise his or her discretion to slow down consideration of a candidate once his or her nomination is sent to the

Hill. Under such conditions, all things equal, we would not expect to see any delays in the selection of nominees for pending vacancies, as the president and the chair should see eye to eye over potential nominees. As the policy views of the president and panel chair diverge, however, we would expect there to be greater differences over the type of nominee selected, and thus the process should drag out as the White House gauges the likelihood of confirmation given the views of the panel chair. Regardless of whether the president heeds the views of the panel chair, the selection should slow down considerably. We would expect to find the following:

> *Committee chair power.* The greater the ideological differences between the president and the committee chair, the longer it will take for a nominee to be chosen to fill a vacancy.

The pace of filling vacancies on the bench should thus be shaped in part by the likelihood of conflict between the president and the head of the Judiciary Committee.

The Impact of Political Parties

The likelihood that a nominee will be swiftly confirmed also depends directly on the Senate's willingness to bring a nominee to the floor for chamber consideration. The majority party leader by precedent holds the right of first recognition on the Senate floor and thus is institutionally empowered to influence the timing of a confirmation decision.[15] The power of the majority party over the consideration of nominations creates a structural incentive for the president to heed the interests of opposition party senators when their party controls the Senate. All else equal, divided party control should slow down the process of selecting a nominee, as the president has an incentive to sound out the views of the Senate majority. When control of the Senate and White House is unified in a single party, the process of selecting nominees will speed up considerably:

> *Party power.* In periods of divided party control, it will take longer to select a nominee to fill a vacancy.

Conditions of divided party control are also likely to affect the ability of home state senators to block nominees they oppose. If nominations, as we show in the next chapter, face tough sledding in periods of divided control, we should expect particularly rough sledding when the home state senator is an ideological foe of the president in a period of divided government. The enhanced leverage of home state senators during periods of divided control creates another structural incentive for the president to negotiate extensively in selecting a nominee. Even if the president's staff does not actually negotiate over the choice of nominees, the process should take longer given the array of differing views about potential nominees. The following interactive effect is thus likely to be visible in filling trial court vacancies:

> *Home state senators in divided government.* It will take longer to select nominees during periods of divided control when a home state senator is ideologically distant from the president.

Presidential Influence

We round out the empirical analysis by including a number of controls for the impact of the president and for the context in which the Senate considers nominees. We control for the popularity of the president, the onset of a presidential election year, and the number of vacancies to be filled. More popular presidents should feel less constrained by Senate opponents in selecting nominees, and thus vacancies should be filled more swiftly as the president's approval rating rises. In contrast, election year dynamics are likely to slow down the process of selecting a nominee. Clearly presidential opponents have an incentive to save vacancies for after a presidential election (in hopes of gaining control of the White House in the intervening election). Presidents, recognizing their diminished leverage in presidential election years, have an increased incentive to consult broadly before making a nomination in those years. Finally, the greater the number of vacancies to be filled, the longer it likely will take to fill them, given the limited time and resources that White House and Justice Department staff have to expend on vetting potential appointees.

Data and Methods

To test our conjectures about the politics of judicial selection, we use the *Final Calendars* of the Senate Judiciary Committee to identify the vacancy and nomination dates for every vacancy on the U.S. district courts between 1947 and 1998.[16] For each observation, we record the date the vacancy occurred and the date on which a nomination was announced.[17] If no nomination is made by the end of the Congress, we add an additional observation for each subsequent Congress until that Congress in which a nomination is announced.[18] So long as there is not a change in control of the White House, the vacancy date on these additional observations remains the original vacancy date. When a new president inherits a vacancy from his predecessor, we recode the vacancy date as the inauguration date for the new president. We do this because we are primarily interested in identifying the institutional and political factors that affect the president's selection process. The inclusion of time that is attributable to the previous administration would introduce measurement error into the dependent variable. On those occasions on which nominees are announced before a seat officially becomes vacant, we set the vacancy date one day before the actual nomination date.[19] Because there are no home state senators for vacancies to the federal District of Columbia District Court, we exclude vacancies to that court as well as to territorial district courts in such territories as Guam or Puerto Rico. Coding decisions yield 2,163 observations over the course of fifty-one years.

Estimation

To test our conjectures about the timing of nominations, we estimate a hazard rate model. Because we have no theoretical expectation regarding the distribution for the time until the event of interest (that is, a nomination) occurs, we use a Cox model of proportional hazards to assess the effect of the covariates on the hazard rate (otherwise described as the conditional probability of failure at time t). The coefficients indicate whether each variable increases or decreases the hazard rate. Roughly speaking, we can interpret an increase (decrease) in the hazard rate as meaning that increases in the value of the variable have the effect of speeding up (or slowing down) the announcement of a nomination. Because we have multiple observations for vacancies if a nominee is not chosen by the end of a Congress, we use robust standard errors clustering on the vacancy to control for correlated errors across multiple observations for a single seat.

Independent Variables

We use a series of dummy variables to tap the dichotomous independent variables. To tap whether or not a home state senator is from the president's party ("senatorial courtesy"), we determine the party of the two home state senators for each vacancy and code whether or not either senator shares the president's party.[20] If at least one of the home state senators is from the president's party, senatorial courtesy is coded 1, 0 otherwise. To isolate home state senators who are ideologically distant from the president, we first determine the ideology of the two home state senators using Poole and Rosenthal's DW-NOMINATE first dimension scores and then calculate the ideological distance between the president and each home state senator.[21] If the farther home state senator is greater than 1 standard deviation above the mean ideological distance, that senator is coded as 1, as an "ideologically distant blue slip senator," 0 otherwise. To mark the incidence of "divided government," we code whether or not control of the Senate and the White House is unified or divided for each Congress during which a vacancy persists without a nominee. We code vacancies that do not have a pending nominee during a "presidential election" year as 1, 0 otherwise.

For the continuous variables, we create three measures. First, to measure ideological differences between the chair of the Judiciary panel and the president ("judiciary chair–president distance"), we calculate the absolute difference between the DW-NOMINATE scores for the president and the panel chair.[22] Second, we use the "president's approval rating" in the year in which the vacancy appeared to tap the president's public standing.[23] Third, to control for the "number of vacancies" to be filled, we determine the total number of vacancies that open up to be filled over the course of each Congress.

Patterns in the Timing of Nominations

Table 3-1 presents descriptive statistics for the variables included in the analysis. The median wait for selection of a nominee during the five decades was 212.5 days, roughly seven months. The vacancy that took the longest to find a suitable nominee lasted 2,070 days. The vacancy on the U.S. District Court for the Western District of Pennsylvania opened in January of 1971, affording President Richard Nixon the opportunity to fill it. Yet a nominee was not selected until March 1978, well after President Jimmy Carter had taken office. In contrast, there were 121 vacancies that lasted just one day, meaning that nominees had already been chosen in anticipation of a judge stepping down from active service.

Table 3-1. *Descriptive Statistics*

Variable	Mean	Std. dev.	Min	Max
Time from vacancy to nomination (days)	284.66	276.24	1	2,070
Senatorial courtesy	0.77	0.42	0	1
Divided government	0.47	0.50	0	1
Ideologically distant blue slip senator	0.19	0.39	0	1
Ideologically distant blue slip senator during divided government	0.10	0.30	0	1
Ideological distance between president and Senate Judiciary Committee chair	0.42	0.34	0.02	0.89
Presidential election year	0.27	0.45	0	1
Presidential approval (percent)	55.35	10.61	28	76
Number of vacancies	128.07	60.20	16	246

Source: Nominations data compiled by authors from U.S. Senate, Committee on the Judiciary, *Legislative and Executive Calendar,* final edition.

In Table 3-2, we estimate two models to explain the timing of judicial nominations.[24] The overall fit of each model is good; we can safely reject the hypothesis in both models that all of the coefficients are jointly 0.[25] In model 1, we find strong support for the simplest version of the received wisdom: A nominee is named more swiftly by the president when a home state senator for the vacancy hails from the president's party. We also find as expected that the overall vacancy load affects the administration's ability to move swiftly to fill existing vacancies. The more seats to be filled, the longer it takes to select nominees to fill them.

Most important, the results in model 2 suggest limits on the impact of senatorial courtesy in face of competing influences on the selection process. To be sure, having a home state senator from the president's party still speeds up the selection process, but the president also appears to be constrained by the involvement of additional senators. First, senators who are ideological foes of the president seem able to slow down the selection process when vacancies occur in their home states—presumably encouraging the administration to consult more carefully when selecting a nominee for federal courts in states represented by Senate foes.[26] There is also some limited evidence that the influence of ideologically distant home state senators is pronounced during periods of divided control. In this specification, control

Table 3-2. *Cox Regression of the Timing of Judicial Nominations, 1947–98*[a]

Variable	Expected sign	Model 1	Model 2
Senatorial courtesy	+	.167**	.129*
		(.069)	(.074)
Divided government	–	--	.003
			(.075)
Ideologically distant blue slip senator	–	--	−.203*
			(0.96)
Ideologically distant blue slip senator during divided government	–	--	.170
			(.130)
Ideological distance between president and Senate Judiciary Committee chair	–	--	−.283**
			(.114)
Presidential election year	–	--	−.619***
			(.070)
Presidential approval	+	--	−.001
			(.004)
Number of vacancies	–	−.004***	−.003***
		(.001)	(.0005)
N		2,163	2,163
Log likelihood		−10,795	−10,735
Chi square		72.58***	199.97***

Source: Nominations data compiled by authors from U.S. Senate, Committee on the Judiciary, *Legislative and Executive Calendar,* final edition.

***$p < 0.001$; **$p < 0.01$; *$p < 0.05$; all one-tailed t tests.

-- = not applicable.

a. Cell entries are coefficient estimates, with robust standard errors, clustered on nominee, in parentheses. Calculated by the authors using *stcox* routine in Stata 8.0. Efron method is used for dealing with ties.

of the Senate by the opposition party does not appreciably slow down the selection process, as shown in the statistically insignificant coefficient for divided government.

We also find that institutional differences between the president and the chair of the Judiciary panel markedly slow down the pace of choosing judicial nominees—something we see playing out clearly when the Democrats regained control of the Senate in the 2006 elections. Taken together, the results suggest that administrations anticipate the likely treatment of their nominees by the Judiciary panel and take the time to consider the broader acceptability of their nominees. When there is no home state senator from the president's party, structural incentives shaped by the Judiciary Committee's influence over the fate of nominees seem to entice presidents to proceed cautiously in choosing nominees. It is important to note that we do not mean to imply that presidents select nominees most preferred by their ideological foes. We mean simply that it appears that the process slows down considerably when administration foes are institutionally empowered by Senate rules or practices.

The results also suggest only limited additional leverage for the president in the selection process. His public standing does not appear to markedly affect the speed with which he fills vacancies, and approaching presidential elections hamper his ability to swiftly select nominees for Senate consideration. Moreover, the sheer volume of vacancies seems to slow down an administration, with heavier loads making it difficult for the administration to choose nominees swiftly.

It is appropriate to interpret these results with some caution. A key assumption of the Cox model is the assumption of proportional hazards.[27] If the assumption holds, then the effect of any given independent variable on the hazard rate is constant over time: For any two values of a covariate, the hazard of failure at time t for one value is proportional to the hazard for the other value. In other words, the ratio of the two hazards will be nonnegative and, of importance, constant. If the assumption holds, the Cox model is an appropriate estimator. If the assumption is violated, one needs to correct for nonproportionality. When we test for nonproportionality with what are known as Schoenfeld residuals, we find that four of our independent variables (those measuring the presence of senatorial courtesy, a presidential election year, the president's approval rating, and the number of vacancies) violate the proportional hazards assumption.[28]

The statistical correction for nonproportionality in this context involves interacting each offending covariate with the natural logarithm of time.[29] This correction is important on both statistical and substantive grounds. In statistical terms, the correction allows the effects of the covariates to vary monotonically with the duration of the vacancy. Substantively, this means that we are able to detect if and how the impact of these key forces changes over the period of time that a vacancy remains unfilled. We elaborate below.

The new parameter estimates appear in table 3-3. Correcting for nonproportionality brings considerable nuance to the original results. First, the

impact of senatorial courtesy is clear, as the presence of a home state senator from the president's party significantly speeds up the process of selecting a nominee. This suggests that presidents are likely to defer to home state
senators from their party, resulting in a swift selection of an agreed-upon
nominee. What is striking is the waning influence of home state partisans
over time, as seen in the coefficient for the covariate's interaction with time.
As a vacancy persists over time without an announced nominee, the presence
of a home state senator from the president's party actually decreases the
hazard of a nominee being chosen—perhaps because opposition from that
senator creates the delay. Once a vacancy has been open for 180 days, the percent change in the hazard of a nomination goes down by some 90 percent.[30]
The revised model also clarifies the impact of the blue slip threat on the
selection of nominees. Overall, ideologically distant home state senators do
not measurably slow down the selection of nominees for vacancies within
their states. But the potential for a negative blue slip from such senators
during periods of divided government markedly affects the selection process,
yielding a 25 percent decrease in the hazard of a nomination being
announced.[31] Diverging policy views between the president and the Judiciary
chair continue to affect the selection process in the new specification, low-
ering the hazard of a nomination by nearly 20 percent.[32] Together, these
results suggest that Senate committee practices significantly constrain the
selection of judicial nominees: presidents have an incentive to consult
broadly when it appears that ideologically distant senators could exploit
institutional rules and practices to block nominees in a subsequent confirmation battle.

The new results also bring some nuance to our interpretation of the
impact of the president. First, in the new estimation, the process of selecting nominees is not appreciably slower in presidential election years. Over
the course of a vacancy, however, the nomination process moves noticeably
slower as the vacancy wears on. Second, and perhaps more important, the
president's public standing seems to confer some advantage on the president
during the process of filling vacancies on the bench. Still, as vacancies stay
open over time, the president's standing has a diminishing impact on the
hazard of naming a nominee. Finally, although a heavy vacancy load does
not initially slow down the selection process, over time high numbers of
vacancies do reduce the hazard of a nomination, suggesting perhaps that a

Table 3-3. *Cox Regression with Log-Time Interactions of Judicial Nominations, 1947–98*[a]

Variable	Coefficient (robust std. error)
Senatorial courtesy	8.759***
	(1.368)
Senatorial courtesy × ln(time)	−1.489***
	(.225)
Divided government	.081
	(.061)
Ideologically distant blue slip senator	.078
	(.092)
Ideologically distant blue slip senator during divided government	−.274*
	(.151)
Ideological distance between president and Senate Judiciary Committee chair	−.325***
	(.105)
Presidential election year	.790
	(.308)
Presidential election year × ln(time)	−.232***
	(.055)
Presidential approval	.034***
	(.003)
Presidential approval × ln(time)	−.065***
	(.002)
Number of vacancies	.016***
	(.002)
Number of vacancies × ln(time)	−.003***
	(.001)
N	2,163
Log likelihood	−8,960.477
Chi square	1,706.53***

Source: Nominations data compiled by authors from U.S. Senate, Committee on the Judiciary, *Legislative and Executive Calendar,* final edition.

***$p < 0.001$; **$p < 0.01$; *$p < 0.05$; all one-tailed t tests, except for variables with ln(time) interactions for which two-tailed tests are used.

a. Cell entries are coefficient estimates, with robust standard errors, clustered on nominee, in parentheses. Calculated by the authors using *stcox* routine in Stata 8.0. Efron method is used for dealing with ties.

long-lasting vacancy receives lower priority from the administration as time passes and no nominee is chosen.

Finally, we lay to rest observations by political scientists and observers that conflict over federal judges emerged abruptly in the 1980s with the debacle of the failed nomination of Robert Bork to the Supreme Court. We find little evidence of what we refer to in chapter 1 as the big bang theory of judicial selection in our analysis of trends in nomination timing. If a momentous event—such as the no-holds-barred confirmation process experienced by Robert Bork in 1987—triggered conflict over lower court judges, then we would expect to find distinct patterns in the duration of vacancies before and after the Bork debacle—to the extent that any such conflict spilled over into the filling of trial court seats. When we divide our data into two samples (the first running from 1947 through 1987 and the second running from 1988 through 1998), we find that the overall fit of each time period's model is good, allowing us to safely reject the hypothesis that all of the coefficients are jointly 0.[33] Although, as we detail below, there are some new developments in the period after the Bork nomination, we find roughly consistent results in both time periods. Most important, home state senators from the president's party have an initial impact on selection, but their influence appears to wane the longer a vacancy remains without a nominee.

What then of the alternative nothing-new-under-the-sun account? Has judicial selection—as Lee Epstein and Jeffrey Segal argue—always been politicized and thus do efforts by the administration to anticipate senatorial preferences constitute an old story?[34] Three pieces of evidence warn against this interpretation. First, as shown in figure 1-3, there was clearly a secular increase in the amount of time it took administrations to choose nominees during the post–World War II period. We can tap this secular increase in the duration of vacancies most directly by controlling for the passage of time in the model. When we do so, we find a negative and statistically significant coefficient for the variable that denotes the Congress in which the vacancy first opened: over time, even controlling for the range of forces that drag out vacancies, there has been a steady increase in how long it takes an administration to announce a nominee.

Second, when we divide the data into two periods, before and after the Bork case, we discover three important changes in the dynamics of selecting nominees during the postwar period. In the latter period (post Bork), ideological differences between the president and Judiciary panel chair and between the president and the ideologically distant home state senator during divided government no longer lead to disproportionately longer vacancies on the nation's trial courts. However, we see a pronounced impact of divided government, finding that the selection of nominees after the late 1980s proceeds more slowly when the opposition party controls the Senate—dropping the hazard of a nominee being selected by nearly 10 percent.

Those results suggest either that the opposition party has become bolder over time in exerting its views about potential nominees or that presidential administrations have become more careful in selecting nominees, understanding the potential for and the incentive of the opposition party to derail nominees that their members oppose. As one close observer of judicial selection during the Clinton and Bush administrations has noted, "The White House under both [administrations] . . . spent a lot of time negotiating with individual senators, including opposition party senators, to find mutually acceptable combinations of nominations."[35] Either account would lead to lengthier vacancies, as interested players dig deep into the backgrounds of judicial candidates and broaden the consultations over potential nominees. Such accounts—which are observationally equivalent and not mutually exclusive—belie the idea that contemporary delays in selecting nominees are an old and persistent story.

In sum, senatorial courtesy works its will quite efficiently in the weeks just following a vacancy. But after those easy nomination choices are made, the dynamics of the selection process take on a new character, as presidents face structural incentives to consult more widely beyond their own partisans in choosing nominees. Constraints imposed by the committee process during a potential confirmation struggle have historically been particularly salient to the president, as ideological foes of the president—whether home state senators or the committee chair—measurably drag out the process of selecting a nominee. Coupled with the newly pronounced impact of divided party control, these results suggest that securing the support of critical senators is the key challenge seen by presidents when negotiating over potential nominees. So long as key senators from the opposition eventually agree to a nomination, administrations seem to calculate that support by the full chamber will follow—as the norm of senatorial courtesy would predict.

Discussion and Conclusions

In April 2001, one of the vetters of judicial nominees from the White House Counsel's Office remarked that "It doesn't do the president any good to send up nominees who are on suicide missions. We have to be sensitive to the winds that blow in the Senate, which is evenly divided. . . . We need to be sure we're doing the right thing politically and philosophically."[36] That observation came before Senator Jim Jeffords of Vermont jumped ship from the Republican conference to give Democrats control of the Senate in May 2001. Even with Republicans in control of the Senate that April, Deputy White House Counsel Timothy Flanigan acknowledged that the political viability of potential nominees was a key consideration. Administrations of late have ample incentive to consider the views of home state senators before naming lower court nominees. As much became clear in May 2001 when Jeffords abandoned the GOP and California Democrat Barbara Boxer announced she would oppose the confirmation of Christopher Cox (R-Calif.) to the Ninth Circuit were he to be nominated by the president.

Granted, Senator Boxer was not always able to derail the selection of Ninth Circuit nominees she opposed (witness the nomination of Carolyn Kuhl in June 2001), but the appreciable delay in naming nominees to vacancies in states represented by ideological foes of the president demonstrates the constraints placed by Senate rules and practices on the president's latitude to select nominees. Even in selecting nominees for the district courts, institutionally empowered senators play a role in the selection process. If their views—and potential opposition—did not matter, we would not expect to see such systematic variation in the duration of judicial vacancies. Presidents seeking to put their stamp on the bench would move swiftly to name nominees. But delays in numerous cases—increasing over the past decades—reinforce our conclusions that the selection of judges is no longer a matter of patronage. The stakes of who sits on the bench are too high for interested senators to give administrations a free pass in selecting judges for lifetime appointments on the bench. Presidents do, of course, ignore the views of senators at times in selecting nominees. But the price of doing so may be high. Carolyn Kuhl was never confirmed to the bench, removing herself from consideration three years later after her nomination was filibustered by Senate Democrats.

The Constitution affords the Senate both the power to advise and to consent. Still, most political observers and scholars tend to focus on the politics of consent rather than on the politics of advice. We suspect this imbalance of attention reflects the high visibility of the confirmation process and the relative ease with which data on confirmation outcomes can be acquired. No doubt, interest groups opposed to pending nominees find it easier to rally opposition around particular nominees than around people who might be selected down the road.

In contrast, the nomination process takes place out of the public eye, making it tougher to systematically explain the politics of selection. When it comes to judicial nominations at the lower court level, the process is often deemed by the received wisdom to be mechanical, if not automatic: presidents simply heed the preferences of the home state senators from their party, giving senators a de facto power to nominate as well as to confirm. It is thus not surprising that with the notable exception of Sheldon Goldman, few have ventured to explore what political forces—if any—structure the selection of lower court judges.

Our results suggest that the received wisdom misses the political dynamics that underlie the selection of trial court nominees. To be sure, the presence of a home state senator from the president's party significantly speeds up the selection process, making it appear that home state senators have a right to name federal judges and that presidents automatically heed their choices. But outside these easy cases for which nominees are swiftly agreed upon, negotiation and consultation appear to be the norm. Bolstered by the blue slip and the majority party's control of the Judiciary Committee and executive session agendas, the opposition party has structural and political leverage to force the administration to consult with senators—or at least to move cautiously in considering potential candidates. Judicial selection is clearly a political process that involves a number of actors using their institutional powers to influence the makeup of the federal trial courts. Senatorial courtesy certainly pervades the process of selecting potential judges, but its limits are clear. Presidents and home state senators do not have a free hand to dictate the choice of lower court nominees: structural incentives force presidents to consult far more widely than the inherited view of judicial selection has led us to believe.

4

The Dynamics of Senate Confirmation

The refrain that advice and consent has always been political—the nothing-new-under-the-sun account—encounters rough sledding when we move our focus to the Senate's record in confirming nominees over the past six decades. As we showed in figure 1-1, confirmation rates for presidents' nominations to the U.S. courts of appeals have steeply declined in recent years. Between 1947 and 1950, all seventeen nominees to the federal appellate bench were confirmed. Between 2001 and 2008, roughly one in two nominees was confirmed (table 4-1). The drop-off is stunning, suggesting a sea change in the Senate's treatment of presidents' nominees for the lower federal courts.

Not only is confirmation less likely for today's nominees, the wait for a positive Senate decision has increased fourfold since the 1940s. In the late 1940s, nominations were pending on average about seven weeks until the Senate confirmed them. The typical wait after George W. Bush took office was six months.[1] That average wait time for the average nomination belies the more extreme experiences of nominees such as Richard Paez, a Clinton nominee to the Ninth Circuit Court of Appeals who waited four years for a Republican Senate to confirm him, and Priscilla Owen, a George W. Bush nominee to the Fifth Circuit Court of Appeals whose nomination was filibustered by Democratic senators and who waited four years for her confirmation vote. If we factor in the experiences of nominees who were never confirmed, the average wait was closer to a year before the Senate rendered its decision or, more often, failed to act before adjourning.

Table 4-1. *Average Confirmation Rate for U.S. Courts of Appeals, by Decade, 1947–2008*

Years	Percentage confirmed (total number of nominations)
1947–50	100 (17)
1951–60	100 (47)
1961–70	95 (85)
1971–80	93 (100)
1981–90	90 (106)
1991–2000	64 (126)
2001–08	48 (123)

Source: Data for the 80th to 107th Congresses compiled by authors from U.S. Senate, Committee on the Judiciary, *Legislative and Executive Calendar,* final edition. Data for 108th to 110th Congresses (through December 18, 2008) compiled by the Department of Justice, Office of Legal Policy (www.usdoj.gov/olp/ [December 18, 2008]).

How do we account for the Senate's uneven performance in confirming federal judges? If senators simply deferred to the choice of the president, we would not expect to see much variation in confirmation rates, and we would expect to see nominees swiftly confirmed, conditional on perhaps nonpolitical forces like the Senate's workload or number of vacancies to be filled. If presidents and senators ceded all decisionmaking to home state senators (or other state politicians) from the president's party for the vacant judgeship, then in a similar fashion, we would not expect to see much variation in the Senate's performance. Both accounts fall short, of course, because we see a near collapse of the confirmation process for appellate court nominations by the end of the George W. Bush administration and a decline even in the confirmation rates for district court nominees over the same period.

Why has confirmation become so much less likely for nominees? Why does it take increasingly longer for the Senate to render these decisions? In contrast to accounts that focus largely on partisan skirmishes over the bench, on "hostage taking" of nominees by iconoclastic senators, or on the lobbying of interest groups keen to influence the selection of judges, we return to our accounting in chapter 2 of the broad array of rules and practices that constitute contemporary advice and consent. We show why and when senators' ideological interests encourage them to exploit the rules of the game to derail nominees they oppose on policy and political grounds. We offer statistical models of the likelihood and timing of confirmation during the postwar period, as well as a broader, synthetic accounting of why, when, and where we see such dramatic change in the tenor and practice of advice and consent over this long period and across the bench. We believe that the results offer a more nuanced and systematic explanation of the impact of Senate rules and practices on the makeup of the federal bench. The rules of the game matter, especially when the policy impact of the federal judiciary is at stake.

Forces Shaping Advice and Consent

In thinking about senators' strategies regarding the treatment of presidential appointments to the bench, we focus on the incentives senators have to affect the fate of nominees and their institutional capacities to do so. Thus we detail the ideological and partisan forces that seem to shape senators' reactions to judicial nominations, as well as the procedural advantages afforded to senators through the rules and practices of advice and consent. We need to understand the interaction of incentives and capacities to explain patterns in the Senate's treatment of nominees during the postwar period.

Partisan and Ideological Incentives

Partisan and ideological conflicts are inextricably linked in the contemporary Congress as the two legislative parties have diverged ideologically in recent decades. Not surprising, Washington pundits assessing the state of judicial selection have often pinpointed poisoned relations between conservative Republicans and President Clinton and between liberal Democrats and President Bush as the proximate cause of the slowdown in advice and consent. They suggest that partisan antagonism between Clinton and far-right conservatives led Republican senators to delay even the most highly qualified nominees. Democrats' blocking of several of Bush's nominees in the One Hundred Eighth Congress (2003–04) was similarly attributed to partisan pique, as liberal Democrats were said to block Bush nominees slated for vacancies that Republicans had prevented Clinton from filling.

Although oftentimes senators have been criticized for allowing partisan gamesmanship to dictate the parties' strategies in attempting to block the opposition party's nominees, these party strategies are also tightly linked to policy differences between the parties over the issues increasingly likely to come before the federal courts. The usual assumption about nominees, of course, is that they are selected in part because their policy views closely reflect the views of the president—insofar as the administration can determine a candidate's views. The rise of ideological differences between the two parties during the past two decades likely has affected the pace and rate of confirming new federal judges, as senators anticipate that Republican-appointed judges will vote more conservatively on the bench and that Democratic-appointed judges will vote more liberally. Party scrutiny of nominees is as much a function of a nominee's policy views as it may be of a party's strategy to elevate judicial selection to a political issue. If so, we would expect to see a relationship between the extent of polarization and the Senate's treatment of nominees:

> *Partisan polarization.* As policy differences between the two parties grow, the confirmation rate of appellate court nominees and the pace of Senate action are likely to slow.

Partisan politics may affect the process of advice and consent more broadly in the guise of divided party government. Because presidents overwhelmingly seek to appoint judges who hail from the president's party, Senate scrutiny of judicial nominees should be particularly intense when two different parties control the White House and the Senate. It is not a surprise then that nominees considered during a period of divided control take significantly longer to be confirmed than those nominated during a period of unified control. Judicial nominees are also less likely to be confirmed during divided government: over the past six decades, the Senate has confirmed on average 87 percent of appellate court nominees considered during a period of unified control, while confirming 70 percent of nominees during divided government. If this general trend holds up over time, we would expect to find the following:

> *Divided government.* Nominations to the appellate courts are less likely to be confirmed in periods of divided party control, and the Senate is likely to take longer to act on those nominations.

If the parties fought over the general tenor of the bench—but not over particular courts of the federal judiciary—we would not expect to see much variation in any given year in the Senate's treatment of nominees to different courts of appeals. All things considered, it would make little difference to senators whether they were considering confirmation of a nominee slated for the Second or Ninth Circuits. But as we saw in table 1-1, the Senate does not appear to treat all circuits alike. Some courts like the Sixth Circuit saw roughly 60 percent of their nominees blocked in recent decades, while other courts like the Seventh Circuit saw most of their nominees confirmed in that period.

The characters of different circuits are not fixed in stone: the composition of the bench tends to vary over time with arrivals and departures of judges nominated by different presidents. Because presidents tend to appoint nominees who share their party affiliation, a fair characterization of a court of appeals is the relative balance of judges appointed by Democratic or Republican presidents. Granted, most cases in the federal appellate courts are heard by randomly generated three-judge panels; an appellate bench rarely meets *en banc*. Still, because three-judge panels are selected from the pool of sitting judges on the bench, the makeup of each of these panels will be shaped in part by the underlying partisan balance of the court.

We draw attention here to the partisan tilt of the court because of its implications for the policy tenor of the decisions that are likely to emerge from the bench. Nominations to courts that are evenly divided are likely to have a more significant impact on the development of the law, as compared with appointments to courts that lean decidedly in one partisan direction or the other. Senators should thus be especially reluctant to confirm nominees to courts when the appointment would tip the court balance in favor of a president from the opposing party. In those cases, the policy views and judicial philosophy of the newly appointed judge could have a marked impact on the nature of the decisions made by that court.

In 2007 half of the twelve federal circuits were technically balanced courts, defined as those appellate courts on which judges appointed by Democratic presidents constitute between 40 and 60 percent of the active judges on the bench in a particular year.[2] Among the balanced courts during the George W. Bush administration was the Sixth Circuit Court of Appeals, straddling populous midwestern states such as Michigan and Ohio. Not only was the bench missing a quarter of its judges—including one seat declared a judicial emergency after sitting empty for several years, but the circuit had also been precariously balanced between the parties for over a decade. We suspect, and test below, that the Senate's sluggishness in filling seats on the Sixth Circuit is in large part due to the even tilt of the court, a feature that increases the strategic importance of the circuit to the parties when considering new judges.

Blocking Clinton's Democratic nominees to the Sixth Circuit in the late 1990s allowed the Senate Republican majority to prevent the Democrats from transforming the party-balanced court into a Democratic-dominated bench. Similarly, once George W. Bush took office, the two Michigan senators (both Democrats) went to great lengths to prevent the Senate from taking action on his nominees for that court. To give these nominees an easy ride to confirmation would only serve to enhance the representation of Republican judges on the bench. The impasse over the makeup of the Sixth Circuit bench ended only when Bush agreed in 2008 to renominate Helene White—a Clinton nominee repeatedly blocked by Republican senators. In return, Democratic senators agreed to support confirmation of Bush's preferred nominee for another Sixth Circuit vacancy, Raymond Kethledge.[3]

In short, the parties in recent years may have taken their battles down to a microlevel, carefully targeting individual courts depending on the ideological tenor of its bench. Such strategies by the parties complicate presidents' efforts to reshape the bench as they see fit, even when their party controls both the White House and the Senate. If balanced courts are generally targeted by the opposition party, we would expect to find the following throughout the postwar period:

> *Party balance.* Nominations to courts with a balanced bench are less likely to be confirmed, and the Senate will take longer to act on these nominations.

Institutional Forces

Partisan and ideological forces likely provide senators with an incentive to probe the opposition party's judicial nominees. But the capacity to derail nominees depends on the rules and practices of advice and consent—a set of institutional tools that distributes power across the institution. Thus to explain the fate of the president's judicial nominees, we need to know something about the institutional arena in which senators dispense their advice and consent.

As we show elsewhere in work with David Primo, multiple potential vetoes can be exploited by senators in seeking to affect the fate of a nominee—including an array of Senate rules and practices wielded in committee and on the floor by individual senators and the two political parties.[4] In theory, nominees only have to secure the consent of a floor majority, as nominations are considered for an up or down vote in the Senate's executive session. In practice, nominees must secure the support of several pivotal Senate players—meaning that more than a simple majority may be needed for confirmation.

The initial institutional hurdle for any nominee is securing approval from the Senate Judiciary Committee. By tradition, senators from the home state of each judicial nominee take the lead on casting first judgment on potential appointees. As we detail in chapter 2, the veto power of home state senators is institutionalized in Judiciary panel procedures. Both of the home state senators are asked their views about judicial nominees from their home state pending before the committee. Senators can return the blue slip demarking their support or objection to the nominee, or they can refuse to return the blue slip altogether—an action signaling the senator's opposition to the nominee. One negative blue slip from a home state senator traditionally was sufficient to block further action on a nominee. As the process has become more polarized in recent years, committee chairs have been tempted to ignore objections from minority party senators. At a minimum, blue slips today weigh heavily in the committee chair's assessment on whether, when, and how to proceed with a nominee, but senators' objections do not necessarily prevent the committee from proceeding.

Historically, large ideological differences between the president and the home state senator for appellate nominees have led to longer confirmation proceedings than normal, suggesting the power of home state senators to affect panel proceedings. Conversely, the strong support of one's home state senator is essential in navigating the committee successfully. Given the often fractured attention of the Senate and the willingness of senators to heed the preferences of the home state senator, having a strong advocate in the Senate with an interest in seeing the nomination proceed is critical in smoothing the way for nominees. If home state senators are able to block nominees they oppose on ideological grounds, we would generally expect to find the following:

Blue slip power. When a home state senator for a judgeship is ideologically distant from the president, nominations will be less likely to be confirmed, and the Senate is likely to act more slowly on the nominations.

Once approved by committee, a nomination has a second broad institutional hurdle to clear: making it onto the Senate's crowded agenda. By rule and precedent, both majority and minority party coalitions can delay nominations after they clear committee. Because the presiding officer of the chamber gives the majority leader priority in being recognized to speak on the Senate floor, the majority leader has the upper hand in setting the chamber's agenda. When the president's party controls the Senate, this means that nominations are usually confirmed more quickly; under divided control, nominations can be kept off the floor by the majority leader—who wields the right to make a non-debatable motion to call the Senate into executive session to consider nominees. That procedural advantage for the majority party enhances the importance of support from the majority leader—and the majority party caucus by extension—in shaping the fate of presidential appointees. This dynamic underlies the divided government hypothesis offered above.

The majority leader's discretion over the executive session agenda is not wielded without challenge, however, as nominations can be filibustered once called up in executive session. The chance that a nomination might be filibustered typically motivates the majority leader to seek unanimous consent of the full chamber before bringing a nomination before the Senate. Such consultation between the two parties means that nominations are unlikely to clear the Senate without the endorsement of the minority party.

The de facto requirement of minority party assent grants the party opposing the president significant power to affect the fate of nominees, even if that party does not control the Senate. As policy differences increase between the president and the opposing party, that party is more likely to exercise its power to delay nominees. Given the high degree of polarization between the two parties today, it is not surprising that judicial nominations have become such a flash point for the parties. As we discuss below, when Democrats lost control of the Senate after the 2002 elections, they turned to new tactics to block objectionable nominees: the filibuster. To be sure, some contentious nominations have in the past been subject to cloture votes. But all of those lower court nominees were eventually confirmed. In 2003, however, numerous of these judicial filibusters were successful. Use of such tactics likely flowed from the increased polarization of the two parties and from the rising salience of the federal courts across the interest group community. As we suggested above in the polarization hypothesis, much of the recent variation in the fate of judicial nominees before the Senate is thus likely driven by ideologically motivated players and parties in both the executive and legislative branches exploiting the rules of the game in an effort to shape the makeup of the federal bench.

Electoral and Other Incentives

We also consider how elements of the political calendar may shape the fate of judicial nominees. It is often suggested that delays encountered by judicial nominees may be a natural consequence of an approaching presidential election. Decades ago, the opposition party in the Senate might have wanted to save vacancies as a pure matter of patronage: that party would have more positions to dole out if it won back the presidency after the election. More recently, the opposition might want to save vacancies, so that a president of their own party might fill the vacancies with judges more in tune with the party's policy priorities.

There is ample evidence of vacancy hoarding in presidential election years in the recent past. For example, with control of both the Senate and the White House up for grabs in November 2008, Democrats had by the spring confirmed only ten of the twenty-one nominations to the federal courts of appeals made by President Bush during the One Hundred Tenth Congress. Nominees for the less controversial federal trial courts did not fare much better in the One Hundred Tenth, with just over 60 percent confirmed before the fall of 2008. More generally, over the past sixty years, the Senate has treated judicial nominations submitted or pending during a presidential election year significantly different from other judicial nominations. First, the Senate has historically taken longer to confirm nominations pending in a presidential election year than those submitted earlier in a president's term. Second, and more notably, these nominees during a presidential election year are significantly less likely to be confirmed. For all judicial nominations submitted between 1947 and 2008, appointees for the courts of appeals that were pending in the Senate in a presidential election year were 35 percent less likely to be confirmed than nominees considered in other years.

The tussle over Senate inaction on courts of appeals nominees in the summer of 2008 gave rise to a perennial Senate debate about the existence of the Thurmond Rule, so named for the late senator Strom Thurmond (R-S.C.). According to media accounts, in July 1980 while attending the Republican National Convention, Senator Thurmond asked the Republican presidential nominee, Ronald Reagan, to contact Minority Leader Howard Baker (R-Tenn.) and other Senate Republicans to request that they attempt to block confirmation of any more judicial appointments before the election; Reagan reportedly agreed.[5] The Senate Republican Conference then dispatched a three-member committee to analyze all of President Jimmy Carter's pending nominations (including judicial appointments) to identify those whose service would overlap with a potential Reagan presidency.[6] However, the Senate Judiciary Committee continued to hold hearings and report nominations well into September. Twelve nominations—eleven for the federal trial courts and one for the appellate courts—were confirmed in September, including ten nominees confirmed en bloc on September 29.[7] Thus, although the Thurmond Rule was said to be born in 1980 in anticipation of a Republican White House, there is little evidence of a blanket work stoppage on the part of the Judiciary Committee in reviewing Carter's nominees that fall.

There is no evidence that the Thurmond Rule ever existed as a formal rule of the Senate Judiciary panel or of the Senate. That has not, however, stopped senators from debating its existence. In 2004 Judiciary Committee chair Orrin Hatch (R-Utah) both denied the existence of the rule on the Senate floor and referred to it during a hearing as something he hoped the committee could overcome.[8] The debate continued in force in 2008, with Republican minority leader Mitch McConnell of Kentucky and Judiciary Committee ranking member Arlen Specter of Pennsylvania claiming that "there is no Thurmond Rule"[9] when criticizing the Democrats for not moving more of President Bush's nominees. Even though there is no formal Thurmond Rule, senators continue to disagree about the date on which the rule kicks in: In 1997 Judiciary Committee ranking member Patrick Leahy (D-Vt.) said the rule applies for the last few months of the president's term; in October 2000, he put the stop date for election-year nomination considerations at "midyear."[10]

The data suggest that in recent presidential election years (1996, 2000, and 2004) the Senate confirmed fewer nominees than in the four previous presidential election years (1980, 1984, 1988, and 1992). In addition, the last three cycles have seen the Senate stop considering judicial nominees earlier in the calendar year—the last confirmation in 2004 was in late June—than in the previous four cycles.[11] Senators, it seems, have ample incentives to drag their feet as a presidential election approaches, even if Senate rules do not formally endorse that practice.[12] If this trend is generalizable over the postwar period, we would expect to find the following:

> *Presidential election years.* Nominations pending during a presidential election year will be less likely to be confirmed, and the Senate is likely to act more slowly on these nominees.

Finally, the evidence arrayed in the three figures in chapter 1 suggests that the confirmation process has become more protracted over time: it takes longer for the president to select nominees and longer for the Senate to confirm, and we see declining rates of confirmation for both levels of the federal bench. Granted, it is difficult to separate the effects of a secular slowdown in the confirmation process from a concurrent rise in partisan polarization. But it is important to keep in mind that ideological disagreement between the parties should only affect advice and consent if the parties hold different views about the courts and their impact on public policy. The rising importance of the federal courts since the 1950s, as interest groups and politicians have used the courts as a means of resolving intractable policy disputes, may well have encouraged the parties to take a more aggressive stance in reviewing nominations made by the opposition party.[13] As the federal courts become more central to the making of public policy, we should expect to find broader and heightened concern amongst politicians and political parties about the makeup of the bench. This gradual and secular change in the confirmation process, if true, undermines empirical support for the big bang account of a sudden, dramatic shift in the practice of advice and consent.

> *Over time trend.* Nominations will be less likely to be confirmed over time, and the Senate is likely to take increasingly longer to act on nominations over time.

Data and Methods

To explain variation in conflict over judicial nominees, we track the fate of all nominations to the federal courts of appeals between 1947 and 2006.[14] We compile data on judicial nominations from the *Final Calendar* printed each Congress by the Senate Committee on the Judiciary.[15] We use two dependent variables. The first indicates whether or not each nominee for the U.S. courts of appeals was eventually confirmed in the Congress in which he or she was nominated. We code "confirmation outcome" as 1 if the nominee failed to be confirmed (0 otherwise). The second dependent variable, "confirmation duration," captures the length of time each nomination was pending before the Senate before being confirmed. For each observation, we record the date the nomination was made and the date on which the Senate acted (and how it acted). If the Senate failed to act by the end of the Congress, we code the final action date as the last day of the Congress. When the Senate fails to act, the nomination dies and must be resubmitted in the next Congress if the president still seeks to see the nominee confirmed.

Estimation

To test our conjectures about the outcome and duration of confirmation contests, we estimate two models. The first is a simple logit model, in which we model the likelihood that a nominee was confirmed during the Congress in which he or she was nominated. The second model is a hazard rate model. As in chapter 3, because we have no theoretical expectation regarding the distribution for the time until the event of interest (a nomination) occurs, we use a Cox model of proportional hazards to assess the effect of the covariates on the hazard rate (otherwise described as the conditional probability of failure at time t). The coefficients indicate whether each variable increases or decreases the hazard rate. Roughly speaking, we can interpret an increase (decrease) in the hazard rate as meaning that increases in the value of the variable have the effect of speeding up (slowing down) Senate action on a nominee. Because we have multiple observations for nominees whose names are submitted to the Senate more than once, we use robust standard errors clustering on the vacancy to control for correlated errors across multiple observations for a single seat.

Independent Variables

We use a series of dummy variables to tap the dichotomous independent variables. To indicate the presence of "divided government," we code whether or not control of the Senate and the White House is unified or divided for each Congress during which a nomination has been submitted to the Senate. We code the annual "party balance" of the cohort of active judges serving on each circuit each year using data compiled by Jonathan Kastellec.[16] We code balanced courts as those on which the proportion of active judges appointed by a Democratic president lies between 40 and 60 percent. To isolate home state senators who are ideologically distant from the president, we first determine the ideology of the two home state senators using Poole and Rosenthal's DW-NOMINATE first dimension score, and then calculate the ideological distance between the president and each home state senator.[17] If the ideological distance between the farther home state senator and the president is greater than 1 standard deviation above the mean ideological distance, that senator is coded 1 as an "ideologically distant blue slip senator," 0 otherwise. We code nominations that are pending during a "presidential election" year as 1, 0 otherwise. To control for the quality of the nominee, we use the majority rating issued for each nominee by the American Bar Association, coding "well-qualified" as 1 (and all other nominees 0).[18]

Finally, we devise a measure of partisan "polarization" to capture the ideological gulf between the two Senate parties. Relying on DW-NOMINATE scores to tap each senator's ideological positions, we calculate the mean ideology of each Senate party in each Congress and take the absolute difference between party means to create a measure of polarization. The variable increases more than double from its nadir in the Eighty-third Congress (1953–54) to its peak in the One Hundred Ninth (2005–06).

Explaining Trends in Advice and Consent

How do we account more systematically for variation in the degree of conflict over judicial nominees? The multiple forces outlined above are clearly at play. For social scientists investigating patterns over time, this raises a key question. Taking these forces together, how well do the trends noted here

Table 4-2. *Likelihood of Senate Confirmation of Nominations to the U.S. Courts of Appeals, 1947–2006*[a]

Variable	Coefficient (robust std. error)
Divided government	−1.106***
	(.342)
Balanced bench	−.484*
	(.283)
Degree of partisan polarization	−9.355***
	(1.168)
Ideologically distant home state senator	−.713*
	(.311)
Nomination pending during a presidential election	−2.245***
	(.288)
Well-qualified nominee	.434
	(.292)
Constant	9.745***
	(.993)
N	524
Log pseudolikelihood	−162.683
Probability Chi square	.000***

Source: Data for the 80th to 107th Congresses compiled by authors from U.S. Senate, Committee on the Judiciary, *Legislative and Executive Calendar*, final edition. Data for 108th to 110th Congresses (through December 18, 2008) compiled by the Department of Justice, Office of Legal Policy (www.usdoj.gov/olp/ [December 18, 2008]).

***$p < .001$; **$p < .01$, *$p < .05$; all one-tailed t tests.

a. The dependent variable is coded 1 if nominee was confirmed in the Congress in which he or she was nominated, 0 otherwise. Parameter estimates are logit coefficients generated by the *logit* routine in Stata 9.0. Independent variables are described in the text.

hold up? Once these forces are subjected to multivariate controls, what can we conclude about the relative impact of partisan, ideological, and institutional forces on the rate and pace of judicial confirmations? Our answers to these questions are consequential as they help us to evaluate how well the president and the Senate discharge their constitutional duties of advice and consent.

The results shown in table 4-2 can help us to disentangle the forces that shape the Senate's treatment of presidential appointees to the bench. First, the degree of partisan polarization matters strongly. As the two parties diverge ideologically, the likelihood of confirmation goes down.[19] The magnitude of the effect is substantial. During the least polarized Senate of the postwar period (the Eighty-third Congress, 1953–54), the likelihood of confirmation was 99 percent for a well-qualified nominee slated for an ideologically balanced court.[20] That same nominee considered in the most polarized Congress (the One Hundred Ninth, 2005–06) had a 63 percent chance of being confirmed. As the two parties take increasingly different positions on major policy issues, they are less and less likely to give the other party's nominees an easy path to the bench. If we make two reasonable assumptions—a president is likely to be off center ideologically when his party is, and a president tries to select nominees who share his policy outlook—then the tandem rise in polarization and decline in confirmation likely reflects the opposition's increased scrutiny of off-center nominees in periods of polarization, all things considered.[21] Given that confirmation rates are rarely 100 percent or 0 percent, the all-things-considered caveat is important. The impact of polarization, in fact, is much stronger than the effect we detect for divided party control. Nominations are significantly less likely to be confirmed in periods of divided government. The magnitude of the effect, however, is less than 10 percent if we assume an average level of polarization under the same conditions noted above.[22]

The statistical results also suggest that home state senators who find themselves ideologically opposed to the president are able to reduce a nominee's chances of confirmation. When the more distant of the two home state senators for a nomination is still reasonably close to the president, the chance of confirmation is more than 90 percent; the chance of confirmation slips by 7 percent when one of the home state senators is ideologically distant from the president (and presumably then from the nominee).[23] Lodging an objection through the blue slip—perhaps because the senator's objection may be backed up by the threat of a party filibuster—confers leverage on a senator seeking to derail a president's pick for a judgeship in the senator's home state. An approaching presidential election also seems to dampen the likelihood of confirmation by nearly 40 percent when control of the White House—and hence the power to select judicial nominees—is at stake.[24]

The partisan balance of the circuit also seems to matter. The likelihood of confirmation drops by 3 percent when senators consider a nomination for a balanced circuit (setting polarization at its average level and the other controls as above). Nominating a candidate for a balanced court in a period of divided government, however, lowers the odds of confirmation precipitously, as it declines by some 12 percent. That finding puts into perspective debates in the late 1990s over the makeup of the Sixth Circuit. In 1997 and 1998 the circuit was nearly evenly balanced between Democrats and Republicans, as Democrats made up roughly 45 percent of the bench. That tight ideological balance led the parties to stalemate over additional appointments to that bench, despite the fact that nearly a quarter of the bench was vacant during that period. Michigan's lone Republican senator blocked Clinton's nominees by exploiting the blue slip in the late 1990s, and the Republican chair of the Judiciary panel recognized his objections. Michigan's two Democratic senators after the 2000 elections then objected to Bush's appointments to the Sixth Circuit. General disagreement over the policy views of the nominees certainly fueled these senators, but their opposition was particularly intense given the stakes of filling the judgeships for the ideological balance of the region's federal bench.

We find only weak evidence that the quality of the nominees, as signaled by the American Bar Association's (ABA) Standing Committee on the Federal Judiciary, has much bearing on confirmation outcomes.[25] One possibility is that the ABA is not viewed across the board as a neutral arbiter of judicial quality: senators may systematically ignore the committee's recommendations. We know for certain that the Bush administration discounted the ratings done by the bar association, as it eliminated in 2001 a fifty-year-old practice that had allowed the ABA to prescreen potential candidates before a nomination was announced.[26] Senator Orrin Hatch also moved in 2001 to abandon the ABA's ratings as part of the Judiciary Committee's review of nominees.[27] Alternatively, judicial qualifications may not be terribly important for most nominees. Very few nominees are actually rated unqualified, and senators may not perceive much of a difference between a nominee deemed well qualified as opposed to qualified. Thus senators' calculations about whether to confirm would be influenced more heavily by other considerations.

Collectively, these institutional and electoral forces matter quite a bit. Imagine a period of unified party control in which the two Senate parties are reasonably close ideologically. If the home state senator is reasonably compatible in ideological terms with the president and if the vacant judge-ship occurs on a court of appeals firmly in one partisan camp or the other, confirmation is all but guaranteed. In contrast, imagine a nomination sub-mitted to the Senate in a period of divided government when the parties are polarized. If that nomination is slotted for a judgeship on a roughly bal-anced court in the run-up to a presidential election, then the chance of confirmation is barely 25 percent.[28] Electoral conditions in the most recent years are, of course, much closer to the latter scenario than the former—helping us to pinpoint obstacles in the pathways of advice and consent. Most important, when we reestimate the model controlling for the passage of time, the results are largely consistent with those reported here.[29] Varia-tion in these electoral, partisan, and ideological forces seems to be as impor-tant as secular change in the practice of advice and consent in explaining confirmation outcomes over the postwar period.

We can also use multivariate methods to evaluate the forces that shape how long it takes the Senate to act on pending nominees. We are interested in how long it takes the Senate to act because the time that elapses serves as a proxy for the degree of conflict over any given nominee. We read quick action by the Senate to indicate widespread support for the nominee; we read slug-gish action to indicate greater opposition to the president's appointee. In table 4-3, we present the results of a duration model, using the same estima-tion procedure introduced in chapter 3. We can read the sign on the coeffi-cients to indicate whether or not increases in the value of the variable increase or decrease what is known as the conditional probability of action: on any given day, what is the likelihood that the Senate has taken action on the nom-inee, given that it has not yet acted? Positive (or negative) and significant coefficients indicate that increases (or decreases) in the variable speed up (or slow down) the pace or, more technically, the "hazard" of Senate action.

The results in the first column of table 4-3 suggest that the Senate moves significantly more slowly in periods of divided party control, in presidential election years, and in Congresses in which polarization is on the rise. These, of course, are the conditions under which a president has an opportunity to tilt an appellate bench in a policy direction that favors the president's agenda while potentially undermining the opposition's. Not surprisingly then, opposition party senators in these Congresses likely take advantage of cham-ber rules and practices to move more slowly in reviewing the nominee—

Table 4-3. *Timing of Senate Action on Nominations to the U.S. Courts of Appeals, 1947–2006*[a]

Variable	Coefficient (robust std. error) 1	Coefficient (robust std. error) 2
Divided government	−.536***	−.327*
	(.118)	(.163)
Balanced bench	−.100	.056
	(.108)	(.142)
Balanced bench during divided government	—	−.342*
		(.213)
Degree of partisan polarization	−5.879***	−5.788***
	(.465)	(.458)
Ideologically distant home state senator	−.045	.174
	(.130)	(.157)
Ideologically distant home state senator during divided government	—	−.595*
		(.277)
Nomination pending during a presidential election	−.882***	−.895***
	(.137)	(.140)
Well-qualified nominee	.095	.083
	(.110)	(.108)
N	524	524
Log pseudolikelihood	−2,187.712	−2,184.308
Probability Chi square	.000	.000***

Source: Data for the 80th to 107th Congresses compiled by authors from U.S. Senate, Committee on the Judiciary, *Legislative and Executive Calendar,* final edition. Data for the 108th to 110th Congresses (through December 18, 2008) compiled by the Department of Justice, Office of Legal Policy (www.usdoj.gov/olp/ [December 18, 2008]).

***$p < .001$; **$p < .01$, *$p < .05$; all one-tailed t tests.

a. Parameter estimates are Cox regression coefficients generated by the *stcox* routine in Stata 8.0.

whether by moving slowly in committee, failing to call up nominees for confirmation on the Senate floor, or in periods of unified control threatening to block confirmation.

It is interesting that the Senate does not move appreciably faster or slower when the president submits a nominee for a balanced appellate court. Nor does the Senate seem to move especially slowly when a home state senator's policy views differ strongly from the president's. If we look at the impact of these factors during periods of divided government, however, the effects are pronounced. First, as shown in column 2 of table 4-3, when a nomination to a balanced bench is forwarded to the Senate in a period when the White House and Senate are led by different parties, the Senate drags its feet appreciably on that nomination.

Second, we find a similar stalling of advice and consent in periods of divided government when an ideological foe of the president is given a blue slip. In these instances, the chair of the Judiciary panel—who may have little incentive to be responsive to the president in a period of divided government—is likely to heed the views of a fellow partisan registered on a blue slip. Democratic foot-dragging on some of President George W. Bush's nominees late in 2001 after Democrats had regained control of the Senate is illustrative. Democratic Judiciary chair Patrick Leahy of Vermont was willing to heed objections from Democrat Barbara Boxer when she refused to return a blue slip for Ninth Circuit nominee Carolyn Kuhl.[30] We can easily imagine that had Republicans not lost control of the chamber, leaving Senator Orrin Hatch (R-Utah) as chair, Boxer's objection might have been brushed aside. This is precisely what happened when Republicans retook control of the chamber in the 2002 elections. Refusal to return the blue slip by Democratic senators did not deter Senator Hatch from reporting several Bush nominations to the floor. Not surprisingly, judicial filibusters of those nominees ensued—contributing to the significant lengthening of the confirmation process in recent years.[31]

The Senate and the "Nuclear Option"

Statistical analysis suggests the enduring impact of partisan, institutional, and temporal forces on the fate of presidential appointments to the federal bench. Still, the falloff in confirmation rates leaves no doubt that advice and consent has changed markedly in recent years. Far more attention is paid to these confirmation battles by the media, and interest in the fate of presidential appointees now extends beyond the home state senators. Both parties—often fueled by supportive groups outside the chamber—have made the plight of potential judges central to their campaigns for the White House and Congress.[32] The salience of judicial nominations to the two political parties—inside and outside of the halls of the Senate—is *prima facie* evidence that there is definitely something new under the sun when it comes to the politics of judicial selection.

The rising salience of judgeships has encouraged senators to innovate as they seek to shape the fate of nominees. These new tactics have prompted charges from critics as being unconstitutional and contrary to the intentions of the Framers of the Constitution. Far from being unconstitutional, we believe these new tactics reflect adjustments by senators in light of a changing electoral and institutional context in which judicial selection takes place.

The key innovation in the confirmation process has been the successful use of filibusters by the minority party on the Senate floor against controversial nominees. By the spring of 2005, Democrats had successfully filibustered ten of President Bush's nominees for the federal courts of appeals, as a nearly united Democratic Party prevented the Republican majority from invoking cloture via Rule 22 to end debate over the nominees. In fact, Democrats had so frustrated the majority party after launching four filibusters that Republicans staged a forty-hour talkathon of their own to highlight Democrats' intransigence. Rather than convincing Democrats to give up their fight, the talkathon ended with Democrats blocking cloture on two more appellate court nominees. Citing the nominees' controversial views on issues including civil rights, environmental policy, and abortion rights of women, Democrats maintained that the Bush nominees held views too far from the mainstream to support confirmation.[33]

Critics of the Democratic-led filibusters charged that the filibusters were unprecedented and unconstitutional. In fact, there is little evidence to sustain such charges. Consider first the question of whether these were the first judicial nominees to be filibustered. Before the One Hundred Eighth Congress filibusters (2003–04), numerous judicial nominations had been subject to cloture votes. Granted, motions to invoke cloture may be filed even in the absence of a filibuster. But given that most judicial nominees are confirmed by unanimous consent, it is reasonable to suspect that efforts to invoke cloture on judicial nominees were precipitated by threatened or actual filibusters on the Senate floor. Certainly the filibuster against the elevation of Abe Fortas to chief justice of the United States in 1968 falls in this category, as President Lyndon Johnson withdrew the nomination after the Senate rejected cloture, 45–43. Between 1967 and 2002, cloture was attempted on seventeen judicial nominations—including the appointments of Stephen Breyer to the First Circuit Court of Appeals and Richard Paez to the Ninth

Circuit (after a four-year wait for confirmation)—a number that rose to twenty-nine by the end of 2004.[34]

So cloture motions on judicial nominations are not unprecedented. And we can assume that the majority party was moved on these occasions to attempt cloture given the continued opposition of minority party senators. Daniel Manion, for example, nominated by Reagan for a court of appeals judgeship in 1986 attracted considerable opposition from Democrats before he was confirmed. What was distinctive about the One Hundred Eighth Congress filibusters, in contrast, was that they were all successful. Apart from the Fortas filibuster, no other judicial nomination filibuster had been successful before Democrats moved to block selected Bush nominees in 2003. To be sure, successful *obstruction* of judicial nominees is not without precedent. Republicans successfully blocked scores of Clinton nominees when they controlled the Senate in the late 1990s. Controlling the agenda of the Judiciary panel, Republicans blocked nominees simply by refusing to hold hearings or to call them up for a vote after they were reported from committee. Successful opposition to confirming new judges is not new, but the tactics of opposition—and their visibility to the public—certainly are.

Even if filibusters against nominations had precedent, Republicans charged that such filibusters were unconstitutional: "The Constitution, fairly read, clearly calls for a majority vote on judicial nominees," argued Senator Jeff Sessions (R-Ala.).[35] If the Constitution is interpreted to require a simple majority vote for confirmation, then any rule or procedure that allows a minority of the body to block a majority from casting a vote on confirmation conflicts with the Constitution. This position led critics of the Democratic filibusters to charge that Rule 22 could not be applied to any nominations. Leaving aside the question of how debate would be conducted on judicial nominations in the absence of any Senate rule other than Rule 22 limiting debate, the plain face of Rule 22 seems to undermine that interpretation. According to Senate rules, a cloture petition can be filed "to bring to a close the debate upon any measure, motion, other matter pending before the Senate." Certainly nominations fall within the broad sweep of Rule 22.

Recognizing the limits of the constitutionality argument, Republican leaders advocated two reforms of the confirmation process in 2003. One reform would have implemented a sliding scale for cloture, successively reducing the number of votes needed to invoke cloture as debate goes on.

Under the proposal, a majority vote could be reached on nominations within two weeks—thus eliminating the filibuster over judicial nominations. In theory, Senate rules can be changed by majority vote. But if the rule change were to be filibustered—which it surely would be—then under Senate rules a two-thirds majority would be needed to break the filibuster. Not surprising, reform of Rule 22 came for naught while the GOP controlled the Senate, which gave up its control after the November elections in 2006.

The Senate majority leader, Bill Frist (R-Tenn.), also proposed in 2003 eliminating filibusters of judicial nominees through a more radical approach dubbed "the nuclear option." Under this approach, a simple majority of the Senate would seek through parliamentary appeals to establish the precedent that filibusters against nominations were unconstitutional. History of cloture reform suggests that such a majority-route to changing Senate rules might technically be possible.[36] But the approach was dubbed the nuclear option because of the anticipated consequences if the attempt were to succeed: Democrats would exploit their remaining procedural advantages and shut down most Senate business. As Senator Chuck Schumer (D-N.Y.) remarked, the nuclear option would "vaporize every bridge in sight—bipartisan or otherwise."[37]

With just a fifty-five-seat majority and decrying the Democrats' tactics as unconstitutional and unprecedented, Republicans' efforts to invoke the nuclear option to end judicial filibusters came to a head in the spring of 2005. With a cloture motion filed on a nomination to the Fifth Circuit Court of Appeals—the nomination of Priscilla Owen, who had been filibustered by Democrats in the previous Congress—Senator Frist declared that should the cloture vote fail, he would put into motion the set of procedural calls envisioned by proponents of the nuclear option.

Enter the Senate's Gang of 14—a group of "moderates, mavericks, and institutionalists."[38] A group of seven Democrats and seven Republicans averted the showdown by signing a "memorandum of understanding on judicial nominations" in May 2005 before the cloture vote could take place. The Gang of 14 promised for the rest of 2005 and 2006 to oppose efforts to invoke the nuclear option, to allow three of the ten filibustered nominations to receive confirmation, and to filibuster judicial nominees only under "extraordinary circumstances." The Gang of 14's agreement averted the showdown, of course, because neither party could proceed without their support. The Democratic leadership could not block cloture without the votes of the seven Democrats; the Republican leadership could not secure the majority vote necessary to invoke the nuclear option without the votes of the seven Republicans. Because Republicans lost their Senate majority in the next elections, the potential threat of the nuclear option dissipated.[39] Democrats in the One Hundred Tenth Congress (2007–08), opposing many of Bush's appellate court nominees, simply refused to bring them up—further evidence that the shape of obstruction in battles over advice and consent will vary with changes in the electoral and institutional contexts.

The New Wars of Judicial Selection

The stalemate over advice and consent in 2005 suggests that the politics of judicial selection continue to change. Although we can attribute variation in the Senate's treatment of judicial nominees during the postwar period to enduring electoral and institutional forces, the character of the process seems qualitatively different today than in the past. To be sure, not every nominee experiences intense opposition, as Democrats acquiesced to more than 300 of President Bush's judicial nominees. But the salience of the process seems to have increased sharply starting perhaps in the early 1980s and continuing with full force under the presidencies of Clinton and George W. Bush.

The rising salience of federal judgeships is visible on several fronts. First, intense interest in the selection of federal judges is no longer limited to the home state senators for the nomination. Second, negative blue slips from home state senators no longer automatically kill a nomination, as recent Judiciary panel chairs have been hesitant to accord such influence to their minority party colleagues. Third, recorded floor votes are now the norm for confirmation of appellate court judges, as nominations are of increased importance to groups outside the institution.[40] And fourth, nominations now draw the attention of strategists within both political parties—as evidenced by President Bush's focus on judicial nominations in stumping for Republican Senate candidates throughout his tenure in office.

How do we account for the rising salience of federal judgeships to actors in and out of the Senate? It is tempting to claim that the activities of organized interests after the 1987 Supreme Court confirmation battle over Robert Bork are responsible. But interest groups have kept a close eye on judicial selection for quite some time. Both liberal and conservative groups were involved periodically from the late 1960s into the 1980s. And in 1984 liberal groups under the umbrella of the Alliance for Justice commenced systematic monitoring of judicial appointments, as had the conservative Judicial Reform Project of the Free Congress Foundation earlier in the decade. Although tactics by interest groups may have fanned the fires over judicial selection in recent years, the introduction of new blocking tactics in the Senate developed long after groups had become active in the process of judicial selection.[41] Outside groups may encourage senators to take more aggressive stands against judicial nominees, but by and large, Senate opposition reflects senators' concerns about the policy impact of judges on the federal bench.

Rather than attribute the state of judicial selection to the lobbying of outside groups, we believe that the politics of judicial selection have been indelibly shaped by two concurrent trends. First, the two political parties are more ideologically opposed today than they have been for the past few decades. Our empirical analysis above strongly suggests that ideological differences between the parties encourage senators to exploit the rules of the game to their party's advantage in filling vacant judgeships or blocking new nominees.

Second, it is important to remember that if the courts were of little importance to the two parties, then polarized relations would matter little to senators and presidents in conducting advice and consent. However, the federal courts today are intricately involved in the interpretation and enforcement of federal law. The rising importance of the federal courts makes extremely important the second trend affecting the nature of judicial selection. When Democrats lost control of the Senate after the elections in 2002, the federal courts were nearly evenly balanced between Democratic and Republican appointees: the active judiciary was composed of 380 judges appointed by Republican presidents and 389 judges appointed by Democratic presidents.[42]

Having lost control of the Senate, distrusting the ideological orientation of Bush appointees, and finding the courts on the edge of partisan balance, it is no surprise that Democrats made scrutiny of judicial nominees a caucus priority starting in 2003 and achieved remarkable unity in blocking nominees they deemed particularly egregious. No small wonder that Republicans responded in kind, threatening recalcitrant Democrats with the nuclear option. Intense ideological disagreement coupled with the rising importance of a closely balanced federal bench has brought combatants in the wars of advice and consent to new tactics and new crises as the two parties struggle to shape the future of the courts. Of course, eight years of Republican rule still left an imprint on the bench: as of September 2008, 60 percent of the 154 active court of appeals judges had been appointed by Republican presidents, up from roughly 50 percent six years earlier.[43]

Candidate Barack Obama said relatively little about federal judges and the confirmation process during the course of the 2008 campaign. As president, Barack Obama's first appellate court nomination—Judge David Hamilton of the U.S. District Court for the Southern District of Indiana—is suggestive of the continuing battles over judicial selection. Although Hamilton had the support of both Indiana senators, including Republican senator Richard Lugar, Judiciary Committee member Jeff Sessions (R-Ala.) decried the nomination, arguing that "I believe the president deserves deference, but he's about used all the deference he's going to get out of me."[44] In short, there is little reason to think that the heat over judicial selection will subside anytime soon, unless the federal courts were to withdraw themselves from the consequential economic, political, and social questions that now come before the courts—an unlikely event.

5 | Constructing the Federal Bench

The contours of the federal judiciary are not fixed in stone. Article III, section 1 of the U.S. Constitution authorizes Congress to design the federal bench and to decide whether and how it should be changed. Such decisions are consequential, not least because they afford a governing majority an opportunity to mold the courts to its advantage. A Republican Congress with a Republican in the White House, for example, could choose to create new trial court judgeships in circuits represented by Republican senators—affording the party an advantage when appointments are made.[1] As we think about the ways in which senators and presidents attempt to shape the federal bench, efforts to expand the federal judiciary deserve attention. Do the parties' incentives to shape the bench also affect decisions about the expansion of the judiciary? What broader set of forces drive the creation of new federal judgeships?

We explore these questions by examining the two most recent major expansions of the U.S. district courts, both of which occurred in periods of divided party control in 1984 and 1990. Why would Congress create new judgeships if the majority party knew that it would not control appointments from the White House? We show that choices made about the location of trial courts are influenced by political and institutional considerations. Electoral incentives, partisan pressures, and constitutional ambition combine to shape the creation of new federal judgeships. Most important, the preferences of the judiciary—as expressed through the policy and rulemaking arm of the federal judiciary, the Judicial Conference—help to shape, but do not dictate, expansion of the bench. Our analytical results suggest the possibilities and the limits faced by legislators as they attempt to expand and potentially reshape the federal bench.

Scholarship on Court Expansion

Some scholars emphasize the role of the political parties in driving the expansion of the judiciary. Among their studies, the most theoretically motivated ones place the tactic of court expansion in a broader political contest to influence the course of judicial doctrine.[2] In short, when an increasing number of federal judges issue decisions that do not conform to the prevailing doctrine set by the Supreme Court, the Court in theory will broaden judicial doctrine to accommodate a broader range of lower court decisions. By giving the lower courts greater doctrinal latitude, the Court can isolate and concentrate on the most nonconforming decisions that make their way to the Court on appeal. Pressure from below in the hierarchy of courts, McNollgast argue, will affect the course of judicial decisionmaking.

In this view, packing the courts by creating new judgeships provides an indirect way for the other branches of government to alter the direction of Supreme Court doctrine. If the costs of securing House, Senate, and presidential support for creating new judgeships are greater than the costs of securing Senate and presidential agreement on filling judicial vacancies, packing of the lower courts should be used extremely rarely and only when the preferences of elected and unelected branches diverge the most. This leads McNollgast to predict that court expansion is most likely to occur at the onset of a durable partisan realignment. Congress expands the bench to encourage change in judicial doctrine from the bottom up.

The involvement of the House in expanding the size of the federal bench leads other scholars to a similar conclusion about the impact of party control: The House and Senate are unlikely to agree to create new judgeships unless the president's party holds majorities in both chambers. Under conditions of unified party control, the House "can rest assured that the 'right' judges will end up on the bench," given the Senate's role in confirming federal judges.[3] Empirical support for the party control hypothesis is mixed. Bench expansion of the trial courts is significantly more likely in periods of divided rather than unified control, as evidenced in the period between 1875 and 1993.[4] But the size of each bench expansion—how many new judgeships are created—tends to be driven by consideration of the judiciary's burgeoning caseloads: As dockets grow, Congress and the president agree to add more judgeships.

These arguments make good intuitive sense, given the incentive of legislators to avoid creating judgeships if their party has little control over who will fill them. Yet existing work leaves unaddressed several critical questions about the dynamics of court expansion. First, as McNollgast acknowledge, their model assumes that the House, Senate, and president are each unitary actors holding a consistent and coherent set of policy preferences. If the House and Senate are instead collections of agents with potentially diverse preferences, then the unitary actor assumption may mask important variation in legislators' incentives. Second, their model provides only a stripped-down view of the legislative process, assuming away the complexities of majority rule institutions—complexities shaped in part by bicameral differences in structural arrangements. If procedural power is allocated differently in the House and in the Senate, then legislators' capacities to shape judgeship bills likely will vary between the two chambers. Third, existing studies offer an impressive historical sweep.[5] Still, they examine only the incidence and size of court expansion. In contrast, we ask *where* new judgeships are created. Once Congress decides to expand the federal bench, which judicial districts—backed by which legislative coalitions—are most successful in securing additional judges? Creating and locating new judgeships, we argue, are inherently political choices that affect the shape of the bench and thus affect the future course of judicial selection.

Creating and Locating New Judgeships

Studies of congressional development highlight a range of forces that influence legislators' choices over institutional arrangements in Congress. Efforts to secure electoral or partisan advantage, particular policy goals, or improved institutional capacity have been shown to shape the dynamics of congressional change.[6] Underlying such studies is the idea that legislators understand the impact of rules on outcomes and thus attempt to calculate the impact of new rules when designing them. Of course, rules and organizational arrangements often have unintended consequences. But legislators still approach the job of designing new institutions by considering the political and policy consequences of these new institutions—even if the consequences are often unachieved.

Our approach to explaining the expansion of the federal bench starts from a similar premise. To the extent that legislators can anticipate the effects of their institutional choices, we view congressional decisions over the shape of the federal courts as strategic efforts by legislators to mold the courts to their policy advantage. Unlike previous efforts to model court expansion that treat Congress as unitary actor, we allow legislators' preferences regarding the courts to vary by institutional and partisan position.[7] Moreover, given that the Constitution empowers Congress and the president to create new judgeships, but gives House members no role in confirming new judges, House and Senate members may hold different preferences about court expansion. Nor are all legislators equally empowered to shape congressional decisions about the structure of the courts. Given bicameral differences in legislative rules and practices, we expect that the capacity of legislators to reshape the bench will vary by institutional and partisan position. Constitutional, partisan, and institutional forces thus constrain the abilities of legislators to mold the courts to their advantage. We elaborate on these considerations and constraints below.

Judicial Capacity

At least since the 1960s when the caseloads of federal courts began to rise exponentially, much of the pressure to enlarge the judiciary has come from the judiciary itself.[8] From the courts' perspective, proposals to expand the federal bench provide an opportunity to meet the needs of sitting federal judges as they attempt to manage often heavy caseloads and sometimes overflowing dockets. The job of determining which courts have the greatest need for more judgeships falls to the Judicial Conference, the administrative and policy arm of the federal bench that is chaired by the chief justice of the United States. Over time, the Judicial Conference institutionalized a process for determining and weighing the needs of the courts; starting in 1964, the conference conducted a quadrennial survey of the federal courts to determine which courts were carrying the heaviest caseloads relative to the size of their bench.[9]

Moving to a biennial survey in 1980, the Judicial Conference now proposes a judgeship request and forwards to Congress every two years its recommendations for which courts should receive additional judges and how many judges each court should receive.[10] Recommendations are based on a survey of the judgeship needs of the courts (including any appellate judgeship requests made by a majority of a circuit's judges) as well as an evaluation of the specific circumstances of each court. A judgeship bill is then drafted for Congress. Thus the judiciary's recommendations for the timing, size, and location of potential bench expansion are routinely conveyed to Congress.[11]

Legislators' views about expanding the courts are likely shaped in part by concerns about the courts' institutional capacity. To be sure, some legislators may be skeptical that creating new judgeships is the appropriate solution for reducing judicial caseloads. Some judges maintain that expanding the bench undermines cohesion and increases uncertainty in the evolution of the law. Moreover, they say, more efficient courts may simply encourage more litigation.[12] Regardless of one's views about whether or not expanding the bench is good public policy, most legislators are likely to believe that expanding the bench will have positive electoral consequences, as legislators can claim credit for taking action that speeds along the courts' handling of federal litigation. On either policy or electoral grounds then, we would expect legislators to take quite seriously the advice of the judiciary on when, where, and to what degree the federal courts should be expanded. This leads us to expect the following:

> *Judicial needs.* The weaker a court's judicial capacity, the more new judgeships it is likely to receive.

Preferences in the House

Still, Congress is not required to heed the advice of the Judicial Conference. More often than not, Congress ignores the routine recommendations for new judgeships originating in the biennial survey and proffered by the Judicial Conference. Typically, Congress declines to advance a judgeship bill and instead periodically addresses the need for new judgeships in an omnibus judgeship bill. Given Congress's discretion over the content of a judgeship bill, we would expect legislators to be guided by their own political and policy motivations—rather than solely by the needs of the courts as expressed in the Judicial Conference's biennial survey. Such motivations are likely shaped by constitutional, partisan, institutional, and electoral considerations—influences that are likely to vary in their weight and impact across the two chambers.

Where members sit is where they stand. From the vantage of the House, legislators have constitutional authority to make decisions about the structure of the bench, but not about who sits on the bench. Previous studies of court expansion have assumed that because of their exclusion from the confirmation process, House members' views about court expansion should depend entirely on their party status. If the House and Senate are controlled by the president's party, expansion will more likely occur, as House members understand that their party will have the opportunity to stack the new seats with ideologically compatible judges. Under such reasoning, it would be irrational for legislators to expand the bench in periods of divided party control.

In fact, Congresses controlled by the opposition party have created new judgeships, even understanding that such moves allow the president's party to further mold the courts to their advantage. This suggests that the expansion of the courts may be valuable to House members, even if they are excluded from advice and consent. We argue that regardless of whether party control is unified or divided, the creation of new judgeships provides an electorally valuable opportunity for credit claiming. Even if new judgeships are not created within one's state or district, House members can claim credit for acting to improve the efficiency of the courts. The addition of a new judgeship to one's own district simply sweetens the opportunity for credit claiming.

Indeed, in 2007 the three Republican House members from Nebraska introduced a bill to create a fourth federal judgeship for the U.S. District Court of Nebraska. "An additional permanent judgeship will help promote efficiency and more timely justice for the people of Nebraska," noted Representative Jeff Fortenberry (R-Neb.) at the time.[13] One might speculate, of course, that three Nebraskan legislators would have little to lose in advocating the creation of a new federal judgeship in a period when a Republican president sat in the White House. However, the Republican threesome reintroduced their bill at the start of the One Hundred Eleventh Congress when a Democrat was poised to enter the White House.[14] Moreover, the senior senator from Nebraska—to whom the new Democratic president might turn for advice in selecting a nominee—was a Democrat, Ben Nelson. Pushing for a new federal judge in a period of unified Democratic control might be seen as working against the legislators' party interests. But they likely did not consider the call for a new judgeship as counter to their own *electoral* interests. The opportunity for credit claiming persists regardless of partisan alignments in the selection process.

We might expect that electoral incentives to pursue new judgeships can be enhanced by institutional position. Jurisdiction over the courts is assigned to the House Judiciary Committee, whose members set the agenda, at least for the House, for when, where, and how many new judgeships are to be created. Given the opportunity to exploit their institutional position, we should expect Judiciary Committee members to be more likely than other members to receive new judgeships within their states and judicial districts, leading to the following conjecture:

> *House Judiciary Committee power.* More new judgeships are likely to be added to courts whose boundaries include congressional districts represented by members of the House Judiciary Committee.

Although majority party members can exercise significant control of the agenda in the House, we doubt that the majority party has a monopoly on securing such "judicial pork." Studies of legislative pork barreling show that the majority party typically shares the largess with minority party legislators; what better way than to buy their support for federal spending bills. The majority party, however, typically reserves a disproportionate share of federal dollars for its members.[15] In creating new judgeships, majority party members can exploit their agenda power in the House to reserve new judgeships for courts in their congressional districts. However, the majority cannot often exclude the minority from sharing judicial pork. Given the geographical structure of the federal judiciary, most federal district courts encompass multiple congressional districts within a state.[16] Any credit claiming opportunity afforded by creating a new judgeship must be shared with the legislators who represent the other congressional districts located within a district court's jurisdictional boundary. In the most recent round of district court expansion in 1990, for example, only 8 percent of the newly created judgeships were added to district courts whose "congressional delegations" consisted of only Democratic majority party members.

We can get a sense of the House majority party's presence across the nation's eighty-nine U.S. district courts by calculating the partisan makeup of the congressional districts located in each trial court's jurisdiction.[17] Figure 5-1 shows the distribution of the partisan balance (percent Democratic) of the eighty-nine district courts' congressional delegations in each of the two years in which judgeship bills were enacted.[18] Although we do not expect to find the minority party squeezed out of new judgeships, we would still expect to see a bonus to those courts with stronger majority party representation in the House. Thus, we expect to find the following:

> *House majority party power.* The greater the concentration of majority party members in a court's congressional delegation, the greater the number of new judgeships that court is likely to receive.

In short, the geographical basis of the judiciary constrains the majority party's ability to exclude minority party members from securing judicial pork. In a period of divided party control, this means that minority party committee members (the president's partisans) should be able to share in the spoils of bench expansion. Ironically, the strategic situation—shaped by the players' constitutional powers—may facilitate bipartisanship in a chamber more often known for its partisan ways of business.

Preferences in the Senate

Constitutional roles should also shape senators' preferences about expanding the federal bench. Unlike House members, whose views about court expansion stem primarily from electoral considerations, senators' views are shaped by their constitutional role in dispensing advice and consent about who sits on the bench. The prevailing wisdom suggests that periods of unified party control produce the strongest incentives for majority party senators to pursue new judgeships. But even in a period of divided government, the president's partisans are likely to push for new judgeships. Given the rules of the Senate, opposition party senators—even when they serve in the minority—likely hold sufficient institutional leverage to push successfully for new judgeships. Failure to accommodate the minority puts at risk the unanimous consent—or under cloture, 60 votes—that the majority party needs to call up a judgeship bill for Senate floor consideration.

Figure 5-1. *Partisanship of U.S. District Courts' "Congressional Delegations," 1984 and 1990*[a]

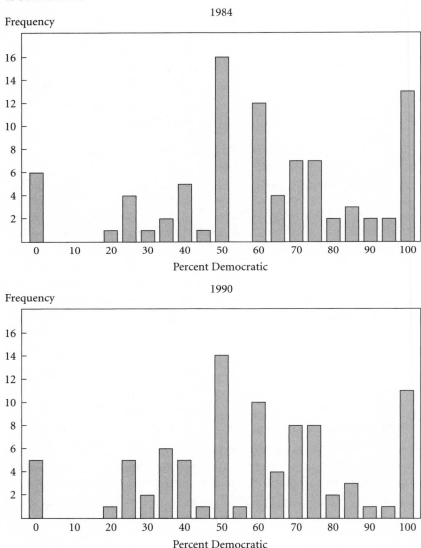

Source: Authors' calculations.

a. The figure shows the distribution of the partisanship (percent Democratic) of the members of Congress representing counties located within each federal district court jurisdictional boundary. See notes 16–18 for an explanation of how the partisanship of each court's "delegation" is identified.

Once the Senate decides to consider a judgeship bill, senators' institutional and partisan positions are likely to affect the allocation of new judgeships across the states. As in the House, membership on the Senate Judiciary Committee provides an advantage to senators seeking to influence which trial courts receive new judgeships. Unlike House members, however, senators' views about new judgeships should be conditioned directly by partisan considerations. Opposition party senators—even those who serve on the Judiciary panel—have little incentive to push for new judgeships for their states when the president is from the other party. Even if electoral credit claiming motivates senators as it does House members, their constitutionally induced preferences should outweigh concerns about electoral advantage. This is especially so for judgeship bills for the U.S. district courts considered in periods of unified party control. It is reasonable to assume that an opposition party senator would have a tough time influencing the selection of trial court nominees in periods of unified control, reducing his or her likelihood of pursuing and securing additional court seats for his or her state.

Not so for senators from the president's party. Regardless of whether they serve in the majority or minority party, the president's partisans on the Senate Judiciary Committee should be more likely than their fellow committee members to secure additional judgeships for the federal courts in their states. Given the role that senators from the president's party play in suggesting and confirming candidates for judicial vacancies within their states, we should expect the president's partisans—but not the opposition party—to aggressively seek new judgeships, even when they do not control the Senate chamber. And given that district courts are located solely within a state's boundaries, the potential partisan impact of creating new judgeships is more pronounced in the Senate. Ironically, because of the structure of the federal judiciary, bench expansion in the Senate—a decidedly more bipartisan chamber than the House—may take on a more partisan cast than it does in the House. Thus we conjecture the following:

> *Senate Judiciary Committee power.* States represented by opposition party senators serving on the Judiciary panel should be less likely to receive additional judgeships; states represented on the committee by governing party senators should be more likely to receive additional judgeships.

Data and Methods

We explore these conjectures about the creation of new judgeships by analyzing the two most recent major judgeship acts to be enacted by Congress and the president: the creation of sixty-one U.S. district court judgeships as part of a bankruptcy reform law enacted in 1984 and seventy-four judgeships in a stand-alone judgeship bill in 1990.[19] Combining the two episodes into a single analysis, we model congressional choices over the creation and placement of new federal trial court judgeships, with the goal of explaining which district courts are most likely to be successful in securing additional judgeships.

Dependent Variable

Our unit of analysis is each of the eighty-nine U.S. district courts, with two observations for each court (reflecting the judgeships bills in 1984 and 1990).[20] Our dependent variable captures the number of new federal district judgeships added by Congress to each United States district court in each of the two years. We identify the location of newly created judgeships from data reported by the Administrative Office of the United States Courts.[21] Those data indicate the number of existing authorized judgeships before each judgeship act, as well as the number of new judgeships added to each trial court in each judgeship bill.

Observations on the dependent variable range from zero (indicating that the trial court received no new judgeships that year) to five (indicating that five new judgeships were created for the court that year). As shown in table 5-1, forty-six of the eighty-nine federal courts (52 percent) received no new judgeships in 1984, while thirty-six out of eighty-nine courts (41 percent) of the courts received no new judgeships in 1990. Only one court—the U.S. District Court for the Central District of California—received five new judgeships in each judgeship bill—making it the fastest growing court in the country.[22]

Independent Variables

We test for the influence of judicial, electoral, institutional, and partisan influences in the following way.

Judicial capacity. When the Judicial Conference considers the need for additional judgeships, its analysis begins with a quantitative case-related

Table 5-1. *Distribution of New Judgeships to the U.S. District Courts, 1984 and 1990*

Number of New Judgeships	Number of court districts, 1984	Number of court districts, 1990
0	46	36
1	33	42
2	6	5
3	2	3
4	0	1
5	2	2

Source: Administrative Office of the U.S. Courts, "History of the Authorization of Federal Judgeships Including Procedures and Standards Used in Conducting Judgeship Surveys" (Washington, 1992).

workload measure. The measure used for evaluating the needs of federal district courts is known as "weighted filings"—an indicator that incorporates information about the number and the complexity of the court's filings. In the 1982 and 1990 Biennial Survey of Judgeship Needs—on which Congress based its consideration of new judgeships in 1984 and 1990—the Judicial Conference's Subcommittee on Judicial Statistics used a standard of weighted filings in excess of 400 per authorized judgeship to indicate a need for additional judgeships for the court.[23] To measure each district court's need for additional judgeships, we measure "weighted needs" as the number of additional judges required to keep each court's workload at 400 weighted filings per judge.[24]

Judiciary Committee membership. Because federal district court boundaries are based on county lines, each trial court's jurisdiction covers one or more congressional districts. We can think of each trial court of having its own congressional delegation in the House and Senate. To determine whether federal district courts that are "represented" by a Judiciary Committee member are more likely to secure additional judgeships, we determine the congressional delegation for each federal district court. To do so, we identify the counties covered by each federal district court and then identify the congressional district(s) located within those counties.[25]

Once each court's House and Senate delegations are determined, we create a variable for each chamber's Judiciary Committee ("HJC" and "SJC") to denote the number of delegation members who sat on the House or Senate Judiciary Committee in the relevant Congress (Ninety-eighth and One Hundred First). We also create dummy variables ("HJC-GOP" and "SJC-GOP") that denote whether or not any of the delegation's Judiciary Committee members hailed from the president's party (that is, whether or not they were Republicans).

Majority party representation. We use the congressional delegation of each district court to determine each court's majority party representation. The variable "House majority power" measures the percentage of each court's House delegation from the majority party. Because we expect senators from the president's party to be more interested than opposition party senators in securing new judgeships, we create a dummy variable, "Senate presidential party," to denote whether or not any of a court's Senate delegation hails from the president's party.

Presidential control. As a control, we include a variable that captures the "percent GOP presidential vote" for the Republican candidate (Ronald Reagan in 1980 and George H. W. Bush in 1988) in the state in which each federal district court is located. We might expect Republican leaning states to be more likely to receive additional judgeships, given that federal judicial candidates are typically drawn from a party's legal elite within each state.

Methods

Because the number of new judgeships allotted to each district court can only be a nonnegative integer, with numerous courts receiving no new judgeships, estimating an event count model is the most appropriate method.[26] Because there are two observations for each court—which are unlikely to be independent—we use robust standard errors clustering on the federal court to account for the lack of independence of the two observations for each court.

Results

Table 5-2 presents descriptive statistics for the variables included in the analysis. Congress allocated from zero to five new judgeships in the 1984 and 1990 bench expansions. By the judiciary's estimate, the number of required judgeships ranged from zero to thirteen, with the U.S. District Court of

Table 5-2. *Descriptive Statistics*

Variable	N	Mean	Std. dev	Min	Max
No. of judgeships added	178	0.764	0.997	0	5
Weighted needs	178	1.056	1.843	0	13
House Judiciary representation	178	0.455	0.745	0	4
GOP House Judiciary representation	178	0.758	0.429	0	1
Senate Judiciary representation	178	0.292	0.492	0	2
GOP Senate Judiciary representation	178	0.146	0.354	0	1
House majority party power	178	0.578	0.271	0	1
Senate presidential party	178	0.725	0.448	0	1
Percent GOP vote in state	178	0.560	0.056	0.423	0.78

Source: Data on judgeships and weighted needs of the courts compiled from Administrative Office of the U.S. Courts, "History of the Authorization of Federal Judgeships Including Procedures and Standards Used in Conducting Judgeship Surveys" (Washington, 1992). See text for other sources.

Pennsylvania, Eastern District (located in Philadelphia) earning the distinction as the most understaffed trial court. With respect to representation on the two Judiciary panels, the median district court had representation on neither the House nor Senate committee. That said, if we combine the Judiciary panel membership variables into a single dummy variable denoting whether or not a district court could claim representation on either panel, we find that just over half of the courts had at least one congressional member on either the House or the Senate Judiciary Committee.

A cursory glance at the data reveals that Congress is not constrained by the Judiciary Conference's assessment of where judgeships are most needed to deal with heavy caseloads. In table 5-3, we compare the number of new district court judgeships created in the 1984 and 1990 expansions (aggregated up to the circuit level) to the number of new judgeships that would be required according to the weighted needs of each circuit.[27] We also calculate a simple ratio of the number of seats created per circuit to the number of seats required based on judicial needs. Were judicial assessments and congressional preferences in sync, the ratio of congressional to judicial seats for most circuits would be close to 1. Clearly, that is not the case, with some circuits showing ratios significantly higher and some significantly lower than 1. In short, some circuits received more seats than they "needed," while others received fewer.

Table 5-3. *Judicial versus Congressional Assessments of District Court Judgeship Needs*

Circuit no.	Judicial assessment	Congressional assessment	Ratio of congressional to judicial assessment
98th Congress			
1	4	3	0.75
2	6	5	0.83
3	3	4	1.33
4	2	3	1.50
5	12	8	0.67
6	10	7	0.70
7	11	7	0.64
8	1	3	0.30
9	8	12	1.50
10	6	4	0.67
11	2	5	2.50
101st Congress			
1	2	3	1.50
2	10	7	0.70
3	19	8	0.42
4	4	5	1.25
5	23	13	0.57
6	17	6	0.35
7	13	3	0.23
8	6	6	1.00
9	16	12	0.75
10	7	6	0.86
11	6	6	1.00

Source: Administrative Office of the U.S. Courts, "History of the Authorization of Federal Judgeships Including Procedures and Standards Used in Conducting Judgeship Surveys" (Washington, 1992). Because the D.C. Circuit does not have home state senators, we drop the circuit from the data analysis. See the text for sources for the independent variables.

In table 5-4, we show the results of a model explaining the distribution of new judgeships to the district courts, pooling the judgeship bills of 1984 and 1990. The overall fit of the model is strong, as we can safely reject the hypothesis that the joint effect of the independent variables is zero. As we explore below, the results largely comport with our expectations about the multiple forces shaping legislators' choices about the bench.

Table 5-4. *Poisson Regression Model: Expanding the Federal Bench,*
1984 and 1990[a]

Independent variable	Coefficient (robust std. error)
Weighted needs of the district court	0.200***
	(0.25)
House Judiciary Committee (HJC) representation	0.327***
	(0.95)
HJC GOP representation (JHC-GOP)	−0.080
	(.204)
Senate Judiciary Committee (SJC) representation	−0.871
	(.341)
SJC GOP representation (SHC-GOP)	0.747*
	(.402)
House majority party representation	−0.046
	(.307)
Senate presendential party representation	−0.064
	(.173)
Percent GOP vote in state	−0.839
	(1.472)
Constant	−0.108
	(0.941)
N	178
Log pseudolikelihood	−172.519
Wald Chi square	152.36
Probability Chi square	0.000

Source: Data on judgeships and weighted needs of the courts compiled from Administrative Office of the U.S. Courts, "History of the Authorization of Federal Judgeships Including Procedures and Standards Used in Conducting Judgeship Surveys" (Washington, 1992). See text for other sources.

***$p < .001$; *$p < .05$; all one-tailed t tests.

a. Dependent variable is the number of new judgeships authorized for each U.S. district court in 1984 and 1990. See text for details. Poisson regression estimates generated via *poisson* routine in Stata 8.2. Robust standard errors in parentheses, clustering on each district court.

First, although Congress is evidently not bound by the recommendations of the Judicial Conference, it clearly responds to signals from the Third Branch about the capacity of the federal courts. The needs of the judiciary do shape congressional decisionmaking about how to expand the federal bench. As indicated by the positive and statistically significant coefficient for "weighted needs," Congress creates more judgeships for those courts whose judges toil under especially heavy caseloads compared with those courts in less dire straits.

Second, the institutional leverage of each court's congressional delegation significantly affects the distribution of new judgeships to the trial courts but in different ways for the two chambers. When courts have representation on the House Judiciary Committee, more federal judgeships are likely to be created for those district courts. Given the potential electoral incentive for legislators to claim credit for creating new judgeships and given the bipartisan character of the vast majority of these delegations, we should not be surprised to find that courts with minority party representation on the Judiciary panel are not likely to secure more judgeships than are courts with Democratic representation on the committee. The null effect for the "HJC-GOP" dummy and the positive and significant effect for the "HJC" variable together suggest that creating new judgeships falls into a well-worn pattern of parochial politics for members of Congress: legislators dole out distributive goodies to members of both political parties. Not surprising then, we find a null effect for the majority party's domination of each court's congressional delegation. Particularism on a bipartisan basis seems alive and well in the distribution of judicial resources within the House.

When courts have representation on the Senate Judiciary Committee, we see a different set of consequences. Having a home state patron on the Judiciary panel does not help the court to attract more judgeships. It is interesting, however, that having a home state patron on the Judiciary panel who hails from the president's party—in this case, Republican senators—increases the number of new judgeships a court is able to secure from Congress. In contrast, Democratic senators—even though they controlled the Senate in 1990—did not have a strong incentive to create new judgeships, as they understood that a Republican president would have been poised to appoint like-minded judicial candidates to the federal bench. The results hold up even after controlling for partisan makeup of the state and the partisanship of each court's congressional delegation in the Senate. Republican-leaning states are not more likely to receive more judgeships; institutional position clearly provides legislators with the necessary procedural leverage to influence expansion of the bench.

Table 5-5. *Simulated Numbers of New Judgeships*

No. of judges required at 400 weighted filings per authorized judge	No. of MCs representing a district court serving on the HJC	No. of GOP representing a district court serving on the SJC	Predicted no. of new judgeships for the district court
0	0	0	0.381
1	0	0	0.466
2	0	0	0.569
3	0	0	0.695
4	0	0	0.849
5	0	0	1.037
1	1	0	0.646
1	0	1	0.938
1	1	1	1.363
2	2	0	1.093
2	2	1	2.038
2	3	1	3.199
0	3	0	1.015
0	3	1	2.144

Source:: Authors' calculations.

HJC = House Judiciary Committee; MC = members of Congress; SJC = Senate Judiciary Committee

The substantive effects of these multiple forces can be evaluated from the data in table 5-5. For each combination of court workload demands ("weighted needs"), court representation on the House Judiciary Committee ("HJC"), and court representation by Republicans on the Senate Judiciary Committee ("SJC-GOP"), we can simulate the number of new judgeships predicted by the model.[28] Because the predicted quantities for each simulation are numbers of new judges, fractional predictions might best be thought of as the probability that a new judgeship will be added for a court.[29]

Perhaps most striking about the simulations is the limited impact of a court's workload-based need for additional judgeships. Lacking congressional committee representation, a district court is likely to secure a new judgeship only if it requires two or more judges to handle overflowing dockets. Requesting just one judgeship leaves the predicted number of judges below .5. Moreover, even if a court does not need additional judge-ships, representation on the House, Senate, or both Judiciary panels is sufficient to create a new judgeship for the court. For example, a court with three members on the House panel and no Republicans on the Senate panel is still likely to secure one new judgeship even in the absence of judicial need.[30] Committee representation seems to have a multiplier effect of sorts, since a court deserving two judgeships that is represented on both the House and Senate panels is likely, according to the model, to secure more than two judgeships. These patterns strongly suggest that only at a certain level are a court's needs sufficient to secure new judgeships, but judicial need for a new judgeship is not necessary for a court to receive additional judges from Congress.

Discussion

The empirical results lend strong support for a model of court expansion in which the structure of the federal judiciary and legislators' incentives and institutional capacity interact to shape the allocation of new judgeships across the bench. Because the majority party in the House can rarely preclude the minority party from sharing credit claiming opportunities created by the generation of new judgeships, bipartisanship tends to suffuse the parochial bargains that underlie House decisions on bench expansion. In contrast, given opposition party senators' reluctance to create judgeships to be filled by the other party's president, bench expansion takes on a more partisan cast in the Senate. Even in periods of divided government, the president's partisans in the Senate have sufficient institutional leverage to extract a disproportionate share of new judgeships for their states. All these calculations, of course, take place under the shadow of the judiciary's caseload-related demands for new judgeships—demands that legislators acknowledge as they pursue their own agendas in shaping the contours of the federal bench.

These findings still beg the question of why legislators allow judgeship bills onto the agendas of the House and Senate in periods of divided party control. Even if legislators extract some political benefits from expanding the bench in periods of divided government, we might expect that the opposition party will keep judgeship expansion off the agenda in periods of divided government. Here, some closer examination of the dynamics of the 1984 and 1990 judgeship acts may shed some light on why bench expansion occurs when the president's partisans lack control of both chambers.

Bench expansion in 1984 occurred in the context of congressional efforts to rewrite the nation's bankruptcy court system.[31] In 1982 the Supreme Court had invalidated a 1978 major overhaul of the bankruptcy system, ordering Congress to act by the end of 1982 to fix the court system. The version of reform preferred by the majority party Democrats in the House was approved by the House Judiciary Committee, but then it stalled in the Rules Committee. Among other provisions, the House bill created life tenure for bankruptcy judges (which was opposed by the Judicial Conference) but did not include any new federal judgeships. The Senate version of the bill endorsed a broader range of bankruptcy reforms, allowed for fourteen-year judge terms, and created seventy-five new federal judges for the district and appellate courts.

With the House and Senate at an impasse over these and other competing bankruptcy measures, the House in the spring of 1984 passed a new version of bankruptcy reform with term-limited judges and other reforms but stripped the bill of the seventy-five new judgeships. Instead, the House added a provision protecting union contracts in the case of company bankruptcy, thereby overturning a 1984 Supreme Court decision opposed by Democrats and their union supporters. Ultimately, the final House-Senate compromise emerged when majority party Republican senators demurred on the pro-union provision in exchange for Democrats accepting new judgeships—now totaling eighty-five new judgeships (including sixty-one for the district courts).[32]

Why did Democrats accede to a Republican Senate's demand for new federal judgeships in a period of divided government? Judgeships were the price House Democrats were willing to pay to secure a reversal of the Supreme Court provision deemed harmful to the Democrats' union base in the run-up to the presidential and congressional elections. House Democrats then extracted extra judgeships as an additional electoral payoff for granting the opposition scores of new judgeships. Finally, Senate Democrats surely understood that confirming new judges late in a presidential election year was unlikely to happen, a valuable consolation prize in the off-chance Reagan failed to be reelected.

The 1990 judgeship bill was less dramatic. Chief Justice William Rehnquist elevated the issue of new judgeships in his year-end report to Congress, raising the specter of federal judges overburdened by the prosecution of drug-offenders after several years of a federal war on drugs.[33] The chair of the House Judiciary Committee, Jack Brooks (D-Tex.), disputed the judiciary's statistics on rising caseloads, opposing efforts to expand the federal bench with a Republican serving in the White House. Senator Joe Biden (D-Del.), chair of the Senate Judiciary Committee, conducted a study of the court management and introduced a bill that mandated court management reforms but ignored the issue of new judgeships.

In marking up the Biden bill, the Senate Judiciary Committee added seventy-seven new federal judgeships. Although minority party Republicans came under attack for adding judgeships to the states represented by Republican senators on the Judiciary panel, the Senate ultimately approved the full slate. In the House, majority party Democrats, apparently not wanting to give Republicans a free hand to expand the bench, marked up their own judgeship bill in response, packing Texas courts with new judgeships, as well as courts located in areas represented by pivotal Judiciary Committee members (both Democrats and Republicans). Ultimately, the House-Senate compromise included all of the new district and appellate judgeships approved by either chamber: sixty-one from the House bill plus twenty-four others from the Senate bill. When it comes to the distribution of judicial pork, legislators have neither the desire nor the need to keep it lean.

Conclusion

By assuming that Congress acts as a unitary actor, prevailing accounts of court expansion underestimate the constitutional and political considerations that shape legislators' views about bench expansion. The constitutionally prescribed powers of legislators to influence the shape and makeup of the bench guide their choices about the structure of the federal courts. House members' exclusion from advice and consent shapes House members' views about creating new judgeships, even in periods when their party does not control the White House. Legislators appear willing to exploit such opportunities for electoral gain, even at the cost of allowing the other party to fill new judgeships with like-minded judges. Given the geographically based structure of the federal bench, however, the House majority party is unable to exclude the minority from sharing the credit claiming that comes with new judgeships.

In contrast, majority party senators in a period of divided government seem at best unenthusiastic participants in efforts to expand the bench. This should not be surprising given the closer approximation of district court boundaries to state lines. Opposition party senators have little to gain from pursuing new judgeships when the White House is controlled by the other party. The needs of the judiciary are certainly recognized when Congress addresses itself to bench expansion. But judicial demands for new judgeships must ultimately compete against electoral and partisan motives that come to the fore when Congress considers when, where, and by how much to expand the bench.

Although our focus has been on the politics and process of allocating new judgeships to the trial courts, one might reasonably wonder why it has been so long since an omnibus judgeship bill has been enacted into law. At least as of this writing in the winter of 2009, the 1990 act was the last successful omnibus effort—despite biennial requests from the Judicial Conference. That is not to say that Congress has stopped creating new judgeships. New judgeships—sometimes in the form of temporary judgeships—have indeed been created since 1990, but not as part of an omnibus bill; the so-called border courts of the Southwest, in particular, have been successful in securing new judgeships to address rising caseloads that have accompanied the federal government's crackdown on illegal immigration. A total of five new judgeships (four permanent, one temporary), for example, were created for the U.S. District Court of Arizona in 1999, 2000, and 2002.[34]

That said, the pursuit of a new omnibus judgeship bill may not have been a high priority for the Judicial Conference. This judgment is based on our scan of the year-end reports that lobbied for increases in judicial salaries and against the creation of an inspector general for the courts—rather than for omnibus expansions of the appellate and district bench. That has not stopped individual courts from lobbying on their own behalf. A former chief judge of the U.S. District Court of Southern California, Marilyn Huff, for example, noted in 2008 that the Judicial Conference—believing it unlikely that Congress would approve an omnibus bill—"gave us permission to do it on our own."[35] Huff recalls "cold-calling reporters for the *Washington Post*" and holding a press conference to push for new judgeships for her border-state court. The institutional interests of the courts as a whole are not necessarily synonymous with the interests of individual courts—especially with respect to the matter of bench expansion.

This study of bench expansion reaffirms the difficulties that majorities face in trying to shape the congressional agenda on the federal courts. Although previous studies of bench expansion implicitly assume that majorities in a period of divided control are able to keep undesired measures off the congressional agenda, such accounts underestimate how signals from the president and the judiciary can push the needs of the bench onto the congressional agenda. Faced with the inevitability of new judgeships, the opposition party attempts to mold the best deal it can, given its institutional capacities and given the constraints of the federal court system that come to affect the ways in which bench expansion unfolds. Although new judgeships may be more likely in periods of unified control, the dynamics of bench expansion under divided government may reveal more about legislators' complex motivations and constraints that come to mold the future shape of the federal courts.

6

The Consequences of Conflict over Judicial Selection

Disagreements over who should serve on the federal bench have their roots in the myriad tensions that arise between the parties and branches over the formation and interpretation of public law. These disagreements have become especially pitched and pronounced in recent years. They have also become consequential in potentially harmful ways. White House foot-dragging in choosing nominees, Senate delays in confirming new judges, and intense political campaigns against judicial candidates deemed out of the mainstream—these developments in advice and consent have downstream effects: they take their toll on judges and on the federal bench. Careful scrutiny of candidates for the bench by the White House and Senate is called for, given the life tenure of judges and the impact of their decisions on the shape of the law. But the costs of contested nominations, we argue, have consequences that bear attention and concern.

We explore two sets of consequences that stem from the current practice of judicial selection. First, we examine the performance of the federal appellate courts over the past three decades, documenting the impact of vacancies on the courts' institutional capacity. The long delays in confirming judges to the bench have immediate consequences for the courts, limiting the courts' ability to keep up with growing caseloads and leaving the courts to scramble for ways to make up the lost manpower. Second, we explore the impact of confirmation conflict on citizens' perceptions of judges and judicial decisions, reporting on the results of a survey experiment we conducted in the fall of 2006. In our experiment, judges who come to the bench via a contested nomination fare worse in the public's eye than do judges who sail through to confirmation. Only strong partisans are encouraged when their party's president selects a contested nominee, suggesting that the parties' advice and consent strategies may be indirectly undermining public confidence in the courts and thus the legitimacy of the unelected branch.

Judicial Vacancies and Court Performance

In 1998 Chief Justice William Rehnquist leveled perhaps the most pointed charge in recent years about the consequences of vacant federal judgeships. In a stinging rebuke of a Republican Senate, Rehnquist observed that slowdowns in the Senate confirmation process had left scores of judgeships empty. "Vacancies cannot remain at such high levels indefinitely," Rehnquist warned, "without eroding the quality of justice."[1] The broader claim is that an understaffed bench—coupled with increasing numbers of civil and criminal cases and the failure to create new judgeships—leads to lengthy delays in court proceedings and mounting caseloads for each judge. Moreover, some critics argue that short-term solutions to vacancies—including the heavy use of visiting judges, including district court judges sitting temporarily as circuit judges—have their own deleterious effects.[2]

Numerous federal judges have echoed Rehnquist's concern. In his annual address to the D.C. Circuit Judicial Conference in 2002, Chief Judge Douglas Ginsburg highlighted the difficulties of maintaining the court when four of its authorized twelve judgeships were empty: "It is clear, however, that if the court does not have additional judges soon, our ability to manage our workload in a timely fashion will be seriously compromised."[3] Ginsburg went on to note that the D.C. Circuit had had to cancel several days of oral arguments, postponing cases several months to the next court session. Slowdowns in confirming federal judges, Ginsburg concluded, are "coming to jeopardize the administration of justice in this Circuit."[4]

Measuring Court Performance

There are numerous ways to measure the institutional performance of the federal bench. Here, we offer two measures of performance that aim to detect how the courts handle their caseloads. As we explain below, we follow the lead of court administrators and judges and rely on court management statistics to provide a rough gauge of the judiciary's capacity to handle the burgeoning caseloads that have confronted federal judges since the 1960s.

Each year, the Administrative Office of the United States Courts requests extensive performance data from each of the federal appellate courts. We use these data, compiled in annual volumes, the *Federal Court Management Statistics,* to devise measures of institutional capacity that we apply to each of the twelve regional federal appellate courts between 1971 and 2002.[5] Although judges and judicial scholars differ about the best ways to measure the institutional capacity of the courts of appeals, several common themes emerge. Most judges agree that a sound measure of court performance should incorporate the amount of time it takes for the court to terminate its cases. Some prefer a measure that captures the time from the filing of the notice of appeal to a final disposition, arguing that that time best reflects the concerns of the plaintiffs seeking court review.[6] Others suggest that the adoption of screening panels and settlement programs for early review of some civil appeals, as well as the courts' relative ability to assemble three-judge panels, means that we should be most interested in the time that elapses from a hearing, or from submission to the panel (when there is no oral argument), to the panel's final disposition. Such a measure arguably best shows the impact of judge power—once the case gets to a panel of judges.

The Administrative Office of the U.S. Courts has compiled information on the duration of the appellate process for each of the courts of appeals, reaching back systematically to 1971.[7] Given our need for a long and consistent time series of data on court performance, we use a measure that captures the "median time elapsed" between filing of a notice of appeal to final disposition. From 1971 through 1981, the office compiled data on the median time in months elapsed from the filing of a complete record until disposition of the case; since 1982, the median time from filing of a notice of appeal to disposition of the case has been tabulated.[8] Thus our first dependent variable taps the median time elapsed (in months) for each court of appeals in each year between 1971 and 2002. The longer the time elapsed, the longer it takes for cases to be resolved and thus—assuming no visiting judges—the fewer the cases the court can dispose of in a given year and the weaker the court's institutional capacity becomes. To control for the change in how median times were computed starting in 1982, we include a dummy variable denoting observations from 1982 to the present.

Our second dependent variable attempts to capture the size of the case-load carried by each judge. Here, we use the pending caseload per judge on each court of appeals at the end of each year in the time series.[9] We assume that courts whose judges have larger caseloads are those whose institutional capacity is most challenged.[10]

Measuring Vacancies and Correlates of Performance

Our key independent variable is the vacancy rate for each court of appeals each year between 1971 and 2002. The most reliable data on federal appel-late bench vacancy rates appear in the *Federal Court Management Statistics.* It reports the number of vacant judgeship-months for each court each year.[11] We divide the number of vacant judgeship-months by total judgeship-months each year (that is, the number of authorized judgeships multiplied by twelve months) to produce a "vacancy rate" for each court each year. If understaffed courts have a harder time keeping up with their respective case-loads, then higher vacancy rates should produce longer case processing times and a higher number of pending cases per judge each year. Granted, such measures do not account for the contributions made by senior judges and visiting judges.

We also include a number of controls. First, we measure the size of each court's annual business with a variable that taps the "number of appeals filed" in each court each year. Second, we create a variable to capture an expansion in the size of the court of appeals bench: a dummy variable indi-cates whether the number of authorized judgeships was increased in that year—"new judgeship added," 1 yes, 0 otherwise. If adding new judgeships exacerbates (or reduces) caseloads or makes the court less (or more) effi-cient, median case processing times and pending appeals per judgeship should both increase (or decrease). Third, we create a variable to tap the per-centage of sitting judges who are newly commissioned for the court, what the judicial literature refers to as a *freshman judge*. We expect that newcom-ers to the bench may take extra time to get up to speed with court practices, as well as with the complexity of the cases before the federal bench. A court of appeals with a higher percentage of freshman judges may show a higher pending caseload and longer case processing times.

Estimation

For each year, we have repeated observations (by year) on the same fixed units (courts of appeals). Given the potential for serial dependence over time and across courts, we estimate a time series, cross-sectional regression, using panel corrected standard errors.[12] To control for temporal autocorrelation, we model the autocorrelation as a panel-specific AR(1) process.[13] We use a lagged dependent variable in each of the estimations to control for serially correlated errors.[14] We also include fixed effects for each court of appeals since an *F* test indicates that we can reject the null hypothesis of no court effects (using the Court of Appeals for the D.C. Circuit as the excluded category). Granted, the fixed effects can tell us whether significant cross-court differences exist, but they cannot tell us why such court differences exist. Most likely those fixed effects are picking up variation across the courts in the use of visiting judges and the nature of the caseloads. Overall, the estimation technique gives us confidence that we have adequately controlled for the types of nonindependence typically encountered in time series cross-sectional data.

The Relationship of Vacancies and Performance

Descriptive statistics appear in table 6-1. Appellate court performance varies considerably. The average court case over the entire time period takes nearly ten months to be disposed of, with the shortest median time less than four months (in the Second Circuit in 1981) and the longest nearly a year and a half in the Ninth Circuit in 1980. Typical appellate courts end the year with roughly 195 cases pending per judgeship, a number that ranges from a low of 43 cases (First Circuit in 1971) to a high of more than 600 appeals per judge (Eleventh Circuit in 1997). The caseload of the appellate bench also varies quite widely, averaging roughly 3,000 cases per court per year; the smallest court docket was 383 cases on the First Circuit in 1971 and the largest (more than 11,000 cases) occurring on the Ninth Circuit in 2002.

We can also get a rough sense of the extent of judicial vacancies during the period. Figure 6-1 provides a useful perspective on vacancy rates, showing the

Table 6-1. *Descriptive Statistics*

Variable	N[a]	Mean	Std. dev.	Min	Max
Median time (in months) per case	372	9.802	3.005	3.800	17.400
No. of pending cases per judge	372	195.193	93.738	43.333	608.293
Percent judgeships vacant	372	0.086	0.087	0	0.624
Were new judgeships added to bench?	372	0.078	0.269	0	1
Percent freshmen judges	372	0.059	0.095	0	.857[b]
No. of appeals filed	372	3,017.253	1,966.392	383	11,421

Source: Administrative Office of the U.S. Courts, *Federal Court Management Statistics*, annual volumes 1971–2002.

a. The *N* for the statistical models is 359. Because the models required lagged values of the dependent variables (which are not available for 1970), we drop the eleven observations for 1971. Because reliable data for the 5th and 11th Circuits are not available for 1981, we lack lagged values of the dependent variables for those two circuits in 1982, thus reducing the *N* by two more cases.

b. The bench with 85.7 percent freshmen judges was the 5th Circuit in 1979. A judgeship act in 1978 nearly doubled the circuit in size from 15 to 26 judgeships; coupled with a vacant judgeship from 1978, twelve new judges started service on the 5th Circuit bench sometime during 1979.

average annual vacancy rate across all of the federal courts. The mean vacancy rate has ranged from a low of 1 percent in 1976 and again in 1984 to a high of nearly 20 percent after the creation of scores of new judgeships in 1978.[15] Most recently, the average vacancy rate across the appellate courts was 8 percent (for the year ending September 2007). Such averages obscure considerable variation across the courts during the time period. As shown in table 6-1, the typical appellate court experienced an 8.6 percent vacancy rate, ranging from a low of no vacancies (occurring in 25 percent of the 372 cases) to a high of 62 percent in the Fifth Circuit in 1979 (stemming from the addition of eleven new judgeships in 1978).[16] Such variation persists in recent years, as seen in the appellate bench vacancy rates for 2002 (figure 6-2). The Second Circuit had the lowest vacancy rate (less than 0.4 percent), while the Sixth Circuit had the highest (47 percent). In the latter case, roughly half of the court's sixteen authorized judgeships sat empty for an extended portion of the year.

To explore the relationship between vacancies and our measures of court performance, we estimate in table 6-2 the impact of judicial vacancies on our two measures of court performance over the thirty-two-year period. In both models, the coefficient for the vacancy rate is positive and statistically

Figure 6-1. *Average Vacancy Rate, U.S. Courts of Appeals, 1971–2002*[a]

Percent bench vacant

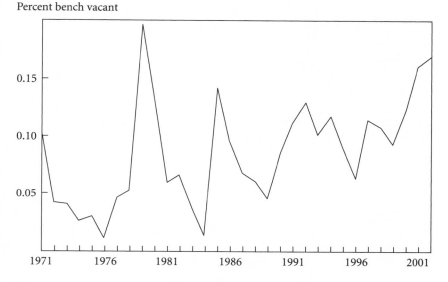

Source: Administrative Office of the U.S. Courts, *Federal Court Management Statistics,* annual volumes 1971–2002.

a. Calculation of vacancy rates is discussed in the text. For each year, vacancy rates for the each of appellate courts are averaged to produce a mean annual vacancy rate for the appellate bench.

significant. The greater the vacancy problem on a court of appeals, the longer it takes for the court to dispose of the cases on its docket and the larger the caseload for each judge is. These results are robust, even after we control for the size of the court's docket and the involvement of judges new to the federal appellate bench that year.

Implications

The organizational stress experienced by the appellate bench during the past couple of decades is a frequent concern of court administrators, legal scholars, judges, and litigants. The number of nationally commissioned studies on the federal court system, as well as on particularly burdened courts of appeals, attests to the warning flags that have been raised in face of mounting caseloads and limited resources.[17] Granted, rising caseloads need not produce heavier workloads; increases in appeals are handled in part by

Figure 6-2. *Vacancy Rates, by U.S. Courts of Appeals, 2002*[a]

Court of appeals

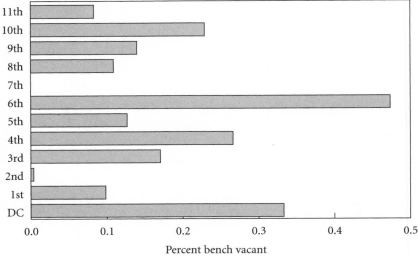

Percent bench vacant

Source: Administrative Office of the U.S. Courts, *Federal Court Management Statistics* (2002).

retired federal judges serving on senior status and by visiting judges. Trun-
cated procedures, including fewer oral arguments and full opinions, also
help to reduce workloads. Federal law allows the chief justice of the United
States to designate and temporarily assign any Article III judge to a district
or appellate court in another circuit, and it also allows chief circuit judges to
assign district judges to serve on the court of appeals in their circuit, and
(less commonly) to assign district and circuit judges in their circuit to sit
temporarily on other courts in the circuit. Most often, visiting judges are district court judges (senior and active) from the subject circuit or are appellate court judges (often senior) from the other circuits. By one estimate,
over the past two decades, visiting judges have participated in roughly 20
percent of all cases decided by merits by the courts of appeals.[18] Still, the
vocal concerns of several chief judges across the appellate bench suggest
that those charged with the efficient functioning of the courts of appeals
worry often about their judges' ability to dispense justice in a timely fashion.

Table 6-2. *Impact of Judicial Vacancies on the Performance of the Courts of Appeals, 1971–2002*

Independent variable	Median time coefficient (pcse) Model 1[a]	No. of pending appeals coefficient (pcse) Model 2[b]
Median time (lag)	.792***	--
	(.037)	
Pending cases per judge (lagged)	--	.646***
		(.048)
Vacancy rate	1.937*	195.35***
	(.654)	(21.096)
New judgeships added	−.343*	−25.570***
	(.158)	(3.919)
Percent freshmen judges	−1.011	30.157*
	(.531)	(15.930)
Post-1982 control	.382*	−4.062
	(.160)	(4.580)
No. of appeals filed	−.000	.010***
	(.000)	(.002)
Constant	2.0214***	27.93***
	(.429)	(7.511)
N	359	359
R^2	0.856	0.941
Wald Chi square	7,387.58***	3,147.31***

Source: Administrative Office of the U.S. Courts, *Federal Court Management Statistics*, annual volumes 1971–2002.

***$p < .001$; *$p < .05$; all one-tailed t tests.

-- = not applicable; pcse = panel corrected standard errors.

a. Dependent variable in model 1 is median time (in months) from filing of briefs until disposition (1971–1981) or median time (in months) from filing notice of appeal to disposition (1982–2002).

b. Dependent variable in model 2 is number of cases pending per authorized judge at the end of each year. Fixed effects for the courts of appeals are estimated but not shown.

Prais-Winsten regression (with pcse) is used to estimate both models via Stata's *xtpcse* routine.

Recent studies of judicial selection have increased our understanding of the causes of institutional and political disputes over the selection of new judges. Such studies, however, have paid scant attention to the consequences of extended judicial vacancies for the institutional capacity of the appellate bench. Even after controlling for the size of a court's caseload and expansions in the number of authorized judgeships for each circuit, extensive and extended vacancies hamper the capacity of the federal bench: Cases take longer to work their way from notice of appeal to final decision, and judges find themselves with rising caseloads. Understaffed in face of rising numbers and complexity of appeals, the federal appellate courts pay the cost for senators' and presidents' unwillingness to compromise in their battles over the makeup of the federal bench.

Confirmation Conflict and Legitimacy of the Bench

Does the conflict over the selection of federal judges have implications for the public's view of the courts? In this section, we report on the results of a survey experiment designed to explore the impact of confirmation votes on the public's perceptions of the courts. We examine the possibility that citizens take cues from the character of Senate debate over nominees, and we show that such conflict affects individuals' views of judges and the decisions they issue from the bench. Given that judges have lifetime appointments to an unelected bench, a confirmation process that weakens citizens' views about judges is worrisome. Rather than instilling confidence in the courts, the current practice of advice and consent may be undermining it.

Before turning to the public's evaluations of federal judges, it is helpful to think about the phenomenon of public criticism of the president. Scholars have carefully delineated the impact of criticism on the president and on his approval ratings. As Richard Brody has shown, the "rally around the flag" phenomenon—the propensity of the American public to support the president in times of crisis, as reflected in high approval ratings—most reflects the lack of criticism of the president by the opposition party in times of crisis.[19] When criticism ebbs, Americans rally around the flag, yielding strong approval ratings for the president. As the crisis recedes, and the opposition resumes its criticism of the president, public approval drops as well.

In contrast, the federal judiciary—in particular, the U.S. Supreme Court— tends to be perceived favorably by voters. It is conceivable that the high approval registered by the public for the Supreme Court is in large part a consequence of the traditional norm of judicial independence. That norm suggests that there should be institutional protections that preclude jeopardizing a judge's lifetime tenure in office because of criticisms. That norm may help to deflect elite criticism of the courts. Of course, the lack of transparency for judicial decisionmaking probably helps to bolster judicial support. As congressional scholars have noted, one reason for Congress's perennially dismal approval ratings is the unabashedly public nature of the legislative process.[20] Voters dislike watching the sausage being made. The black box character of decisionmaking on the Supreme Court (and on the lower federal courts, even further out of the public eye) no doubt reduces dissent about the courts. Out of the public view and potentially bolstered indirectly by the norm of judicial independence, the federal judiciary typically enjoys high and sustained levels of support.

But what happens when nominees and judges become the target of a party's criticism for their policy views or for their decisions on the bench? In that case, the public's views of the bench are likely affected. Although an extreme and singular example, the Supreme Court's *Bush* v. *Gore* decision in 2000 reduced support for the court among supporters of presidential candidate Al Gore.[21] We have evidence from a study by James Gibson that also suggests that the public reacts negatively when judges are portrayed as political. Using an experimental survey, Gibson shows that campaign ads that attack candidates in state judgeship elections weaken the public's perceptions of judges' evenhandedness.[22] There is also some experimental evidence to show that the way in which Supreme Court decisionmaking is depicted for the public makes a difference in their views about the Court. A case decided on the grounds of competing legal principles elicits high marks for the Court from individuals; a case decided after a process of political bargaining reduces public support for the Court.[23]

A Survey Experiment

Given the rise in conflict over lower court nominees and judges over the past decade, could polarized debate over the makeup of the lower federal bench affect the public's views of judges and the courts? To test for the impact of contentious confirmation contests, we designed and implemented a survey experiment as part of the Cooperative Congressional Election Study, an internet survey put into the field in the fall of 2006.[24] In the survey, 1,000 respondents were randomly divided into six different groups. The groups were treated as shown in table 6-3. Respondents were arranged into groups that vary by the president who nominated the judge (George W. Bush, Bill Clinton, or no president mentioned) and by the outcome of the confirmation vote

Table 6-3. *Treatment and Control Groups for Survey Experiment*

Group	Nominating president	Confirmation vote
1st	George W. Bush	53–47
2nd	Bill Clinton	53–47
3rd	George W. Bush	unanimous
4th	Bill Clinton	unanimous
5th	no president mentioned	53–47
6th	no president mentioned	unanimous

Source: Internet survey in 2006 as part of the Cooperative Congressional Election Study (http://web.mit.edu/polisci/portl/cces).

(53–47 or unanimous). Once separated into groups, all survey respondents were given the following scenario about a real case decided by a fictitious federal judge, Ralph Jones:

> Federal judge Ralph Jones recently struck down a law that prohibited the sale of guns within one mile of any school. In the ruling, Jones argued that "although protecting children from firearms may be a justified policy, under the Constitution, Congress does not have the right to mandate local zoning codes."

Respondents were then asked two questions. Do you agree with Judge Jones's opinion in the case? To what degree do you trust Judge Jones to make decisions that are right for the country as a whole?[25]

The experimental results shown in table 6-4 are striking, as they show a strong and negative impact of a contested confirmation vote on respondents' views about the judge and his decisions, controlling for respondents' partisanship. Because the decision might be viewed as anti–gun control, being exposed to information about confirmation conflict did not seem to affect Republicans' views of the judge. Individuals who are more likely to be inclined against gun control are arguably more likely to identify with the Republican Party. Thus Republicans' policy views on the subject at hand might have been strong enough that their views of the judge were insulated from a confirmation vote treatment effect. In fact, confirmation conflict in this case might have served as a signal to anti–gun control Republican respondents that this judge was worth fighting for, thus driving up Republicans' trust in his decisionmaking. Democrats overall show lower levels of

Table 6-4. *Impact of Confirmation Conflict, by Party*
Percent

Partisanship of respondent	Treatment: unanimous vote (agree with Jones)	Treatment: contested vote (agree with Jones)	Treatment: unanimous vote (trust Jones)	Treatment: contested vote (trust Jones)
Democrat	58	53	40	29
Republican	75	76	56	69
Independent	70	60	63	40

Source: Internet survey in 2006 as part of the Cooperative Congressional Election Study (http://web.mit.edu/polisci/portl/cces).

enthusiasm for Judge Jones's decision, and those exposed to confirmation conflict harbor even dimmer views of the judge's decision and significantly lower trust in the judge.

The reactions of self-identified independents are especially noteworthy. The support of independents for the judge is generally high. But when exposed to a report of confirmation conflict, the percentage of independents agreeing with Jones's decision dropped ten points, and the percentage trusting Jones dropped twenty points. This suggests that Senate disagreements about judges send a signal to independents, which they interpret as a warning about the judge and his potential decisions. That signal is potentially one of immoderation, as the confirmation vote suggests that only a bare Senate majority believes the judge well suited for a lifetime appointment. In contrast, independents exposed to a signal of unanimous support for a judge infer moderation (or potentially independence) from the bipartisan character of the nominee's Senate support.

How Much Does Confirmation Conflict Matter?

We can go a step further in analyzing the impact of confirmation conflict by moving to a multivariate context. To bolster our confidence in the causal impact of a contested vote, we control for the several forces likely to affect respondents' views about and trust in Judge Jones. First, we create a dummy variable denoting whether the respondent was treated to a "contested vote," coded as 1, or was not treated to a contested vote, coded as 0. Second, we create a "Bush treatment" dummy to mark respondents who were told that

Judge Jones was nominated by President Bush, coded as 1, 0 otherwise, and a "Clinton treatment" dummy for those who were told that Jones was nominated by President Clinton. (The excluded group consists of those respondents for whom the nominating president was not identified.) Third, we create dummy variables to denote a "strong Democrat" and a "strong Republican" (the excluded group is independents) and then interact the strong partisan dummies with the corresponding Bush or Clinton treatment variable. These allow us to isolate strong identifiers in each party who were told that their own party's president nominated Judge Jones. Strong partisans should view contested nominees selected by their party's president more favorably than do weak partisans and others. Finally, we control for respondents' views about gun control. Elsewhere in the survey, respondents were asked whether or not they owned a gun. We infer opposition to gun control among those respondents who claimed to own a gun (37 percent); we infer support for gun control among respondents who responded that they did not own a gun (62 percent).[26] "Gun owners" are coded 1 (0 otherwise).[27]

We estimate two statistical models to determine the influence of these forces on respondents' views about Judge Jones. The dependent variable in column 1 of table 6-5 is whether or not the respondent agrees with Judge Jones's decision. The dependent variable in column 2 is whether or not the respondent trusts Judge Jones to make decisions that are right for the country.[28] The models allow us to predict the likelihood that an individual will agree with or trust Judge Jones. We find similar results for both estimations. Citizens are likely to view a judge less favorably once they are informed about the level of conflict in the Senate over the judge's confirmation. Contested votes depress support for a judge, even after controlling for the respondents' partisanship, the appointing president, and the respondents' views about guns.

We can get a better sense of the depressive impact of a contested vote by simulating two confirmation scenarios. In the first, the respondent (a non-gun-owning independent or moderate partisan) is told that a Bush nominee was confirmed unanimously. In the second, a similarly situated respondent is told that a Bush nominee was confirmed in a contested vote. The difference is remarkable: the likelihood of agreeing with the judge's decision drops some 10 percent, while the likelihood of trusting the judge drops 20 percent.[29] Of note, the predicted probability of trusting the judge, even when

Table 6-5. *Estimating the Impact of Confirmation Conflict on Support for Federal Judges*

Independent variable	Agree with Judge Jones coefficient (robust std. error) Model 1[a]	Trust Judge Jones coefficient (robust std. error) Model 2[b]
Gun owner	.316***	.495***
	(.117)	(.177)
Contested vote treatment	−.146[†]	−.245[†]
	(.109)	(.166)
Bush treatment	−.246*	−.343[†]
	(.144)	(.213)
Clinton treatment	−.078	−.464*
	(.143)	(.218)
Strong DEM * Clinton treatment	.589*	1.981***
	(.308)	(.572)
Strong GOP * Bush treatment	.785***	1.296***
	(.326)	(.482)
Strong DEM	−.561***	−1.100***
	(.179)	(.263)
Strong GOP	−.104	−.265
	(.164)	(.233)
Constant	.498***	.312[†]
	(.126)	(.202)
N	589	267

Source: Authors' calculations based on Cooperative Congressional Election Study Internet 2006 survey (http://web.mit.edu/polisci/portl/cces).

***$p < .01$; *$p < .05$; [†]$p < .1$; all one-tailed t tests.

a. Dependent variable in model 1 is whether or not the respondent agrees with Judge Jones's decision.

b. Dependent variable in model 2 is whether or not respondent trusts Judge Jones to make the right decisions for the country.

Results estimated in Stata's *probit* routine, robust standard errors in parentheses.

told of a unanimous confirmation vote, is more than 10 percent lower than the predicted probability of agreeing with the judge's decision. This is not surprising, given that the trust question inevitably elicits considerations beyond the actual policy question at issue in the local zoning case decided by the judge.

We recognize that there are limitations to our ability to generalize from experimental results. The causal inferences we draw about the impact of confirmation support on individuals' views about federal judges are robust, given the experimental design of the study that bolsters the internal validity of the study. And in methodological terms, the results are generalizable; they should have strong external validity, again given the experimental design. But we recognize that these are ultimately experimental results and are based on an Internet survey. Still, many citizens are exposed to news stories about confirmation conflict; the salience of judicial filibusters in the spring of 2005 is surely evidence of the public's growing awareness of Senate fights over judges. But many likely know little about the Senate's treatment of judicial nominees, suggesting that the impact of confirmation conflict is conditional on the extent to which the public learns and is motivated to learn about battles over the bench. As the two parties and organized interests have increasingly focused in recent years on debates over judicial selection, we suspect that a wider share of the public will be susceptible to what we view as potentially harmful effects of drawn-out battles over controversial nominees.

Citizens' support for and trust in federal judges are conditional on what they know about a judge's pathway to the bench. The spillover effects of confirmation conflict—reflecting disagreements that mirror the parties' disagreements over policy issues before the bench—are substantial and consequential. It matters how the Senate conducts itself when presented with contentious nominees, and thus it matters when a president nominates candidates for the bench who are likely to be unacceptable to a partisan opposition. Nominees that engender pitched battles—rightly or wrongly—ultimately may put the legitimacy of the unelected bench at risk.

7 | Reforming Advice and Consent

Cooperation and conflict over the shape of the federal bench have been enduring themes over the course of the history of the judiciary. Some argue that contemporary judicial selection reflects an old story of perennial disputes over the makeup of the bench: selecting judges has always been a political exercise. Others point to an abrupt change in the practice of advice and consent, the result of the battle over confirming Robert Bork to the Supreme Court in the 1980s, typically held to be the "big bang" of contentious judicial selection. We argue instead that understanding the dynamics of judicial selection requires us to think historically, analytically, and broadly about the institutional context in which advice and consent take place. Taking account of the multiple and evolving avenues of Senate resistance—coupled with an understanding of the rise of polarized parties whose members care about the decisions of the federal courts—provides the basis for explaining patterns in judicial selection over the postwar period. As we argue in this chapter, thinking institutionally also paves the way for considering pragmatic reform of the rules and practices of advice and consent.

Advantages of an Institutional Perspective

An institutional perspective affords us leverage in studying advice and consent in three ways. It allows us to recast the received wisdom about judicial selection, it gives us insight into the adoption and evolution of organizational arrangements in the Senate, and it provides a constructive way to think about potential reforms of advice and consent. We explore each of these in turn.

Recasting the Received Wisdom

By focusing on the ways in which Senate rules and practices distribute power unevenly across the institution, an institutional perspective encourages us to rethink the conventional wisdom that has emerged about judicial selection in recent years. Most accounts of the difficulties encountered by judicial nominees place the blame first and foremost on the behavior of political parties in the Senate or party activists outside the Senate. As John Maltese has argued, "Polarized politics led to confirmation battles and confirmation gridlock because judicial appointments were thought by participants in the process to have a potentially profound impact on public policy. . . . As long as the balance of power remains divided, the process promises to be a contentious one."[1]

There is no doubt that the ideological polarization of the parties that has occurred steadily over the past two decades plays an important role in explaining why the confirmation process has become so contentious in recent years. Both parties understand the importance of federal courts to the making of public law; the parties have divergent views about appropriate policy in a range of salient areas; and they assume (not always correctly) that judges' decisions differ significantly depending on whether Democratic or Republican presidents appoint them. Thus the selection of judges for lifetime positions on the bench features high on the list of items that the parties will disagree about. Of course, we see episodic conflict over the selection of executive branch nominees—for example, John Bolton's twice failed nomination to be the U.S. ambassador to the United Nations. But the lifetime tenure of judges and the jurisdictional reach of the federal appellate courts clearly raise the stakes for partisans when they consider presidential nominations for the bench.

Polarization is a necessary part of explaining the rise of conflict, but it is not sufficient. In a purely partisan account, we lose sight of the ways in which Senate rules and practices allocate procedural advantage to different senators—institutional tools that can be used to have an effect on both the president's selection of nominees and the fate of nominees once submitted to the Senate. Senators can exploit various tools when they oppose nominees on ideological grounds, when they seek leverage over the president or their colleagues on unrelated measures, and when they find old avenues of resistance closed off by new innovations in the practice of advice and consent. These tools include home state senator advantage conferred via the blue slip, the ability to filibuster nominations through the chamber's Rule 22, the ability of opposition senators to place anonymous holds on nominees by threatening to deny consent to call up nominations, and the tools (however limited) of agenda control that endow majority party leaders in committee and on the floor.

These tools are not wielded as blunt instruments across all nominees. Senators choose their targets carefully, typically saving their ammunition for nominations slated to fill vacancies on balanced appellate courts and for nominations in the run-up to a presidential election. Moreover, senators have honed their tools of resistance and released them prospectively—at times threatening to block a nomination if the president selects a nominee without regard to the views of the home state senator.

Without this medieval allocation of procedural rights across the chamber, senators opposing nominees would have little opportunity to influence the selection of nominees or to block candidates they oppose. The president would simply aim to obtain the consent of the median senator, thus securing confirmation in an up or down vote on the floor. Although nominations do have to attract the support of the median, they must also gain the consent of the two home state senators, of the Judiciary Committee and its chair, the median of the majority party empowered to call up a nomination in executive session, and a typically bipartisan supermajority of sixty votes on the chamber floor. Senators understand these hurdles and exploit them when they cannot tolerate nominees they deem to be too far from the mainstream, when they seek to preserve the seat for a favored nominee, or when they prefer to keep the seat vacant for other reasons. Tracking the confluence of ideological and political tendencies and institutional rules and practices is essential to explaining patterns in the selection of nominees and in the rate and pace of Senate confirmation.

The Path Dependency of Advice and Consent

Thinking institutionally about judicial selection is valuable in a second way because it encourages us to consider advice and consent as a set of inherited institutional practices that have evolved over time. The contemporary practice of advice and consent does not follow a script laid out by the Framers. As we explored in chapter 2, the design of the federal judiciary was contested by the first members of Congress in 1789, with Federalists and anti-Federalists disagreeing over the proper extent of federal court jurisdiction and how closely federal court procedures and boundaries should track state court procedures and state borders. The decisions over federal court boundaries were consequential as they eventually elevated home state senators into becoming the natural arbiters of who would serve in judicial posts from their states. Even with the creation of the courts of appeals in 1891, home state senators retained their leverage over appointments, since each appellate seat eventually became associated with a particular home state within the multistate circuit.[2] Finally, it took the Senate until 1913 to create the blue slip, the key procedural practice that empowers home state senators—even if initially senators did not seem to have intended the blue slip to serve as a formal veto tool for senators.

These innovations—the emergence of home state senators as the first movers on judicial nominations and the creation of the blue slip—influenced the future course of judicial selection. And as senators have innovated with the practice of advice and consent, subsequent presidents and Senate majorities have had to grapple with the broad and increasingly interconnected array of procedural rights that shape the fate of nominees before the Senate. Advice and consent continues to evolve, as the recent confrontation over the nuclear option suggests. As we suggest in chapter 4, Republican efforts to curtail the blue slip at the start of George W. Bush's administration simply encouraged Democrats to try new tactics of resistance, leading to almost a dozen judicial filibusters against Bush's appellate nominees. As Senator Barbara Boxer (D-Calif.) said when Hatch ignored her dissenting blue slip, "This decision to move forward without both home-state senators' approval will have ramifications for years to come."[3]

The development of advice and consent is instructive to political scientists interested in the creation and evolution of institutional arrangements. First, to the extent that we can generalize from senators' experiences with advice and consent, it seems that politicians rarely design institutions rationally and with a clear understanding of their consequences. More often, institutions are the product of political compromise, and they acquire unanticipated consequences.[4] The Framers did not set out to empower home state senators; such powers emerged as a consequence of decisions about the courts made for other reasons. Second, the evolution of advice and consent suggests the path-dependent character of congressional rules and institutional arrangements more generally. Once the notion of home state senator power became entrenched—first in the norm of senatorial courtesy and then in the informal practice of the blue slip—it became extremely difficult to uproot it. In this way, we can think of the rules and practices of judicial selection as a classic case of path dependence. Choices made in the past over institutional design continue to shape and constrain the choices that senators have today about the rules and practices of judicial selection.[5]

Is Reform Possible?

Third, placing our emphasis on the institutional framework of the Senate allows us to think constructively about the potential for reform of advice and consent. We are not naïve about reforming the Senate. The high threshold of Rule 22, which requires a two-thirds vote to end debate over resolutions to change the rules, stands as a significant barrier to reforming the Senate and how it dispenses advice and consent. Absent crisis or a widespread recognition that the current system of rules is broken and needs to be changed, efforts to reform the Senate typically fail.[6] Still, the practice of advice and consent is not fixed in stone, as our overview of its evolution suggests. Senators do at times consider changes in how the institution works, or fails to work, as evidenced by episodic reform of Rule 22 over the course of the twentieth century and more recently by the attempt to ban judicial filibusters in 2005 via the nuclear option. Harnessing changes in the rules to senators' and presidents' incentives, we will argue, is essential for designing institutional reforms of advice and consent that have greater chances of adoption.

Reforming Advice and Consent

We consider three potential reforms of judicial selection, offering our assessment of the benefits and drawbacks of each: the adoption of commissions at the state level to encourage the nomination of more widely accepted candidates; a nonstatutory fast track for nominations somewhat akin to those adopted for certain trade, budget, and other measures; and changes to the threshold for confirming nominees. We make a case for the first two reforms, providing some evidence of the positive impact of commissions and suggesting how fast-track rules could be attractive to senators if coupled with the adoption of commissions. Finally, we question the arguments made in favor of imposing a supermajority threshold on the grounds of unintended consequences: Raising the bar for confirmation, we suggest, risks making the problems of judicial selection even worse.[7]

Commissions to Suggest Potential Nominees

Presidents and senators have sometimes used commissions to recruit and recommend candidates for federal district court judgeships and, during the Carter administration, courts of appeals judgeships. The heyday of such commissions was the 1970s, when both of Florida's senators created the first one in 1974.[8] Thirty other commissions were created by 1979, spurred largely by President Jimmy Carter's 1977 executive order establishing the U.S. Circuit Judge Nominating Commission and by Carter's letters to each senator asking them to appoint commissions to help identify district court nominees. Carter intended first to encourage the use of commissions to evaluate potential candidates and later to seek more women and minorities for federal judicial service.[9] By the mid-1980s, it appears that only senators from the states of Florida and Wisconsin were still using commissions to review and recommend candidates for the lower federal bench. One review that studied the operations and impact of the original commissions during the Carter administration gave the commissions a mixed grade, noting that the commissions were more likely to have recommended "superior" candidates.[10] Still, the study noted that given the preponderance of Democrats recommended by the commissions and then nominated by President Carter, the early operation of these commissions "may simply represent a form of merit selection of Democrats, by Democrats."

The count of old and new commissions as of early 2009 stands at twelve states: California, Connecticut, Florida, Georgia, Hawaii, Michigan, North Carolina, Pennsylvania, Texas, Vermont, Washington, and Wisconsin—five of these commissions have been newly created after Democrats regained the White House in 2008.[11] During the Bush administration, commissions in California, Colorado, Hawaii, Washington, and Wisconsin followed a bipartisan model, ensuring an even or near-even balance of commission members appointed by Democrats and Republicans. Bipartisan commissions are especially attractive to a state's Senate delegation when both of them are not from the president's party—such as California's Senate delegation during the Bush administrations.[12] By creating a bipartisan commission in California, for example, Senators Dianne Feinstein and Barbara Boxer made it more likely that candidates acceptable to themselves would also be acceptable to the president.[13] Perhaps not surprisingly, when Democrats regained control of the White House in 2009, the California senators disbanded the bipartisan commission. Instead, each senator formed her own selection commission for each of the state's four federal districts; the commissions were to alternate in recommending potential candidates to President Obama for federal judgeships, U.S. marshals, and U.S. attorneys. In contrast, in states with commissions that are not explicitly noted to be bipartisan, we suspect that the makeup of the commission more closely reflects the partisanship of the state's Senate delegation. We cannot be sure, since the partisanship of the commission is rarely explicitly documented and there is some precedent for senators to select a commission member from the other party. Still, in the absence of counter evidence, we suspect that these other commissions are filled on a partisan basis.

Are there discernible effects of the use of commissions on either the rate or pace of confirmation for lower court nominees? We have only a limited history over which to evaluate commission effects. Because we need to control as much as possible for the nature of the selection process and the electoral and political contexts, we isolate nominations to the U.S. district courts made by President George W. Bush during the One Hundred Eighth (2003–04) and One Hundred Ninth (2005–06) Congresses, both periods when Republicans controlled the White House. During these two Congresses, there were 156 nominations made to the federal district courts; in forty-two of these nominating opportunities, selection commissions in five states were in operation, and they recommended nominees either to the senior home state senator from the president's party or directly to the White House.[14]

To determine whether or not the adoption of a commission could affect the fate of nominees, we need to isolate nominations made for judgeships in states represented by two Democrats; given a Republican White House and Senate in those Congresses, we do not look at the fate of nominations in states whose Senate delegations included a Republican, as the Republican senator or senators in those states likely would have recommended nominees who could pass muster with the White House and Senate GOP colleagues, even in the absence of a selection commission. We then compare the rate and pace of confirmation for nominees from states using commissions compared with the rate and pace of confirmation for nominees from states that did not employ a commission.[15] If the adoption of a commission by a senator makes it more likely that opposition party senators will approve the nomination (and thus not attempt to block the nomination through a blue slip, hold, or filibuster), then we should see nominations move more swiftly through the Senate and encounter higher rates of confirmation when commissions are in place at the state level.

We find evidence that suggests the positive impact of nominating commissions. Across the One Hundred Eighth and One Hundred Ninth Congresses, there were a total of seventy-four nominations made to federal trial courts located in states represented by two Democratic senators. Of those seventy-four, twenty-seven nominations were made in states with commissions in operation.[16] As shown in table 7-1, the confirmation rate for district court nominations in these states showed a twelve-point percentage increase when senators used a commission, jumping from 66 to 74 percent.[17] If we drop the most contentious state (California), the confirmation rate increases even more steeply, by about 35 percent. There may also be an impact of commissions on how long it takes the Senate to act. Nominees from Democratic-represented states that used commissions waited on average 137 days for Senate action, or just under five months; nominees from Democratic states that did not use commissions waited nearly twice as long for the Senate to act.[18]

A full analysis of the impact of selection commissions requires more data, preferably after the newest commissions have been in operation for several years and across a new administration. We do not know from our initial analysis, however, much about the nature of the candidates recommended by commissions, except for their acceptability to both parties when the structure of the commission is bipartisan.[19] In addition, future analysis will need to grapple with the questions of why, when, and under what conditions senators are likely to create commissions in the first place. Selection bias may be at work here, leading states with less contentious political

Table 7-1. *Selection Commissions and Nominations to the U.S. District Courts, 2003–06*[a]

Was a commission used by one or both senators?	Confirmation rate percent (no. of nominations)	Average number of days elapsed between nomination and Senate disposition[b]
Yes	74 (27)	137
No	66 (47)	240

Source: Authors' calculations.

a. Includes only nominations to states represented by two Democratic U.S. senators.

b. For failed nominations, final date of Senate action is the date a nomination was withdrawn or the date that the Senate adjourned at the end of the session of the Congress.

climates to adopt selection commissions. Given the ideological differences of organized Democrats and Republicans in California, as well as in Florida, our sense is that no single explanation can account for the decision to appoint a commission.

That said, political incentives are often at the heart of senators' efforts to appoint commissions. In 1997, for example, Senator Slade Gorton (R-Wash.) was the senior senator of the delegation when Republicans controlled the Senate. With a Democrat in the White House and Gorton opposed to the proposed nominees, the senator exploited the blue slip to block the Democratic nominees until his fellow senator, Democrat Patty Murray, agreed to appoint a bipartisan panel to screen and recommend nominations for the White House's consideration.[20] Clearly, senators' political and policy objectives shape their views about appropriate selection methods, which suggests that not all senators will eagerly adopt a commission unless there is an additional strong incentive to do so. When such commissions are in place, however, we see a different course of advice and consent for nominations from those states.

A Judicial Fast Track

In the wake of Democratic filibusters of several appellate court nominees, Republican majority leader Bill Frist of Tennessee in 2003 advocated two reforms of the confirmation process. One reform would have implemented a sliding scale for cloture on nominations, successively reducing the number of votes needed to invoke cloture as debate goes on. Frist's plan closely resembled a plan advocated by Senators Tom Harkin (D-Iowa) and Joe

Lieberman (D-Conn.) in 1995. Under Frist's proposal, the first attempt to invoke cloture would require sixty votes, or three-fifths of the Senate. If the majority failed to muster sixty votes, the number of senators required to invoke cloture would be reduced by three for each subsequent cloture motion. By ratcheting down the number of votes required to limit debate, a majority vote would be sufficient to invoke cloture on nominations on the fourth cloture motion—thus eliminating the filibuster of judicial nominations.

Supporters of the sliding scale provision argued that it reconciled the Senate's tradition of extensive deliberation with the constitutional requirement of majority rule.[21] Adoption of the Frist proposal, however, was never likely. Although the Constitution permits a majority of the Senate to establish its own rules, Senate rules and precedents make procedural changes themselves subject to a filibuster. If the rule change were to be filibustered— which it surely would have been—then under Senate rules a two-thirds majority would have been needed to break the filibuster.[22] Considering that the Republicans lacked sixty votes within their ranks, reform of the cloture threshold was dead on arrival that Congress. Making little progress, Frist turned to the nuclear option as we recounted in detail in chapter 4—a more contentious episode that ultimately ended in failure as well.

A close cousin of the diminishing cloture threshold would be a process whereby the Senate would provide judicial nominations with the type of fast-track consideration that has become common for treaty ratifications and even recommendations for defense base closings. Fast-track authority for these other policy areas has been set statutorily by the Senate, limiting overall debate time on measures and guaranteeing an up or down vote at the end of the allotted time. By creating a nonstatutory fast track for judicial nominations, filibusters would no longer be possible. But passage of a bill establishing fast track for nominations would itself be subject to a filibuster, meaning that the Senate is unlikely to adopt this proposal alone under the current polarized environment. With the stakes of judicial appointments perceived as being high, the minority party is unlikely to agree to a procedural reform that diminishes its existing ability to influence the course of advice and consent.

Democrats in 2003 advocated other solutions to the confirmation malaise. Most notable among them was a solution advocated by Senator Charles Schumer (D-N.Y.) that he believed would enhance the Senate's provision of advice to the president.[23] Under his proposal, senators would designate bipartisan commissions to identify qualified candidates for the federal bench. Presidents would then select their appointees from the pool of candidates endorsed by the bipartisan group. Such a selection process would encourage presidents to select more moderate nominees. Schumer was confident that the Senate would treat such nominees more expeditiously. In reaction, the Bush administration asserted that such a mechanism would usurp the constitutional authority of the president to choose judges.

A potential solution to the partisan and institutional wars that have been waged over judicial selection would be to try, on a pilot basis, a hybrid solution that matches elements of the Schumer and fast-track proposals. The process would start by the Senate detailing procedures for states to establish acceptable bipartisan commissions. The Senate would then treat nominees selected via the selection commission more expeditiously than other nominations. If the president selected a judicial candidate from a list of candidates recommended by a bipartisan commission, then the nominee would be afforded fast-track protection during the confirmation process. As such, the commission proposal would overcome problems that were inherent in experiments with selection commissions during the late 1970s. If the president chose instead someone not recommended by a bipartisan commission, fast-track protection would not apply. Presumably, presidents would make a strategic choice of which route to follow for each nomination. If the stakes for the appointment were high, a strategic president would probably opt to rely on the recommendations of a bipartisan commission avoiding the likely long delay in these circumstances. In other cases, for less salient appointments, the president might reasonably try his luck without seeking protection of fast track. By providing both parties and both branches with an incentive to participate, the hybrid proposal might be attractive enough to secure supermajority support for adoption.

Shy of meaningful procedural innovations, the only other vehicle for overcoming nomination gridlock would be for the Senate to agree, on a case-by-case basis, to consider the packaging of nominations. If nominees were packaged to include both liberal and conservative judicial candidates, Democratic senators would likely tolerate conservative nominees favored by recent Republican presidents, and vice versa. Still, when President George W. Bush attempted such a strategy with his first set of nominations in the spring of 2001—with the Senate under control of the Democrats—it failed. Bush's package included two African American Democrats, some moderate conservatives, and some hard right conservatives. Democrats promptly confirmed the Democrats but not the hard right conservatives.

Moreover, the proposal raises two broader problems. First, some presidents are unlikely to be interested in nominating centrist judges, preferring candidates from either the conservative or liberal wings of the party. Second, such a process may enhance the probability of selecting judges who are ill-suited for lifetime appointments on the federal bench. In *Federalist* No. 76, Alexander Hamilton supported the notion of having nominees selected by one person rather than a collegial body because the choice made by one was likely to be better than the choices by "a body of men who may each be supposed to have an equal number; and will be so much the less liable to be misled by the sentiments of friendship and of affection." Hamilton thought that if a group of politicians made the nominations, they would inevitably distribute the positions equally among them. Hamilton did not want judicial nominees filled on the basis of logrolling among politicians who each held a "diversity of views, feelings, and interests, which frequently distract and warp the resolutions of a collective body." Clearly, if judicial nominees were routinely considered as part of a package, the result might be a judiciary stacked with extremists who individually make decisions that do not take into consideration the diversity of views about the law and its application.

Requiring Sixty Votes for Confirmation

One other potential reform of judicial selection merits reflection. In contrast to recent efforts to reduce the number of votes required to cut off debate on nominations, prominent legal scholars have suggested that the threshold for confirmation be increased. As Judith Resnick has argued, "A supermajority rule of sixty could . . . create incentives for the President to put forth individuals about whom a broad consensus of approval exists."[24] Although the Senate's Rule 22 currently requires sixty votes to cut off debate on a motion to confirm a nominee, the Resnick proposal would require sixty votes for the actual vote to confirm. Looking at the decade between 1993 and 2003, Resnick notes that relatively few nominees have been confirmed with fewer than sixty votes. In part because she believes that "the

Senate has been too accommodating, approving too many candidates, too quickly," Resnick suggests that the overall impact of the rule would be benign, if not beneficial.[25]

We view the imposition of a supermajority requirement differently. Our hunch is that the unintended consequence of raising the threshold for confirmation would reduce the rate of confirmation and would not necessarily encourage the selection of nominees with broad Senate support. First, under the Senate's Rule 22, there is a de facto supermajority requirement already in place. However, because nominees can be confirmed on a simple majority vote, a successful filibuster to prevent an up or down vote to confirm requires intensity on the part of senators; otherwise they would not carry the costs of mounting and sustaining a filibuster, often in face of stringent criticism from the president and organized interests. If a supermajority vote is implemented for confirmation, the costs of filibustering will go down as the minority now only needs to vote together rather than to sustain a campaign against the nominee. Moreover, so long as the Senate lacks a previous question motion (which puts the Senate in the position of requiring unanimous consent to call up a nominee in executive session), senators' ability to place anonymous holds on nominees would remain. The blue slip practice would also remain in place, suggesting that home state senators might still attempt to kill nominations at the committee stage.

Second, the moderating effect of supermajority rules is unclear. More likely, the effect of a supermajority rule on the ideology of the candidates selected by the president is conditional on the underlying distribution of opinion in the Senate.[26] In a Senate in which ideology follows a bell-shaped curve—with a large moderate center and narrow tails—a supermajority rule will most likely encourage the president to select a nominee closer to the middle of the ideological spectrum. In a Senate in which the ideological distribution is bipolar—as we have had for the past two decades—there is far less incentive for a president seeking confirmation of his nominees to select someone from the ideological center. Attracting the vote of the sixtieth senator requires moving to the sixtieth percentile of the Senate; that is unlikely to be someone at the center of public opinion, at least as arrayed in the contemporary Senate. A supermajority threshold might also encourage logrolling among senators, each of whom is seeking to help favored nominees secure confirmation—reminding us of Alexander Hamilton's concern about the harm posed by allowing groups of politicians to select nominees. This possibility further undermines the likelihood that requiring sixty votes would encourage the selection of moderate nominees.

Third, would presidents truly attempt to nominate candidates who can secure the support of the sixtieth senator? As some legal scholars have argued, "the President would change the nature of his nominations in the shadow of the new rules of the confirmation game, selecting persons who are more likely to be able to secure a Senate supermajority."[27] This may well be right, but it assumes that a president's only strategy is to fill the federal bench in a timely manner. The record of many recent nominations, however, is that presidents may want as well to use nominations to signal their ideological and policy commitments to organized interests and to conservatives or liberals within the legal profession. Certainly the effort in the Reagan administration—aided by the newly formed Federalist Society—to nominate candidates with conservative, ideological records attests to the use of nominations by presidents to pursue a policy agenda.[28] President Bush's similar efforts—renominating candidates whom Senate Democrats had previously filibustered—suggests that a supermajority requirement would not necessarily tame a president into making consensus appointments.

Conclusions

In the run up to the 2008 presidential elections, the nomination and confirmation of judges for the lower federal courts ground to a halt. Reflecting on the impasse, Senator John Cornyn (R-Tex.) observed that Democrats were playing "a short-sighted game, because around here what goes around comes around. . . . When the shoe is on the other foot, there is going to be a temptation to respond in kind."[29] The senator's point was certainly on the mark, as one party's intolerance of the other party's nominees has of late typically been answered in turn when the parties swap positions in the Senate. But the obstruction of judicial nominees is nested within a larger game over the makeup of the court and future contests over the shape of public law. Placing constraints on the opposition's long-term impact on the courts and the development of the law has been construed by senators as a benefit worth the cost of weathering subsequent obstruction of one's own nominees.

We believe still that the costs of a judicial selection process infused with political partisanship and ideology are steep and potentially too great to bear. First, judicial legitimacy is potentially harmed. As Fifth Circuit Court of Appeals judge Carolyn King has observed, "Judicial independence is undermined . . . by the high degree of political partisanship and ideology that currently characterizes the process by which the President nominates and the Senate confirms federal judges." Such a process, King continues, "conveys the notion to the electorate that judges are simply another breed of political agents, that judicial decisions should be in accord with political ideology, all of which tends to undermine public confidence in the legitimacy of the court."[30] As our experimental evidence showed in chapter 6, the public's agreement with a federal judge's decisions and more important the public's *trust* in the judge to make the right decisions are diminished in the face of a confirmation contest perceived to be polarized and conflicted. King, incidentally, is considered a Republican jurist whose nomination was suggested to President Carter by the merit selection commission operating in Texas in the late 1970s.[31]

Second, King raises a pointed charge about the potential impact of an appointment process that seeks to select nominees on the basis of their commitments to particular policy positions or ideological outlook. There is a "grave danger to the rule of law," posed by a politicized selection process. "A judge who has been selected primarily for his perceived predisposition to decide cases in accordance with a particular political ideology may be consciously or subconsciously influenced to decide cases in accordance with that ideology, rather than in accordance with an impartial and open-minded assessment of what the law actually is."[32] King's concern—particularly pointed coming from a sitting appellate court judge—is that the polarization of the appointments process may be undermining the very act of judging. Given the very high per judge caseloads on most courts of appeals and given what legal scholar Stephen Burbank calls "hard-wired judges" on either the right or the left, the risk is that appellate court decisions may not be "true to the rule of law."[33] How widely Judge King's sentiment is shared within and beyond the Fifth Circuit is beyond our focus here, but her vantage point as former chief judge of the Fifth Circuit and her nearly three decades on the appellate bench should encourage scholars and observers of judicial selection and the courts to take note of her concern and warning.

Third, as we demonstrate in chapter 6, an understaffed bench cannot be expected to keep up with the heavy caseloads experienced by the courts in most of the circuits. Foot-dragging in the White House in selecting nominees and stalemate on the Hill over potential judges leave dozens of federal judgeships vacant at a time of generally heavy and rising caseloads—albeit vacancy rates have ebbed quite a bit from their heights during the Clinton and Bush administrations. And when judgeships sit vacant, it takes longer for sitting judges to dispose of cases. Vacancies, even after controlling for a range of forces likely to affect a court's ability to handle its caseload, harm the timely performance of the federal appellate courts.

Fourth, the cumbersome and uncertain nomination and confirmation process might impose too high a cost on potential nominees, leading them to avoid public service. That is certainly how Miguel Estrada felt, nominated to the U.S. Court of Appeals for the District of Columbia by President Bush in 2001 and again in 2003, both times filibustered by Democrats who unsuccessfully sought access to the legal memoranda he wrote during his service in the Solicitor General's Office during the Clinton administration. With his future caught up in a gridlocked confirmation process, the lure of a lifetime appointment on the federal bench no longer seemed worth the cost. As he stated in his letter to the president requesting that his nomination be withdrawn, "I believe that the time has come to return my full attention to the practice of law and to regain the ability to make long-term plans for my family."[34] How widespread such sentiment is felt is difficult to determine, but a long, drawn-out confirmation process with uncertainty of Senate action may be discouraging promising federal judges from seeking public service on the bench.

Finally, recurring battles over advice and consent are harmful for the Senate as an institution and for its members. The breakdown in the confirmation process over the course of the Bush administration sheared what had already been a tenuous relationship between the two Senate parties. The parliamentary standoff over the nuclear option in 2005 is no doubt the clearest indication of the disintegration of political trust between the parties. Also unsettling was a debacle over the actions of Judiciary Committee staff a year earlier. Several Republican committee staff found themselves in criminal jeopardy after hacking into the computers of Democratic staff and discovering strategy memos on the president's judicial nominations.[35] In response, one of the Republican staffers under investigation unapologetically asserted that the real crime is the "corruption" associated with Democratic tactics for blocking conservative judicial nominees.[36]

The breakdown in party relations might seem old hat for veteran observers of the House of Representatives. But in the Senate—where unanimous consent is essential to make the body function—partisan disagreements can make the Senate unmanageable. One Democratic senator, reacting to the investigation of Republican committee staff, decried what he called a "breach of trust"—critical for securing bipartisan consent in the Senate.[37] Such breaches occur not only because of contentious staff relations but, more important, from disagreements over how judicial selection should be practiced in the White House and on Capitol Hill.

Because senators' views about advice and consent are conditioned by their institutional positions, we are not hopeful that changes in party control ushered in with the elections of 2008 will channel disagreements over nominations in a more productive manner. Indeed, in the opening salvo of the One Hundred Eleventh Congress, Republican senators warned in a letter to Senate Democrats and newly elected President Barack Obama that Republicans would filibuster any nominees who did not pass muster with the Republican Conference and about whom the White House had not consulted.[38] Despite Republicans' recognition that the confirmation process by 2009 had "become needlessly acrimonious," no signs of a thawing in partisan relations were evident in the spring of 2009. To the president's credit, his first judicial nomination—selecting David Hamilton for an opening on the Seventh Circuit Court of Appeals—attracted the support of both Indiana senators, Democrat Evan Bayh and Republican Richard Lugar.[39] Still, the opposition party raised red flags about the nominee's past work for the American Civil Liberties Union, leaving in doubt at this writing when and how the Senate might act on the nomination.

If presidents alone could alter the course of advice and consent, we would be hopeful from Obama's first judicial choice—attracting support from the Democratic and Republican home state senators—that improvements in the practice of advice and consent were on the horizon. That is probably too simple a prescription for improving the confirmation process. Equally important is reducing the partisan and ideological heat over judicial nominations that has encouraged senators from both political parties to exploit Senate rules and practices—often derailing nominations along the way. How well senators are able to repair the partisan breaches of Senate trust will tell us much as we look ahead about whether the breakdown in consent over lifetime appointments to the bench will have temporary or more lasting and harmful effects.

Notes

Chapter One

1. See Administrative Office of the United States Courts, *2007 Annual Report of the Director* (Washington), table: "Judicial Caseload Indicators," p. 13 (www. uscourts.gov/judbus2007/2007judicial%20business.pdf [December 17, 2008]). Technically, the data cover the period October 1, 2006, through September 30, 2007.

2. Statistics for Supreme Court opinions in October 2006 appear in "The Statistics," *Harvard Law Review* 121, no. 1 (November 2007): 436–49.

3. Supreme Court confirmation statistics are drawn from Lee Epstein, Thomas G. Walker, Nancy Staudt, Scott Hendrickson, and Jason Roberts, "The U.S. Supreme Court Justices Database" (Northwestern University School of Law, 2007) (http:// epstein.law.northwestern.edu/research/justicesdata.html [December 17, 2008]).

4. We exclude the U.S. Court of Appeals for the Federal Circuit (created in 1982) from our purview, because of its fixed jurisdiction that focuses primarily on appeals arising under U.S. patent laws.

5. As cited in Carl Hulse and David Stout, "Embattled Estrada Withdraws as Nominee for Federal Bench," *New York Times,* September 4, 2003.

6. Legal studies addressing judicial selection are surveyed, for example, by Stephen B. Burbank, "Politics, Privilege, and Power: The Senate's Role in the Appointment of Federal Judges," *Judicature* 86, no. 1 (July–August 2002): 24–27. On the impact of presidential agendas, see Sheldon Goldman, *Picking Federal Judges* (Yale University Press, 1997); on the role of interest groups, see Lauren Cohen Bell, *Warring Factions* (Ohio State University Press, 2002); Nancy Scherer, *Scoring Points* (Stanford University Press, 2005).

7. John Anthony Maltese, "Anatomy of a Confirmation Mess: Recent Trends in the Federal Judicial Selection Process," JURIST Online Symposium (University of Pittsburgh School of Law, April 15, 2004) (http://jurist.law.pitt.edu/forum/Symposium-jc/Maltese.php#2 [October 24, 2008]).

8. See, for example, Wendy L. Martinek, Mark Kemper, and Steven R. Van Winkle, "To Advise and Consent: The Senate and Lower Federal Court Nominations, 1977–1998," *Journal of Politics* 64, no. 2 (2002): 337–61.

9. See Benjamin Wittes, *Confirmation Wars: Preserving Independent Courts in Angry Times* (Lanham, Md.: Rowman and Littlefield, 2006), p. 59.

10. See Scherer, *Scoring Points*; Cohen Bell, *Warring Factions*.

11. Lee Epstein and Jeffrey Segal, *Advice and Consent: The Politics of Judicial Appointments* (Oxford University Press, 2005), p. 4.

12. Epstein and Segal, *Advice and Consent*, p. 3.

13. See, for example, Martinek, Kemper, and Van Winkle, "To Advise and Consent."

14. On the historical expansion of the federal judiciary, see Deborah J. Barrow, Gary Zuk, and Gerald S. Gryski, *The Federal Judiciary and Institutional Change* (University of Michigan Press, 1996).

15. At the lower court level, exceptions include Tonja Jacobi's formal, theoretic treatment of senatorial courtesy. See Tonja Jacobi, "The Senatorial Courtesy Game: Explaining the Norm of Informal Vetoes in 'Advice and Consent' Nominations," *Legislative Studies Quarterly* 30, no. 2 (May 2005): 193–217.

16. For a recent statistical modeling of voting on the courts of appeals, see Erin B. Kaheny, Susan Brodie Haire, and Sara C. Benesh, "Change over Tenure: Voting, Variance, and Decision Making on the U.S. Courts of Appeals," *American Journal of Political Science* 52, no. 3 (July 2008): 490–503.

Chapter Two

1. As cited in David Firestone, "With a New Administration, Partisan Battle Resumes over a Federal Appeals Bench," *New York Times*, May 21, 2001, p. A13.

2. The recent history of the Court of Appeals for the Fourth Circuit is detailed in Firestone, "With a New Administration, Partisan Battle Resumes over a Federal Appeals Bench."

3. For a history of the Fourth Circuit, see "History of the Federal Judiciary," Federal Judicial Center website (www.fjc.gov/history/home.nsf [October 27, 2008]).

4. The actual motion to go into executive session—the procedural context in which nominations are considered—is a nondebatable motion in Senate rules,

meaning that the motion cannot be filibustered. By precedent set in 1980, the majority leader can offer a single motion to go into executive session and to call up a particular nomination for debate. See Stanley Bach, "The Senate's Compliance with Its Legislative Rules: The Appeal of Order," *Congress and the Presidency* 18, no. 1 (1991): 77–92.

5. "Madison," in *The Records of the Federal Convention of 1787,* May 29, vol. 1, edited by Max Farrand, rev. ed. (Yale University Press, 1966), pp. 20–21 (Orig. pub. 1911).

6. "Madison," in *The Records of the Federal Convention of 1787,* June 5, vol. 1, pp. 119–20.

7. Ibid., quotation on p. 120.

8. "Journal," in *The Records of the Federal Convention of 1787,* June 5, vol. 1, p. 116; "Madison," in *The Records of the Federal Convention of 1787,* June 5, vol. 1, p. 120.

9. Forrest McDonald, *Novus Ordo Seclorum: The Intellectual Origins of the Constitution* (University Press of Kansas, 1985). State population figures in this chapter are taken from 1790 census data, available from the U.S. Census Bureau, *United States Summary,* table 16 (www.census.gov/population/censusdata/table-16.pdf [April 14, 2005]).

10. "Madison," in *The Records of the Federal Convention of 1787,* June 5, vol. 1, p. 119.

11. Compare "Journal," in *The Records of the Federal Convention of 1787,* June 13, vol. 1, p. 224, with "Madison," June 13, vol. 1, p. 232.

12. "Madison," in *The Records of the Federal Convention of 1787,* June 13, vol. 1, pp. 232–33.

13. Ibid., p. 233.

14. James E. Gauch, "Comment: The Intended Role of the Senate in Supreme Court Appointments," *University of Chicago Law Review* 56 (Winter 1989): 348–50; Daniel Wirls and Stephen Wirls, *The Invention of the United States Senate* (Johns Hopkins University Press, 2004), pp. 114–15.

15. Although Ghorum was recorded as first in calling for the "advice and consent" language, Alexander Hamilton already had proposed in a lengthy speech on June 18 that the executive and the Senate jointly appoint "supreme judicial officers." He also provided for "all other officers" not mentioned elsewhere in his plan to be appointed by the executive "subject to the approbation or rejection of the Senate," a formulation similar to Ghorum's. On Hamilton's proposal, see "Madison," in *The Records of the Federal Convention of 1787,* June 18, vol. 1, p. 292; "Yates," in *The Records of the Federal Convention of 1787,* June 18, vol. 1, pp. 300–01; on Ghorum's, see "Madison," in *The Records of the Federal Convention of 1787,* July 18, vol. 2, p. 41.

16. "Madison," in *The Records of the Federal Convention of 1787*, July 18, vol. 1, pp. 42–43.

17. "Madison," in *The Records of the Federal Convention of 1787*, July 21, vol. 2, pp. 80–81.

18. Ibid., p. 81.

19. "Madison," in *The Records of the Federal Convention of 1787*, July 18, vol. 2, p. 44.

20. Ibid., p. 44.

21. "Madison," in *The Records of the Federal Convention of 1787*, July 21, vol. 2, p. 83.

22. "Madison," in *The Records of the Federal Convention of 1787*, July 18, vol. 2, pp. 42–43.

23. Gauch usefully notes the absence of substantive debate on these issues in his "Comment," pp. 342–43.

24. "Madison," in *The Records of the Federal Convention of 1787*, July 18, vol. 2, p. 42.

25. Ibid., pp. 42-43.

26. "Madison," in *The Records of the Federal Convention of 1787*, July 21, vol. 2, p. 81.

27. "Journal," in *The Records of the Federal Convention of 1787*, August 31, vol. 2, p. 473, and September 4, vol. 2, p. 495.

28. "Madison," in *The Records of the Federal Convention of 1787*, September 7, vol. 2, pp. 538–40.

29. U.S. Constitution, Article II, section 2, clause 2.

30. One of the Committee of Detail's drafts holds (though subsequently crossed out) that judges of "such inferior tribunals, as the legislature may appoint" would be appointed by the Senate, just as would judges of the "one supreme tribunal"; see "Committee of Detail," in *The Records of the Federal Convention of 1787*, vol. 2, p. 146. A later draft states that the Senate will appoint Supreme Court justices and the executive will appoint all "Officers of the United States . . . not otherwise provided for by this Constitution"; see "Committee of Detail," in *The Records of the Federal Convention of 1787*, August 6, vol. 2, pp. 169–71.

31. Wirls and Wirls, *The Invention of the United States Senate*, p. 122.

32. Wirls and Wirls, *The Invention of the United States Senate*, chapter 5.

33. "Madison," in *The Records of the Federal Convention of 1787*, September 7, vol. 2, pp. 538–39.

34. "Madison," in *The Records of the Federal Convention of 1787*, September 7, vol. 2, p. 539.

35. David A. Strauss and Cass R. Sunstein make roughly the same point in their piece "The Senate, The Constitution, and The Confirmation Process," *Yale Law Journal* 101 (May 1992): 1491–524: 1498.

36. See a discussion of the appointments clause in the ratification debates in Gauch, "Comment," pp. 354–55.

37. On the broader battle over the scope of state agency, see David Brian Robertson, *The Constitution and America's Destiny* (Cambridge University Press, 2005).

38. On the key debates over the Federal Judiciary Act of 1789, see Charles Warren, "New Light on the History of the Federal Judiciary Act of 1789," *Harvard Law Review* 37, no. 1 (November 1923): 49–132. See also Russell R. Wheeler and Cynthia Harrison, *Creating the Federal Judicial System*, 3rd ed. (Washington: Federal Judicial Center, 2005).

39. On the ways in which jurisdiction over federal questions was slowly given to the federal courts over the course of the nineteenth century, see William Wiecek, "The Reconstruction of Federal Judicial Power, 1863–1875," *American Journal of Legal History* 13 (1969): 333–59. See also Howard Gillman, "How Political Parties Can Use the Courts to Advance Their Agendas: Federal Courts in the United States, 1875–1891," *American Political Science Review* 96, no. 3 (September 2002): 511–24.

40. On the ties of federal courts to the states, see Wheeler and Harrison, *Creating the Federal Judicial System,* pp. 6–7.

41. On the changing character of litigation in the federal courts in the nineteenth century, see Tony Allan Freyer, "The Federal Courts, Localism, and the National Economy, 1865–1900," *Business History Review* 53 (1978): 343–63.

42. See Gillman, "How Political Parties Can Use the Courts to Advance Their Agendas," p. 514.

43. In 1869 a judgeship was created for each of the existing nine circuit courts. These designated circuit court judges heard cases with the district judge for the court and the designated justice for the circuit (or in combination). See Federal Judicial Center, "U.S. Circuit Courts and the Federal Judiciary" (Washington) (www.fjc.gov/history/home.nsf [December 15. 2008]).

44. Nomination information for confirmed nominees is drawn from the Federal Judicial Center, "Judges of the United States Court: Biographical Directory of Federal Judges," "History of the Federal Judiciary" website (www.fjc.gov/history/home.nsf [October 28, 2008]). To determine failed nominations (which are not recorded in the "Biographical Directory"), we searched the *Senate Executive Journal* for each Congress. The 159 nominations count includes all nominations to the U.S. district courts, other than nominations to courts for the District of Columbia. We tally the District of Columbia court nominations separately in this chapter because

of the mix of local and federal jurisdictions assigned by various judiciary acts to the District of Columbia courts. The history of the District of Columbia courts is summarized by the Federal Judicial Center, as cited above. There were an additional thirty-one nominations to the U.S. circuit courts in that period.

45. We searched the codebooks of Senate roll call votes for each Congress between 1789 and 1946 to determine the number of recorded votes on judicial nominations. Codebooks are available at ⟨http://voteview.com⟩.

46. See, for example, Joseph Harris, *The Advice and Consent of the Senate* (University of California Press, 1953), p. 40.

47. See Wirls and Wirls, *The Invention of the United States Senate*, p. 177.

48. See Harris, *The Advice and Consent of the Senate*, and Clara Hannah Kerr, *The Origin and Development of the United States Senate* (Ithaca, N.Y.: Andrus & Church, 1895).

49. Kermit Hall, *The Politics of Justice* (University of Nebraska Press, 1979).

50. Andrew Jackson to John Coffee, December 28, 1830, in Andrew Jackson Papers, Library of Congress, as cited in Hall, *The Politics of Justice*, p. 19.

51. Inter-University Consortium for Political and Social Research (ICPSR), "United States Congressional Roll Call Voting Records, 1789–1996," [computer file] ICPSR00004, vote 33, 23rd Congress (Ann Arbor, Mich.: ICPSR, and Washington: Congressional Quarterly, 1997).

52. ICPSR, "United States Congressional Roll Call Voting Records, 1789–1996," vote 44, 29th Congress.

53. The overview of presidential ambitions is drawn from Hall, *The Politics of Justice*.

54. On the motivation for and application of the expansion of federal judicial power after the Civil War, see Wiecek, "The Reconstruction of Federal Judicial Power, 1863–1875"; Freyer, "The Federal Courts, Localism, and the National Economy, 1865–1900."

55. See Gillman, "How Political Parties Can Use the Courts to Advance Their Agendas."

56. The Senate also considered twenty-seven nominations to the trial court designated for the District of Columbia.

57. The count excludes twenty-seven nominations to the District of Columbia's trial court.

58. Divisive factions within the governing majority—even during periods of unified control—also spelled trouble for presidential appointees, especially given President Andrew Johnson's testy relations with fellow Republicans during the late 1860s. For example, only two of Johnson's five nominations to the federal district courts in the Fortieth Congress were confirmed—for a 60 percent failure rate.

59. "Letter to Senator Kennedy from Judiciary Committee staff re: senatorial courtesy," January 22, 1979, in *Selection and Confirmation of Federal Judges: Hearing before the Committee on the Judiciary, United States Senate,* part 1, p. 2, 96 Cong. 1 sess. (Government Printing Office, 1979).

60. See, for example, Brannon Denning, "The 'Blue Slip': Enforcing the Norms of the Judicial Confirmation Process," *William and Mary Bill of Rights Journal* 10, no. 1 (December 2001): 75–102; Benjamin Wittes, *Confirmation Wars: Preserving Independent Courts in Angry Times* (Lanham, Md.: Rowman and Littlefield, 2006).

61. See Elliot Slotnick, "Reforms in Judicial Selection: Will They Affect the Senate's Role?" *Judicature* 64, no. 2 (August 1980): 60–73.

62. Harris, *The Advice and Consent of the Senate,* p. 224.

63. See Michael W. Giles, Virginia A. Hettinger, and Todd Peppers, "Picking Federal Judges: A Note on Policy and Partisan Selection Agendas," *Political Research Quarterly* 54, no. 3 (2001): 623–41.

64. See Lewis A. Froman Jr., "Organization Theory and the Explanation of Important Characteristics of Congress," *American Political Science Review* 62, no. 2 (June 1968): 518–26.

65. See, for example, Sarah A. Binder, *Minority Rights, Majority Rule: Partisanship and the Development of Congress* (Cambridge University Press, 1997); Douglas Dion, *Turning the Legislative Thumbscrew: Minority Rights and Procedural Change in American Politics* (University of Michigan Press, 1997).

66. See Jack Knight, *Institutions and Social Conflict* (Cambridge University Press, 1992).

67. Raymond L. Solomon, "The Politics of Appointment and the Federal Courts' Role in Regulating America: U.S. Courts of Appeal Judgeships from T. R. to F. D. R.," *American Bar Foundation Research Journal* 9, no. 2 (1984): 285–344.

68. Solomon, "The Politics of Appointment and the Federal Courts' Role in Regulating America," pp. 314–20.

69. The same cannot be said for Wilson's anomalous choice of noted reactionary James McReynolds for the Supreme Court.

70. See E. E. Schattschneider, *The Semi-Sovereign People: A Realist's View of Democracy in America* (New York: Holt, Reinhart, and Winston, 1960).

71. See Harris, *The Advice and Consent of the Senate*; Harold Chase, *Federal Judges: The Appointing Process* (University of Minnesota Press, 1975). Chase probably has in mind the blue slip when he states that the "committee automatically checks with the senators of the state where the nominee will hold his post," but he does not discuss the practice further (p. 20).

72. Alan Neff, *U.S. District Judge Nominating Commissions: Their Members, Procedures and Candidates* (Chicago: American Judicature Society, 1981), p. 146.

73. *Selection and Confirmation of Federal Judges: Hearing before the Committee on the Judiciary, United States Senate,* part 1.

74. Richard Madden, "Javits Delaying a Judgeship Here," *New York Times,* December 14, 1967, p. 82.

75. Obnoxious indeed. The nominee, former Texas governor James Allred, had resigned a federal district judgeship to run against O'Daniel. Allred's subsequent nomination to the Fifth Circuit Court of Appeals was said to be a "'political payoff' for his attempt to unseat the Anti-New Deal Democrat [O'Daniel]." See "O'Daniel Considers Allred 'Obnoxious,'" *Washington Post,* March 16, 1943, p. 8.

76. The first negative blue slip—or at least failure to return the blue slip to the committee—by an opposition party senator appears to have occurred in 1926. Republican Calvin Coolidge's nomination of William Josiah Tilson was reported adversely from the Senate Judiciary Committee in June of 1926, and Tilson was never confirmed after receiving two recess appointments to the Middle District of Georgia. Both home state senators from Tilson's home state of Georgia were Democrats.

77. National Archives and Records Administration (NARA), "Record Group 46," Records of the U.S. Senate, Committee on the Judiciary (SJC) (hereafter NARA: SJC).

78. Under S. Res. 464 (96 Cong.), Senate committees have the authority to restrict access to records of individuals for fifty years. Thus the nomination files kept for each of the nominees referred to the Senate Judiciary Committee between 1958 and the present are closed by order of the Judiciary Committee.

79. Based on the nomination files, Mitchel Sollenberger dates the origins of the blue slip to 1917. See Mitchel Sollenberger, *The History of the Blue Slip in the Senate Committee on the Judiciary, 1917–Present,* CRS Report for Congress RL32013 (Washington: Congressional Research Service, 2003).

80. According to Sollenberger's review of the nomination files, the format of the blue slip remained unchanged between 1917 and 1922. At that time, a deadline was added for senators to return the blue slip (seven days from a senator's receipt of the blue slip). Also, because Charles Culberson (D-Tex.) chaired the committee in the Sixty-third, Sixty-fourth, and Sixty-fifth Congresses, we can infer that the blue slips from the Sixty-fifth Congress (reproduced in figure 2-2) closely resemble those used in the Sixty-third Congress. At least starting in the Sixty-fifth Congress, the term *blue slip* came from the color of the paper on which the slips were printed.

81. NARA: SJC, blue slip in "Nomination folder for George W. Jack," 65 Cong.

82. See William Ross, *A Muted Fury: Populists, Progressives, and Labor Unions Confront the Courts, 1890-1937* (Princeton University Press, 1994); Gillman, "How Political Parties Can Use the Courts to Advance Their Agendas."

83. On Senate reforms in 1913, see Gerald Gamm and Steven S. Smith, "Policy Leadership and the Development of the Modern Senate," in *Party, Process, and Political*

Change in Congress, vol. 1: *New Perspectives on the History of Congress,* edited by David W. Brady and Mathew D. McCubbins (Stanford University Press, 2002), pp. 287–311; Walter Oleszek, "John Worth Kern: Portrait of a Floor Leader," in *First Among Equals: Outstanding Senate Leaders of the Twentieth Century,* edited by Richard A. Baker and Roger H. Davidson (Washington: Congressional Quarterly, 1991), pp. 7–37.

84. See Scott James, *Presidents, Parties, and the State: Electoral College Competition, Party Leadership, and Democratic Regulatory Choice, 1884–1936* (Cambridge University Press, 2000).

85. On Wilson's approach to filling the federal courts, see Ross, *A Muted Fury*; Solomon, "The Politics of Appointment and the Federal Courts' Role in Regulating America."

86. Committee membership was determined from David Canon, Garrison Nelson, and Charles Stewart, "Historical Congressional Standing Committees, 1st to 79th Congresses, 1789–1947," Senate, 63rd Congress (http://web.mit.edu/17.251/www/data_page.html [November 9, 2006]). Augustus Bacon (D-Ga.) died in office and was replaced on the committee by another Georgia Democrat, Hoke Smith. Nor did the Southern Democratic bias on the Judiciary Committee simply reflect prevailing ratios on Senate committees. Sixty percent of Appropriations Democrats hailed from the South, and only 35 percent of Finance Committee Democrats came from the South. Moreover, just 45 percent of Democrats in the Sixty-third Congress were from the Deep South (plus Tennessee).

87. See James, *Presidents, Parties, and the State.*

88. On Wilson's relations with southern legislators, see C. Vann Woodward, *Origins of the New South, 1877–1913* (Louisiana State University Press, 1951); Elizabeth Sanders, *Roots of Reform: Farmers, Workers, and the American State, 1877–1917* (University of Chicago Press, 1999); James, *Presidents, Parties, and the State.*

89. See James, *Presidents, Parties, and the State,* pp. 185–87.

90. See Gerald Gamm and Steven S. Smith, "The Rise of Floor Leaders in the United States Senate, 1890–1915." Paper presented at the Conference on Party Effects in the United States Senate, Duke University, April 7–8, 2006.

91. See Donald Ritchie, ed., *Minutes of the U.S. Senate Democratic Conference: 1903–1964* (Government Printing Office, 1999), p. 79.

92. *New York Times,* "Democrats Agree to Lobby Inquiry," May 29, 1913, p. 1.

93. *New York Times,* "Democrats Agree to Lobby Inquiry."

94. See Jason Roberts and Steven S. Smith, "The Evolution of Agenda-Setting Institutions in Congress: Path Dependency in House and Senate Institutional Development," in *Party, Process, and Political Change in Congress,* vol. 2: *Further New Perspectives on the History of Congress,* edited by David W. Brady and Matthew D.

McCubbins (Stanford University Press, 2007), pp. 182–204. A unanimous consent agreement sets the parameters for floor debate and schedules floor votes for legislative measures and nominations on the Senate floor. Given the lack of a majority cloture rule (or any cloture rule before 1917), unanimous consent of all senators was required to set the parameters of floor debate and to schedule votes.

95. Adoption of the blue slip, in this context, is a prime example of institutional development that follows from the layering of reforms on top of one another. See Eric Schickler, *Disjointed Pluralism* (Princeton University Press, 2001).

96. See Franklin Burdette, *Filibustering in the Senate* (Princeton University Press, 1940), chapter 4.

97. See Nelson W. Polsby, "The Institutionalization of the U.S. House of Representatives," *American Political Science Review* 62, no. 1 (March 1968): 144–68; Gregory Wawro and Eric Schickler, *Filibuster* (Princeton University Press, 2006); Eric Rauchway, "The Transformation of the Congressional Experience," in *The American Congress: The Building of Democracy,* edited by Julian E. Zelizer (Boston: Houghton Mifflin Co., 2004), pp. 319–34.

98. See Sollenberger, *The History of the Blue Slip in the Senate Committee on the Judiciary, 1917–Present.*

99. U.S. Congress, *Senate Executive Journal,* 65 Cong. 1 sess., April 24, 1917.

100. Hardwick dutifully returned a blue slip with his positive endorsement. Smith again did not appear to return his blue slip, leading the committee to note on the transmittal paper for the nomination that the nomination of Beverly Evans was "authorized to be reported favorably by Senator Fletcher . . . in case word comes from Senator Smith of Georgia that he has no objection." See NARA: SJC, "Papers Pertaining to above Nomination, Beverly D. Evans Folder."

101. See Paul Pierson, *Politics in Time: History, Institutions, and Social Analysis* (Princeton University Press, 2004), p. 104.

102. Edward Sait, *Political Institutions: A Preface* (New York: Appleton-Century, 1938), p. 529.

103. See also Kathleen Thelen, *How Institutions Evolve: The Political Economy of Skills in Germany, Britain, the United States, and Japan* (Cambridge University Press, 2004).

104. In 2003 the chair of the Senate Judiciary Committee conducted a hearing on a Sixth Circuit Court of Appeals nomination even though two negative blue slips had been returned by the Michigan senators. See Jennifer Dlouhy, "Blue Slip or Not, Hatch Holds Judiciary Panel Hearing on Bush Court Nominee," *CQ Today,* July 30, 2003.

105. For a formal, theoretic treatment of the impact of uneven salience of nominees across the Senate, see Tonja Jacobi, "The Senatorial Courtesy Game: Explaining

the Norm of Informal Vetoes in 'Advice and Consent' Nominations," *Legislative Studies Quarterly* 30, no. 2 (May 2005): 193–217.

106. Most recently, see Martin Shapiro, "Comment," in *Red and Blue Nation? Consequences and Corrections of America's Polarized Parties*, vol. 2, edited by Pietro S. Nivola and David W. Brady (Brookings, 2008), pp. 134–41.

107. Shapiro, "Comment," p. 135. Having said that, as Robert Kagan has argued in *Adversarial Legalism* (Harvard University Press, 2001), Congress certainly played a role in forcing the federal judiciary into the fights over implementing regulatory statutes starting in the 1960s.

Chapter Three

1. Vacancy data are maintained by the Administrative Office of the U.S. Courts. See (www.uscourts.gov/judicialvac.html [July 8, 2008]).

2. Editorial, "A Thoughtful Refusal to Confirm," *New York Times*, March 15, 1980.

3. Harold Chase, *Federal Judges: The Appointing Process* (University of Minnesota Press, 1972), p. 7.

4. Robert A. Carp and Ronald Stidham, *Judicial Process in America*, 5th ed. (Washington: Congressional Quarterly Press, 1983).

5. Carp and Stidham, *Judicial Process in America*, p. 230.

6. Sheldon Goldman, *Picking Federal Judges: Lower Court Selection from Roosevelt through Reagan* (Yale University Press, 1997), p. 173.

7. See Goldman, *Picking Federal Judges*, p. 211.

8. Al Kamen, "Clinton Nominates Hatch Friend to Bench," *Washington Post*, July 28, 1999, p. A8.

9. The fury over Judiciary panel chair Orrin Hatch's (R-Utah) proposal at the beginning of the Bush administration in 2001 to only recognize negative blue slips from Republicans is testament to the tradition of respecting negative blue slips from all senators. As Senator Chuck Schumer (D-N.Y.) reacted to the proposed change, "Each senator from each state will lose a grand prerogative." See Elizabeth Palmer, "'Blue Slip' Issue Claims First Casualties as Democrats Walk Out of Meeting on Justice Department Nominees," *CQ Weekly*, May 4, 2001, p. 1020. The Democratic minority leader at the time promised to filibuster any nominee who was opposed by a Senate Democrat.

10. Chase, *Federal Judges*, pp. 9–10.

11. See Helen Dewar, "Daschle Warns GOP on Judicial Confirmations," *Washington Post*, May 3, 2001, p. A14.

12. Elizabeth Palmer, "Senate GOP Backs Down from Dispute over Handling of Nominees," *CQ Weekly*, June 9, 2001, p. 1360.

13. Here, we assume that there is at least one home state senator from the president's party, or two home state senators from the president's party who have worked out an arrangement in which one of the senators gets to recommend nominees for vacant judgeships in their state.

14. See Mitchel A. Sollenberger, *The History of the Blue Slip in the Senate Committee on the Judiciary, 1917–Present*, CRS Report for Congress RL32013 (Washington: Congressional Research Service, 2003).

15. Nominations are considered when the Senate is convened in executive session, a time when non-germane amendments are impermissible. Thus, the majority party leader's control of the floor agenda cannot be circumvented by opposition party members seeking confirmation for preferred nominees.

16. We supplement these calendars where necessary with data from the Federal Judicial Center's Federal Judges Biographical Database ("History of the Judiciary," www.fjc.gov). We thank Peter Wonders and Bruce Ragsdale for their assistance with these data.

17. If no nomination was made during the Congress in which the vacancy first occurred, we record the last day of the session as the date on which the vacancy was no longer "at risk" of having a nomination forwarded during that Congress.

18. If a nominee is announced by the president but is not confirmed during that Congress (and thus is resubmitted by the president at the start of the next Congress), we do not create an additional observation. Although technically Senate rules require a new nomination each session, renomination of pending nominations during the second session of a Congress is typical.

19. We estimate the models with Stata's *stcox* routine, which does not allow an observation to both enter and exit the data at the same time. Thus we adjust the vacancy date by one day before the nomination date.

20. We determine the relevant home state senators and their parties from Poole's DW-NOMINATE file for the First through the One Hundred Sixth Congresses (http://voteview.com [November 4, 20008]). In many Congresses, more than two senators served from a single state, owing to a death or resignation of a senator before the end of a Congress. In these cases, we determine which two senators were serving when the vacancy opened.

21. DW-NOMINATE scores are estimates of legislators' ideal points derived from a spatial model of voting. For the original presentation of NOMINATE scores, see Keith T. Poole and Howard Rosenthal, *Congress: A Political-Economic History of Roll Call Voting* (Oxford University Press, 1997).

22. Committee chairs are determined from Garrison Nelson, *Committees in the United States Congress, 1947–1992,* vol. 1 (Washington: Congressional Quarterly Press, 1993). Halfway through the Eighty-fourth Senate (1955–56), Judiciary chair Harley Kilgore (D-W.Va.) died in office, with James Eastland (D-Miss.) succeeding him as chair in early 1956. The distance between the president and the chair thus varies across the two committee chairs for the Eighty-fourth Senate.

23. See Lyn Ragsdale, *Vital Statistics on the Presidency: Washington to Clinton* (Washington: CQ Press, 1998); Frank Newport, "Bush's Favorable Rating Running Higher than Job Approval" (www.gallup.com/poll/9598/Bushs-Favorable-Rating-Running-Higher-Than-Job-Approval.aspx [June 16, 2008]).

24. To deal with the presence of observations with tied survival times, we estimate the Cox model using the Efron method of handling tied values. Alternative methods for handling ties do not appreciably affect the estimates.

25. Analysis of Cox-Snell residuals for the model in column 2 reinforces the overall good fit of the model. Analysis of Martingale residuals is also instructive. The plots of deviance residuals based on the Martingale residuals suggest that the Cox model in column 2 slightly underestimates the probability of a nominee being announced when vacancies are filled quickly and slightly overestimates the probability of a nominee being selected when vacancies take longer to be filled. Still, there is little evidence that influential observations are uniquely driving the results. Estimating the model with and without outlier observations (those with deviance residuals greater than 2 or less than –2) yields substantively similar results. Diagnostic tests for Cox proportional hazard models are outlined in *Base Reference Manual* (Stata Press, 2007).

26. The parameter estimate is also statistically significant for other specifications of ideologically distant home state senators.

27. The methodological problem of nonproportional hazard ratios is identified and explored in Janet Box-Steffensmeier and Christopher Zorn, "Duration Models and Proportional Hazards in Political Science," *American Journal of Political Science* 45, no. 4 (October 2001): 972–88. Below, we follow their advice for how to detect and correct for nonproportionality.

28. We also reject the null hypothesis of proportional hazards for the global test across all covariates.

29. According to Box-Steffensmeier and Zorn cited above, this is the preferred method and functional form for estimating the Cox model in the presence of non-proportional covariates.

30. The expected percent change in the hazard rate is calculated via the *adjust* routine in Stata 9.0. This simulation compares the hazard rate of a nominee being

announced at day 30 and day 180 of a vacancy. We assume a period of divided government and a presidential election year. All continuous variables are set at their mean values.

31. The expected percent change in the hazard rate is calculated assuming a presidential election year, divided government, and the presence of a home state senator from the president's party. Continuous variables are set at their means.

32. The expected percent change in the hazard rate is calculated for 1 standard deviation below and above the mean distance between the president and Judiciary chair, assuming divided government, a home state senator from the president's party, and a presidential election year. All continuous variables are held constant at their means.

33. Results available from authors.

34. For the broader argument of how judicial selection has always been political, see Lee Epstein and Jeffrey A. Segal, *Advice and Consent: The Politics of Judicial Appointments* (Oxford University Press, 2005).

35. See Benjamin Wittes, "Comment," in *Red and Blue Nation? Consequences and Correction of America's Polarized Politics,* vol. 2 (Brookings, 2008), p. 145.

36. George Lardner Jr., "'Careful' Judicial Vetting Process," *Washington Post,* April 19, 2001, p. A17.

Chapter Four

1. In calculating the typical wait during the Bush administration, we determine the average length of time between nomination and confirmation per nomination, rather than per nominee. Because some candidates are renominated in successive Congresses until they are confirmed, the average wait time per nominee (as opposed to nomination) may be longer than six months.

2. The count of twelve courts of appeals includes the D.C. Circuit but excludes the Federal Circuit (given its limited jurisdiction). Data on the partisan balance of active judges on each court of appeals are available in Jonathan Kastellec, "Panel Composition and Voting on the U.S. Courts of Appeals over Time," paper presented at the annual meeting of the American Political Science Association, Chicago, Illinois, August 30, 2007.

3. Senator Patrick Leahy, the Democratic chair of the Senate Judiciary Committee in 2008, offers a summary of the impasse and its resolution here: (http://leahy.senate.gov/press/200804/041508a.html [January 28, 2009]).

4. The relative impact of these multiple potential vetoes is explored in David M. Primo, Sarah A. Binder, and Forrest Maltzman, "Who Consents? Competing Pivots in Federal Judicial Selection," *American Journal of Political Science* 52, no. 3 (July 2008): 471–89.

5. Denis Steven Rutkus and Kevin M. Scott, "Whether the Senate, in the Judicial Confirmation Process, Customarily Observes the 'Thurmond Rule,'" memorandum (Congressional Research Service, July 10, 2008), prepared for the Senate Republican Conference Forum "Protecting American Justice: Ensuring Confirmation of Qualified Judicial Nominees," July 14, 2008, p. 5.

6. Martin Tolchin, "Republicans Fight Carter Nominees," *New York Times*, September 14, 1980, p. A31.

7. Statement by Denis Steven Rutkus, specialist on the federal judiciary, Government and Finance Division, Congressional Research Service, before the Senate Republican Conference Forum "Protecting American Justice: Ensuring Confirmation of Qualified Judicial Nominees," July 14, 2008, p. 3.

8. Rutkus and Scott, "Whether the Senate, in the Judicial Confirmation Process, Customarily Observes the 'Thurmond Rule,'" p. 5.

9. Keith Perine, "Senate Republicans Gather to Press for More Appellate Court Confirmations," *CQ Today*, July 14, 2008.

10. Geoff Earle, "Senators Spar Over 'Thurmond Rule,'" *The Hill*, July 21, 2004, p. 4.

11. Rutkus and Scott, "Whether the Senate, in the Judicial Confirmation Process, Customarily Observes the 'Thurmond Rule,'" pp. 10–12.

12. The source of foot-dragging, of course, should vary by partisan position. In periods of unified party control, we would expect the opposition party to attempt to slow down the process. In periods of divided government, we would expect the Senate majority to take its time on the White House's nominees.

13. See Robert Kagan, *Adversarial Legalism: The American Way of Law* (Harvard University Press, 2001); Martin Shapiro, "Comment," in *Red and Blue Nation? Consequences and Correction of America's Polarized Politics*, vol. 2, edited by Pietro S. Nivola and David W. Brady (Brookings, 2008), pp. 134–41; Gordon Silverstein, *Law's Allure: How Law Shapes, Constrains, Saves, and Kills Politics* (Cambridge University Press, 2009).

14. Because there are no home state senators for nominations to the Court of Appeals for the District of Columbia (and thus no opportunities for a home state senator to invoke the blue slip to affect the fate of those nominees), we estimate the models below excluding nominations to the D.C. Circuit. The results are largely the same when we include nominations to the D.C. bench and drop the home state senator variable.

15. Nominations data for the One Hundred Eighth and One Hundred Ninth Congresses (2003–06) are drawn from the Department of Justice's Office of Legal Policy website (www.usdoj.gov/olp/). We exclude the appellate court for the Federal Circuit on account of its limited jurisdiction.

16. See Kastellec, "Panel Composition and Voting on the U.S. Courts of Appeals over Time."

17. We determine the ideologies of the relevant home state senators and their parties from Poole's DW-NOMINATE file for the First through the One Hundred Sixth Congresses (http://voteview.com). In many Congresses, more than two senators served from a single state, owing to death or resignation before the end of a Congress. In these cases, we determine which two senators were serving when the nomination was made. DW-NOMINATE scores are estimates of legislators' ideal points derived from a spatial model of voting. For the original presentation of NOMINATE scores, see Keith T. Poole and Howard Rosenthal, *Congress: A Political-Economic History of Roll Call Voting* (Oxford University Press, 1997).

18. ABA ratings for the One Hundred First through the One Hundred Ninth Congresses are drawn from ABA's website: (www.abanet.org/scfedjud/ratings.html). ABA ratings for the previous Congresses were graciously provided by Shelly Goldman.

19. The impact of polarization on the likelihood of confirmation is robust across the time period studied. If we look only at the period before the election of Ronald Reagan (1947–80), increases in polarization reduce the chances of confirmation, as does the misfortune of being a nominee pending during a presidential election year.

20. The simulation assumes a period of unified party control outside of a presidential election, and the absence of an ideologically extreme home state senator. The simulations are conducted with Stata's *mfx* command, setting the level of polarization at its least and greatest values and the other variables at the specified values.

21. The generation of DW-NOMINATE scores for presidents lends empirical support for the first assumption (see www.voteview.com for presidential NOMINATE scores). The latter assumption is central to almost all formal treatments of presidential appointment politics. See, for example, Primo, Binder, and Maltzman, "Who Consents?"

22. We assume a well-qualified nominee for a balanced court, not pending during a presidential election year.

23. We assume a well-qualified nominee for a balanced court, during divided government but outside of a presidential election year. We set the level of polarization at its postwar average to conduct the simulation.

24. We assume the same conditions as in the previous simulations, with no ideologically extreme home state senator.

25. The *p* value for a one-tailed *t* test is .065.

26. On the elimination of prescreening by the ABA, see Kelly Wallace and Major Garrett, "White House Ends ABA's Role in Screening Judicial Nominees," CNN.com, March 23, 2001 (http://archives.cnn.com/2001/LAW/03/22/bush.ABA/index.html [January 28, 2009]).

27. But note that despite these Republican moves, Democrats still insisted on viewing the ABA report before voting on a nominee.

28. Both simulations assume that the nominee has been rated highly by the ABA and that the home state senator is not extremely ideologically different from the president. We set the level of polarization at 1 standard deviation below and above the mean value of polarization.

29. We include a "Congress" variable that notes the number of the Congress in which the nomination was submitted to the Senate. Note that the more sophisticated controls we include in previous iterations of this research (including fixed effects for each president) yield substantively similar results as those reported here. See Sarah A. Binder and Forrest Maltzman, "Senatorial Delay in Confirming Federal Judges, 1947–1998," *American Journal of Political Science* 46, no. 1 (January 2002): 190–99.

30. Blue slips were made public for the first time by the Senate in the One Hundred Seventh Congress. The record of blue slips for that Congress is maintained here: (www.usdoj.gov/olp/blueslips1107.htm [July 27, 2008]).

31. This example suggests that the blue slip may serve more as an advisory or informational tool for chamber leaders, rather than as a formal and absolute veto power for home state senators. The blue slip is ultimately an effective tool because it can be backed up by the threat of a Senate filibuster. On the relative effectiveness of the blue slip compared with other potential veto powers, see Primo, Binder, and Maltzman, "Who Consents?"

32. Involvement of interest groups in lower court judicial selection reaches back decades, but a marked increase in their organized involvement occurred in the early 1980s. See Gregory A. Caldeira and John R. Wright, "Lobbying for Justice: The Rise of Organized Conflict in the Politics of Federal Judgeships," in *Contemplating Courts,* edited by Lee Epstein (Washington: CQ Press, 1995), pp. 44–71. See also Lauren Cohen Bell, *Warring Factions: Interest Groups, Money and the New Politics of Senate Confirmation* (Ohio State University Press, 2002); Nancy Scherer, Brandon L. Bartels, and Amy Steigerwalt, "Sounding the Fire Alarm: The Role of Interest Groups in the Lower Court Confirmation Process," *Journal of Politics* 70, no. 4 (2008): 1026–039.

33. One nominee, Miguel Estrada, was opposed because the White House refused to grant Senate Democrats access to his writings from when he worked in

the solicitor general's office; without those memos, essentially no paper trail existed with which to confirm Estrada's ideological views.

34. See Richard S. Beth and Betsy Palmer, "Cloture Attempts on Nominations," CRS Report for Congress RL32878 (Washington: Congressional Research Service, April 22, 2005).

35. As cited in Jeffrey Toobin, "Advice and Dissent: The Fight over the President's Judicial Nominations," *New Yorker,* May 26, 2003, p. 42.

36. On the politics of the nuclear option, see Sarah A. Binder, Anthony J. Madonna, and Steven S. Smith, "Going Nuclear, Senate Style," *Perspectives on Politics* 5, no. 4 (December 2007): 729–40. For a broader treatment of filibuster reform, see Sarah A. Binder and Steven S. Smith, *Politics or Principle? Filibustering in the United States Senate* (Brookings, 1997).

37. As cited in Helen Dewar, "GOP Votes to Break Nominee Filibusters: Democrats Appear Able to Block Plan," *Washington Post,* June 25, 2003, p. A21.

38. David Nather, "Senate Races against the Nuclear Clock on Judges," *CQ Weekly,* May 28, 2005, p. 1440.

39. We say "potential" threat because it is not clear that a majority for the nuclear option ever existed. On the broader institutional implications of the nuclear option and the degree of threat posed by such innovations, see Binder, Madonna, and Smith, "Going Nuclear, Senate Style."

40. The introduction of recorded floor confirmation votes has been attributed to a decision of the Senate Republican conference in 1997, amidst conservatives' complaints that the Judiciary Committee was confirming too many of President Clinton's judicial nominees. Judiciary Committee chair Orrin Hatch, eager to defeat a change in the committee's blue slip practice advocated by his fellow GOP senators, suggested instead that Republicans demand recorded floor votes on President Clinton's judicial nominees. The episode is recounted in Ed Henry, "His Power Being Judged, Hatch Beats Back Leaders," *Roll Call,* May 1, 1997.

41. Tactics of two leading interest groups are detailed in Bob Davis, "Objection! Two Old Foes Plot Tactics in Battle over Judgeships," *Wall Street Journal,* March 2, 2004, p. A1.

42. See Alliance for Justice Judicial Selection Project, *2001–2 Biennial Report,* appendix 3 (2002) (www.allianceforjustice.org). This report is on file with the authors. Data exclude judges who serve on the U.S. Court of Appeals for the Federal Circuit and drop judgeships that stood vacant at the time of the Alliance report at the close of 2002.

43. Data on the partisan balance of the appellate courts in the fall of 2008 are drawn from the website of the Federal Judicial Center, "History of the Federal Judiciary" (www.fjc.gov). We exclude judges who serve on the U.S. Court of Appeals for the Federal Circuit.

44. Bart Jansen, "Democrats Chafe at Delayed Nominations," *CQ Today,* April 24, 2009.

Chapter Five

1. Note, in contrast, that when Congress writes legislation to create new judgeships for the courts of appeals, Congress allocates new judgeships to particular courts, but not, by statute allocation, judgeships to particular states within the circuit.

2. See McNollgast (Mathew D. McCubbins, Roger G. Noll, Barry R. Weingast), "Politics and the Courts: A Positive Theory of Judicial Doctrine and the Rule of Law," *Southern California Law Review* 68 (1995): 1631–683.

3. John M. de Figueiredo, Gerry Gryski, Emerson Tiller, and Gary Zuk, "Congress and the Political Expansion of the U.S. District Courts," *American Law and Economics Review* 2, no. 1 (2000): 107–25. As quoted on pp. 113–14.

4. De Figueiredo, Gryski, Tiller, and Zuk, "Congress and the Political Expansion of the U.S. District Courts." See also Jon Bond, "Politics of Court Structure: The Addition of New Federal Judges, 1949–1978," *Law & Policy Quarterly* 2 (April 1980): 181–88.

5. See, for example, Deborah J. Barrow, Gary Zuk, and Gerard S. Gryski, *The Federal Judiciary and Institutional Change* (University of Michigan Press, 1996).

6. For a synthetic overview, see C. Lawrence Evans, "Politics of Congressional Reform," in *The Legislative Branch,* edited by Paul J. Quirk and Sarah A. Binder (Oxford University Press, 2005), pp. 490–593.

7. See de Figueiredo, Gryski, Tiller, and Zuk, "Congress and the Political Expansion of the U.S. District Courts"; Bond, "Politics of Court Structure."

8. See Richard A. Posner, *The Federal Courts: Challenge and Reform,* rev. ed. (Harvard University Press, 1999).

9. Administrative Office of the U.S. Courts, Statistics Division, Analysis and Reports Branch, "History of the Authorization of Federal Judgeships Including Procedures and Standards Used in Conducting Judgeship Surveys," mimeo (Washington, 1992) (on file with the authors).

10. The exact process is explained in "Prepared Statement of Judge Dennis Jones, Appendix 2" in "Federal Judiciary: Is There a Need for Additional Federal Judges?" hearing before the Subcommittee on Courts, the Internet, and Intellectual Property, U.S. House Committee on the Judiciary, 108 Cong. 1 sess., June 24, 2003, pp. 17–18.

11. We need to draw a distinction here between designation of new seats to the trial and appellate courts. The Judicial Conference specifies the particular district court for which it is requesting additional judgeships (for example, Southern District of New York), but it does not specify for courts of appeals judgeships *which*

states should receive the new judgeship within the circuit. The process of assigning new judgeships to particular states within the circuit process appears to be informal, as states lay claims to new seats depending on the current allocation of seats across the states in a circuit. We leave for future analysis the process and politics by which new judgeships are claimed by states within each circuit.

12. Judge Gerald B. Tjoflat of the Eleventh Circuit is a prominent opponent of expanding the size of the bench, in particular his own Eleventh Circuit Court of Appeals. See Arthur D. Hellman, "Assessing Judgeship Needs in the Federal Courts of Appeals: Policy Choices and Process Concerns," *Journal of Appellate Practice and Process* 5, no. 2 (Fall 2003): 239–70.

13. "Terry, Fortenberry, & Smith Push for Fourth Federal Judge," *American Chronicle*, January 5, 2007 (www.americanchronicle.com/articles/printFriendly/18688 [January 30, 2009]).

14. See H.R. 349, introduced January 8, 2009, in the U.S. House of Representatives (http://thomas.loc.gov [February 2, 2009]).

15. Steven J. Balla, Eric Lawrence, Forrest Maltzman, and Lee Sigelman, "Partisanship, Blame Avoidance, and the Distribution of Legislative Pork," *American Journal of Political Science* 46 (July 2002): 515–25.

16. The average size of a district court's "congressional delegation" in this period was six members of Congress. The smallest delegations are, of course, located in states with a single district court and a single member of Congress (for example, Vermont, Delaware, and Alaska). The district court with the largest congressional delegation in this period (twenty-five members of Congress) was the U.S. District Court for the Central California District. We detail below the process for mapping congressional districts into district court boundaries.

17. The counties in each congressional district are located using *Congressional Districts in the 1980s* (Washington: CQ Press, 1983). For courts whose county boundaries straddle multiple congressional districts, we include all relevant congressional districts in determining the makeup of each court's congressional delegation.

18. More specifically, the two panels of figure 5-1 display histograms for the partisan makeup of the courts' congressional delegations in 1984 (Ninety-eighth Congress) and 1990 (One Hundred First Congress). The modal court district's representation in both Congresses was roughly split between the parties.

19. Technically, in 1984 eight of these new judgeships were designated as "temporary" judgeships, and in 1990 thirteen were designated as temporary. In practice, however, the 1990 judgeship act made all of the 1984 temporary judgeships permanent, while creating thirteen new temporary judgeships. Definitions of temporary judgeships have tended to be interpreted to mean that when a judge holding a temporary judgeship steps down that vacancy cannot be filled. If a judge serves for

twenty-five years, "temporary" is not so temporary. Thus we count temporary judgeships as permanent ones, and we do not count as new judgeships those temporary judgeships converted to permanent status. On the definition and treatment of temporary judgeships, see Administrative Office of the U.S. Courts, "History of the Authorization of Federal Judgeships Including Procedures and Standards Used in Conducting Judgeship Surveys." In addition to the new trial court judgeships, both measures also created new federal appellate court judgeships: twenty-four such judgeships in 1984 and eleven in 1990. The analysis here concentrates on the creation of district court judgeships, given senators' expectations of greater influence over the selection of nominees.

20. We limit our analysis to U.S. district courts in the United States that are represented in the Senate, excluding federal trial courts in Puerto Rico, Guam, the Virgin Islands, the Northern Marianas Islands, and the District of Columbia.

21. See Administrative Office of the U.S. Courts, "History of the Authorization of Federal Judgeships Including Procedures and Standards Used in Conducting Judgeship Surveys."

22. Two additional U.S. district courts received five new judgeships each, but only in one of the two judgeship bills: The U.S. District Court for the Northern District of Illinois received five new judgeships in 1984, and the U.S. District Court for the Southern District of Texas received five new judgeships in 1990.

23. The 1984 judgeship act (P.L. 98-353) was based on the 1982 survey; the 1990 judgeship act (P. L. 101-650) was based on the 1990 survey. In both surveys, the case weights were based on a 1979 District Court Time Study conducted by the Administrative Office of the U.S. Courts. By counting the number and mix of different case types, the weighted filings measure is designed to determine the demands on judges' time imposed by the particular mix of cases on a court's docket. The accuracy of the weighted filings measure is explored in "Statement of William O. Jenkins," in *Federal Judgeships: General Accuracy of District and Appellate Judgeship Case-Related Workload Measures,* GAO-03-937T (U.S. General Accounting Office, June 24, 2003).

24. Judgeship recommendations by the Judicial Conference also incorporate information about factors unique to individual courts. We rely on the weighted filings measure because it provides a uniform measure of court needs.

25. The counties in each congressional district are located using *Congressional Districts in the 1980s.* For courts whose county boundaries straddle multiple congressional districts, we include all relevant congressional districts in determining the makeup of each court's congressional delegation.

26. We estimate a Poisson regression model after rejecting a more general specification of negative binomial regression. When we estimated a negative binomial regression model, we nested the Poisson regression model as a restricted case (without the

clustering option). We could not reject at a .05 level of significance the restriction that the overdispersion parameter (alpha) equaled zero.

27. Because the D.C. Circuit does not have home state senators, we drop the circuit from the data analysis.

28. Predicted numbers of new judgeships are generated via the *mfx* routine in Stata 8.2. All of the other variables are held constant at their means.

29. The concept of a "fractional judge" is not such a far-fetched idea. At times, Congress has created roving judgeships, whose occupants divide their time in fixed percentages across multiple courts within a state. Oklahoma, for example, for many years had two judgeships split between the three district courts in the state—thus providing in effect a "two-thirds" judge for each trial court.

30. Perhaps not surprising, court representation on the Senate panel by a member of the president's party is more valuable than representation on the House panel by a member of either party. Assuming a court's workload merits an additional judgeship, the likelihood of securing a new judge with Senate representation is .938, compared to .645 with House representation.

31. Details about passage of the 1984 and 1990 judgeship bills are drawn from *Congressional Quarterly Almanac* (Washington: CQ Press, 1984 and 1990).

32. Democrats insisted on language providing that no more than forty judges could be filled before January 21, 1985 (the end of President Reagan's term). Ultimately, Senate Democrats blocked all appointments in the fall of 1984, rendering the dispute over the limitation moot. See Helen Dewar, "Democrats Block Federal Judgeship Nominations," *Washington Post,* September 7, 1984, p. A10.

33. Linda Greenhouse, "Chief Justice Makes Plea for More Federal Judgeships to Help in Fight against Drugs," *New York Times,* January 1, 1990, p. A10.

34. See Federal Judicial Center, "U.S. District Court of Arizona Legislative History" (www.fjc.gov/public/home.nsf/hisc [February 2, 2009]). For a full accounting of new district court judgeships since 1990, see Administrative Office of the U.S. Courts, "U.S. District Courts Additional Authorized Judgeships" (www.uscourts.gov/history/districtauth.pdf [February 2, 2009]).

35. Judge Huff's remarks were made at the "'New Media' and the Courts Symposium," Rehnquist Center at the University of Arizona, September 9, 2008. Video link (www.rehnquistcenter.org/MediaConference/agenda.cfm [February 2, 2009]).

Chapter Six

1. Quote is from the chief justice's "1997 Year-End Report on the Federal Judiciary," as cited in John H. Cushman Jr., "Senate Imperils Judicial System, Rehnquist Says," *New York Times,* January 1, 1998, p. A1.

2. On the implications of the use of visiting judges, see James J. Brudney and Corey Ditslear, "Designated Diffidence: District Court Judges on the Courts of Appeals," *Law and Society Review* 35, no. 3 (2001): 565–606.

3. Granted, the comment from Judge Ginsburg was also a plea for confirming more of President Bush's pending nominees. Ginsburg's address is reprinted in "A Judiciary Diminished Is Justice Denied: The Constitution, The Senate, and The Vacancy Crisis in the Federal Judiciary," hearing before the House Committee on the Judiciary, Subcommittee on the Constitution, 107 Cong. 2 sess., October 10, 2002 (http://judiciary.house.gov/Legacy/82264.PDF), pp. 75-76. Copy on file with the authors [February 2, 2009].

4. "A Judiciary Diminished Is Justice Denied," p. 76.

5. We start the data in 1971, since that is as far back as the Administrative Office of the U.S. Courts has compiled consistent data across the variables of interest in the analysis below. We include the eleven appellate courts and the D.C. Circuit Court of Appeals but exclude the U.S. Court of Appeals for the Federal Circuit because of its limited jurisdiction. As noted in detail in note 7, the Eleventh Circuit was created in 1981 with division of the Fifth Circuit into two separate circuits.

6. See the arguments in U.S. Senate, Subcommittee on Administrative Oversight and the Courts of the Committee on the Judiciary, *Chairman's Report on the Appropriate Allocation of Judgeships in the United States Courts of Appeals,* 106 Cong. 1 sess. (March 1999).

7. The Eleventh Circuit Court of Appeals was created by Congress in October 1981 when the Fifth was divided into two circuits. Fifth Circuit data for 1980 apply to the pre-split circuit. Because of limited data on the Fifth Circuit for 1981 reported in the *1982 Federal Court Management Statistics* (Administrative Office of the U.S. Courts), we drop the Fifth Circuit in 1981 from the analysis. Data for the Eleventh Circuit are included for the period 1982–2002.

8. The filing of the notice of appeal is simply the first step for litigants seeking to appeal a decision from the trial court. Submission of the complete record occurs after the filing of the notice of appeal.

9. The size of the caseload and the amount of time expended on the median case are related, given that both tap an overextended court. The two variables do not run completely in tandem, however; they correlate only at .65.

10. Granted, this may be a risky assumption because the mix of cases varies from court to court. The D.C. Circuit Court of Appeals, for example, has a disproportionate share of administrative law cases, while the Court of Appeals for the Eleventh Circuit has a heavier load of easier-to-dispose criminal cases. Still, on a per judge basis, the D.C. appellate court appears to have a lighter overall caseload. Unlike the U.S. district courts—for which the Administrative Office of the U.S. Courts has

developed a weighted case load measure, there is no such weighted caseload measure for the courts of appeals (whose judges have refused to submit to a time study).

11. "Vacant judgeship-months" indicate the total number of months that vacancies occurred in any authorized judgeship position on each appellate court that year.

12. We estimate the model via Stata's *xtpcse* routine to deal with the likelihood of panel heteroskedasticity (that is, the chance that the error variance could vary across courts). On the choice of panel corrected standard errors, see Neal Beck and Jonathan Katz, "Time-Series-Cross-Section Issues: Dynamics," paper presented at the 21st Annual Summer Meeting of the Society for Political Methodology, Stanford, California, July 29–31, 2004 (http://as.nyu.edu/docs/IO/2576/beckkatz.pdf [October 29, 2008]).

13. PSAr(1) assumes first-order autocorrelation within panels but calculates a panel-specific autocorrelation parameter.

14. See Nathaniel Beck, "Time-Series-Cross-Section Data: What Have We Learned in the Past Few Years?" *Annual Review of Political Science* 4 (2001): 271–93. Beck (p. 279n) suggests using a Lagrange multiplier test to test whether the error process (once the lagged variable is included) is temporally independent. The *p* value for that test shows that we cannot reject the null of no serial autocorrelation. The need to include lagged values of the dependent variable forces us to drop data from 1970.

15. We calculated an average monthly vacancy rate for each court each year that is based on the vacant judgeship months data. An average annual vacancy rate for the federal courts is calculated across the twelve courts (including the D.C. Circuit Court of Appeals) each year.

16. By the end of 1979, twelve new judges had received their commissions for the Fifth Circuit, still leaving a high vacancy rate for the court that year (based on months any judgeship went unfilled). The next highest vacancy rate occurred in the Sixth Circuit in 2002 (.47), stemming from nomination and confirmation delays rather than from the addition of new judgeships. Given the division of the Fifth Circuit into two circuits in 1981, we rerun the analysis below dropping both circuits. The results reported below do not change significantly when the circuits are dropped.

17. See, among others, Long Range Planning Committee, *Long Range Plan for the Federal Courts* (Judicial Conference of the United States, December 1995), and Commission on Structural Alternatives for the Federal Courts of Appeals, *Final Report* (Washington, December 1998).

18. The estimate appears in James Brudney and Corey A. Ditslear, "Designated Diffidence: District Court Judges on the Courts of Appeals," *Law and Society Review* 35, no. 3 (2001): 801-42. It is difficult to quantify the contributions made by senior judges in alleviating rising caseloads. The Administrative Office of the U.S. Courts

notes each year how many senior judges served on each court, but senior judges can select which case types they want to participate in. (Then again, the court can determine what work it does not want them doing.) There are some strong incentives for seniors to carry a reasonable load because they are required to do the equivalent of 25 percent of a full load to be eligible for any salary increases. Chief Judge Ginsburg of the D.C. Court of Appeals estimated that the combined service of the court's two part-time senior judges added up to the load of one full-time judge. See "A Judiciary Diminished Is Justice Denied." Without data on the numbers of cases handled by senior judges, it is difficult to estimate how much work has been shouldered by senior judges during the period studied here.

19. Richard Brody, *Assessing the President: The Media, Elite Opinion and Public Support* (Stanford University Press, 1991).

20. See John Hibbing and Elizabeth Theiss-Morse, *Congress as Public Enemy: Public Attitudes Towards American Political Institutions* (Cambridge University Press, 1995).

21. See Vincent Price and Anca Romantan, "Confidence in Institutions Before, During, and After 'Indecision 2000,'" *Journal of Politics* 66 (August 2004): 939–56.

22. James L. Gibson, "Challenges to the Impartiality of State Supreme Courts: Legitimacy Theory and 'New-Style' Judicial Campaigns," *American Political Science Review* 102 (February 2008): 59–75.

23. Vanessa A. Baird and Amy Gangl, "Shattering the Myth of Legality: The Impact of the Media's Framing of Supreme Court Procedures on Perceptions of Fairness," *Political Psychology* 27 (2006): 597–614.

24. The 2006 survey is described at CCES's website (http://web.mit.edu/polisci/portl/cces/). Both internal validity (the causal inferences we draw from isolating cause and effect with regard to the impact of a confirmation vote on perceptions of judges) and external validity (our ability to generalize from our sample to the larger population) are enhanced by use of the nationwide survey experiment. On the limitations of survey experiments and the endurance of treatment effects, see Brian J. Gaines, James H. Kuklinski, and Paul J. Quirk, "The Logic of the Survey Experiment Reexamined," *Political Analysis* 15, no. 1 (2007): 1–20.

25. In the cross-tabulations in table 6-4, "agreeing with" and "trusting in Judge Jones" are recoded into dichotomous variables. Individuals who strongly agree or agree with Judge Jones or strongly agree or agree that Jones can be trusted to make decisions that are right for the country are coded 1; individuals who disagree or disagree strongly with Judge Jones or disagree or disagree strongly that Judge Jones can be trusted are coded 0.

26. We dropped the fifteen respondents (1.7 percent of the sample) who said that they were "not sure" whether they owned a gun. To be sure, people who do not

own a gun could still oppose gun control; we are reasonably confident, in contrast, that most gun owners oppose gun control measures.

27. We limit the controls to those forces most likely to affect one's views about court decisions from the lower federal bench.

28. The *N* is much smaller for the trust model, as a substantial number of individuals responded "neither" when asked whether they trusted or did not trust Judge Jones.

29. We simulate the likelihood of agreeing with and trusting the judge via Stata's *mfx* routine. Predicted agreement with the judge drops from 60 to 54 percent; predicted trust in the judge drops from 49 to 39 percent. We report here the percentage drop in the predicted level of support for the judge.

Chapter Seven

1. See John Anthony Maltese, "Confirmation Gridlock: The Federal Judicial Appointment Process under Bill Clinton and George W. Bush," *Journal of Appellate Practice and Process* 5, no. 1 (Spring 2003) (www.law.ualr.edu/publications/japp/journals/tocvol5.1.asp [October 30, 2008]).

2. Today, by statute, each state within a court of appeals circuit is represented on the circuit bench. However, such a requirement did not exist when the courts of appeals were first created in 1891.

3. Jonathan Groner and Jason Hoppin, "Senate Democrats Grill 9th Circuit Nominee," *Recorder*, April 2, 2003.

4. On the matter of rationality and institutional design, see Paul Pierson, *Politics in Time: History, Institutions, and Social Analysis* (Princeton University Press, 2004).

5. On path dependence, institutional design, and unintended consequences in the design of legislative institutions, see Sarah A. Binder, *Minority Rights, Majority Rule: Partisanship and the Development of Congress* (Cambridge University Press, 1997).

6. On the history of the Senate filibuster and senators' mixed efforts at reform, see Sarah A. Binder and Steve S. Smith, *Politics or Principle? Filibustering in the U.S. Senate* (Brookings, 1997).

7. Several alternative proposals have also been offered in recent years, which include setting term limits for federal judges (intended to reduce the stakes of each lifetime appointment) and requiring party balance on federal courts (as is often provided for in statute for some regulatory commissions). Such a change would have precedent: The Court of International Trade (since it was reconstituted in 1980 from the U.S. Customs Court) is required by statute to have no more than five judges from the same political party. See the Federal Judicial Center's website "Courts of the Federal Judiciary" (www.fjc.gov/public/home.nsf/hisc [February 18, 2009]).

8. The American Judicature Society offers a brief early history of commissions on its website (www.judicialselection.us/federal_judicial_selection/federal_judicial_nominating_commissions.cfm?state=FD [February 18, 2009]).

9. The experiences of these early nominating commissions are assessed in Larry Berkson, Susan Carbon, and Alan Neff, "A Study of the U.S. Circuit Judge Nominating Commission," *Judicature* 63, no. 3 (September 1979): 104–29.

10. See Berkson, Carbon, and Neff, "A Study of the U.S. Circuit Judge Nominating Commission."

11. But note that the number of commissions was fluid at the start of 2009, with numerous senators creating commissions after Obama took office. We suspect that senators' decisions to form commissions—even in states with two Democratic senators—may have been intended to signal to the president that the senators aimed to fully exercise their power to advise the president about nominations.

12. Note that the partisanship of a commission is not fixed in stone. Upon the election of Barack Obama, the two Democratic senators from Wisconsin altered the makeup of their selection commissions—as provided for in the commission's charter—undercutting the influence of the commission's Republican members. See Diana Merrero, "Sensenbrenner Says Senators Snubbed Him on Judicial Nominations," *Journal Sentinel* (Milwaukee, Wisconsin), January 30, 2009, p. A5.

13. The commission was also charged with recommending U.S. attorneys for the state of California. Political appointees in the Department of Justice apparently sought to do an end run around the commission by recruiting candidates directly. Monica Goodling's efforts on this and other hiring practices drew the scrutiny of Justice Department investigators in the summer of 2008, who concluded that the decision of DOJ staff to base hiring practices on political and partisan considerations violated civil service laws. On the attempted end run around the California commission, see Richard B. Schmitt, "Justice Aide Took Lead to Replace Prosecutor," *Los Angeles Times,* May 23, 2007, p. A1 (http://articles.latimes.com/2007/may/23/nation/na-goodling23 [August 5, 2008]).

14. The states with operating commissions in place and that had a district court with at least one vacancy to be filled during the One Hundred Eighth and One Hundred Ninth Congresses included California, Florida, Georgia, Texas, and Washington. Wisconsin had a commission in place, but there were no district court appointments to the federal court in Wisconsin during either Congress.

15. The unavoidable limitation in studying the impact of selection commissions is that we do not know for sure whether or not the candidates nominated by the president were in fact recommended by a selection commission operating in the state. In some cases, for example, we know that President Bush selected a nominee who had not been on the list of nominees recommended by a commission. In the

summer of 2008 in Colorado, for example, the president selected three nominees from Senator Tom Allard's (R-Colo.) list of seven recommended candidates; only two of the three nominees, however, had passed muster with the junior senator's, Ken Salazar (D-Colo.), selection commission. See Tillie Fong, "Salazar, Ritter Split on Judge Pick," *Rocky Mountain News,* July 11, 2008, p. 8 (www.rockymountainnews. com/news/2008/Jul/11/salazar-ritter-split-on-judge-pick/ [March 27, 2009]). Thus, while we attribute differences in the rate and pace of nominations from states with and without commissions to the impact of the commission, we cannot know for sure that confirmation differences occur because of the preclearance afforded by the use of a commission. If the president does not select from a commission's list and yet the nomination still moves more quickly or successfully than nominations from non-commission states do, some other factor likely accounts for the differences.

16. During the One Hundred Eighth Congress, commission states with two Democratic senators included California, Florida, and Washington; in the One Hundred Ninth, only California and Washington.

17. The difference is statistically significant at $p < .1$ (one-tailed t test).

18. In calculating the average time for Senate action, we include both confirmed and failed nominations. Time elapsed for a failed nomination runs from the day the nomination was referred to the Senate until the day that the nomination was rejected (rarely), withdrawn (occasionally), or left unconfirmed in the Senate at the end of the Congress (the modal outcome). The differences reported are statistically significant at the $p < .01$ level (one-tailed t test).

19. A recent preliminary study by Russell Wheeler of George W. Bush's district court appointees suggests that appointees from states using commissions were less likely to identify themselves as Republicans or as active party members than were appointees from noncommission states. That finding may stem from the greater likelihood of commission state appointees to be former judges, compared with non-commission state appointees.

20. See Joel Connelly, "Senate Votes Today on Delayed Appeals Court Nomination; Gorton Deal Breaks Political Logjam," *Seattlepi.com,* October 6, 1998 (http:// seattlepi.nwsource.com/archives/1998/9810060083.asp [August 7, 2008]).

21. See John C. Eastman, "Filibuster Preservation," *National Review Online,* May 15, 2003 (www.nationalreview.com/script/printpage.p?ref=/comment/comment-eastman 051503.asp [October 30, 2008]); Sarah A. Binder and Steven S. Smith, "Filibusters: A Great American Tradition," *Atlanta-Journal Constitution,* May 25, 2003 (www. brookings.edu/opinions/2003/0525governance_binder.aspx [October 30, 2008]).

22. Although three-fifths is sufficient to invoke cloture on a nomination filibuster, the cloture threshold for a motion to change the rules is two-thirds.

23. The reform was discussed during the program "Politics and Justice," PBS's *NewsHour with Jim Lehrer,* May 8, 2003 (www.pbs.org/newshour/bb/congress/jan-june03/judicial_05-08.html [March 27, 2009]).

24. See Judith Resnick, "Judicial Selection and Democratic Theory: Demand, Supply, and Life Tenure," *Cardozo Law Review* 26, no. 2 (2005): 579–647; p. 638.

25. Resnick, "Judicial Selection and Democratic Theory," p. 638.

26. On the potential for the filibuster to moderate legislative measures, see Binder and Smith, *Politics or Principle?*

27. John O. McGinnis and Michael B. Rappaport, "Supermajority Rules and the Judicial Confirmation Process," *Cardozo Law Review* 26, no. 2 (2005): 544–78; p. 551. Note that McGinnis and Rappaport endorse a supermajority threshold to confirm Supreme Court nominees but not to confirm lower court nominees. They argue that the diversity that comes to the lower bench with a simple majority threshold is valuable for the development of the law: "A few outlying judges can provide both discipline and insight through dissents" (p. 546).

28. On the contributions of the Federalist Society to the recruitment and vetting of conservative jurists, see Steven M. Teles, *The Rise of the Conservative Legal Movement: The Battle for Control over the Law* (Princeton University Press, 2008).

29. As quoted in James Rowley, "Senate Standstill to Let Obama or McCain Tip Balance on Courts," *Bloomberg News,* August 7, 2007 (www.bloomberg.com/apps/news?pid=20601087&sid=aPaxOvQrYI7k&refer=home [March 27, 2009]).

30. Carolyn Dineen King, "Challenges to Judicial Independence and the Rule of Law: A Perspective from the Circuit Courts," Hallows Lecture, Marquette University Law School, February 20, 2007 (http://law.marquette.edu/s3/site/images/alumni/HallowsLecture2007.pdf [August 8, 2008]), pp. 11, 24.

31. At the time of her selection, she was considered an independent.

32. King, "Challenges to Judicial Independence and the Rule of Law," pp. 27–28.

33. King, "Challenges to Judicial Independence and the Rule of Law," p. 27.

34. Neil A. Lewis, "Stymied by Democrats in Senate, Bush Court Pick Finally Gives Up," *New York Times,* September 5, 2003, p. A1 (http://query.nytimes.com/gst/fullpage.html?res=9C04E2DE1E38F936A3575AC0A9659C8B63 [August 7, 2008]).

35. Charlie Savage, "U.S. to Probe Taking of Computer Files: GOP Staff Leaked Democrats' Memos," *Boston Globe,* April 27, 2004 (www.boston.com/news/nation/washington/articles/2004/04/27/us_to_probe_taking_of_computer_files/ [March 27, 2009]).

36. Manuel Miranda, "What Wrongdoing?" *National Review Online,* March 11, 2004 (www.nationalreview.com/comment/miranda200403111041.asp [March 27, 2009]).

37. Statement of Senator Patrick Leahy, Senate Judiciary Committee, Executive Business Meeting, February 12, 2004 (http://leahy.senate.gov/press/200402/021204a. html [March 27, 2009]).

38. Senate Republican Communications Center, "Letter to the President on Judges," Republican.Senate.gov website "The Leader Board," March 2, 2009 (http:// republican.senate.gov/public/index.cfm?FuseAction=Blogs.View&Blog_ID=3c5224 34-76e5-448e-9ead-1ec214b881ac&Month=3&Year=2009 [March 6, 2009]).

39. See David Ingram, "Obama Announces First Judicial Nominee," *The BLT: The Blog of Legal Times,* March 17, 2009 (http://legaltimes.typepad.com/blt/2009/03/ obama-announces-first-judicial-nominee.html [March 27, 2009]).

Index

ABA. *See* American Bar Association

Actor-centered functionalism, 54

Adams, John Quincy, 30

Administrative Office of the Courts, 129

Advice and consent: constitutional provision, 18–19; contemporary practices, 55–57; evolution, 17–18, 97–98, 146; Founders' intentions, 19, 22, 24, 25–26; institutional perspective, 10–11, 17–18, 143–47; in nineteenth century, 29–35; path dependency, 145–47; potential reforms, 147–48. *See also* Confirmation process; Judicial selection process

Alliance for Justice, 102

American Bar Association (ABA), Standing Committee on the Federal Judiciary, 94

American Civil Liberties Union, 159

Anti-Federalists, 28, 29, 146

Appellate judges: policy views, 83; Republican appointments, 77, 102, 103; senators' influence on nominations, 77; visiting judges, 128, 134. *See also* U.S. courts of appeals

Appellate judges, confirmation process: ABA ratings of nominees, 94; confirmation rates, 2–3, 79, 90–91; duration, 4–5, 79, 90; factors in duration, 81–89, 95–97; failed nominations, 15–16, 158; filibusters, 16–17, 79, 97, 98–101, 146, 158; recorded roll call votes, 101. *See also* Confirmation process

Baker, Howard, 88

Bankruptcy courts, reform of, 123

Bayh, Evan, 159

Beveridge, Albert, 38

Biden, Joseph, 124

Big bang theory of judicial selection conflicts, 7–9, 75, 89

Binder, Sarah A., 85

Blue slips: as absolute veto, 35–36, 50, 52–54, 55; agenda control function, 39–40; archival evidence of use, 40–45, 50–52; committee action on negative, 50, 52, 65; confirmation process duration and, 85–86; emergence in *1913*, 41–43, 45–52, 146; evolution, 55, 146; explanations of origins, 37–40, 45–52; format of early, 43–45; future use, 155; influence of minority party senators, 36, 38, 43, 48, 52, 63, 85–86, 101; influence on duration of nomination process, 73;